SURVIVAL SONGS

Conchita Piquer's *Coplas* and Franco's Regime of Terror

STEPHANIE SIEBURTH

Survival Songs

Conchita Piquer's *Coplas* and Franco's Regime of Terror

UNIVERSITY OF TORONTO PRESS
Toronto Buffalo London

Toronto Buffalo London
www.utppublishing.com

ISBN 978-1-4426-4473-1

Library and Archives Canada Cataloguing in Publication

Sieburth, Stephanie Anne, author
Survival songs : Conchita Piquer's coplas and Franco's regime of terror / Stephanie Sieburth.

(Toronto Iberic)
Includes bibliographical references and index.
ISBN 978-1-4426-4473-1 (bound)

1. Piquer, Conchita, 1908–1990 – Criticism and interpretation. 2. Coplas – Spain – History and criticism. 3. Coplas – Spain – Psychological aspects – History – 20th century. 4. Popular music – Spain – History and criticism. 5. Popular music – Spain – Psychological aspects – History – 20th century. 6. Psychic trauma – Spain – History – 20th century. 7. Political persecution – Psychological aspects – Spain – History – 20th century. 8. Spain – History – 1939–1975. I. Title. II. Title: Conchita Piquer's coplas and Franco's regime of terror. III. Series: Toronto Iberic

ML3714S53 2014 781.6200946 C2014-901328-0

University of Toronto Press acknowledges the financial assistance to its publishing program of the Canada Council for the Arts and the Ontario Arts Council, an agency of the Government of Ontario.

Canada Council for the Arts Conseil des Arts du Canada

This book has been published with the help of a grant from the Federation for the Humanities and Social Sciences, through the Awards to Scholarly Publications Program, using funds provided by the Social Sciences and Humanities Research Council of Canada.

University of Toronto Press acknowledges the financial support of the Government of Canada through the Canada Book Fund for its publishing activities.

For my mother, Renée Sieburth, and in memory of my grandmother, Friedel Schimmel.

Contents

Acknowledgments

I am very grateful to all those who gave their permission for the reproduction of lyrics and images in this book. Special thanks go to Manuel López-Quiroga for his marvellous gift of three songbooks of Conchita Piquer, for his generosity in allowing me to reproduce León and Quiroga's lyrics, and for his help in locating other heirs. Photojournalist Eloy Alonso González generously allowed me to include his photographs of the exhumations of the bones of Franco's victims. Although I was unable to include their images in the end, I am very grateful to Concha Márquez Piquer and Ramiro Oliveros for sharing some of their photographs with me, and for their generous gift of Concha's memoirs. I also appreciate my e-mail dialogue with Salvador Valverde, who generously sent me information about his father's life and crucial collaboration with León and Quiroga prior to his exile in 1939.

I offer my warmest thanks to my editor at the University of Toronto Press, Siobhan McMenemy, for her strong faith in the project, her suggestions for improvements, and her skilful guidance throughout the process. I am also indebted to the anonymous readers for the press, who have made this a much stronger book through their comments.

Deans William Chafe and George McClendon, Department Chairs Margaret Greer and Michèle Longino, and Jean O'Barr as Director of Women's Studies, all helped me obtain leave time at crucial moments in the development of this project. Department Chair Roberto Dainotto gave me his unfailing encouragement and support in the final stages.

I could not have written this book without the help of psychotherapists and academic psychologists. In North Carolina, Terry Vance, Bob Vaillancourt, and the Tuesday group prepared me to make the processing of feelings the topic of this book. Terry Vance consulted with me throughout the project, sharing her bibliography and her clinical experience with role-play, helping me deepen my analysis of the emotional processes occurring in each song, and keeping me going with her strong faith in the project. At Duke, qualitative psychologist Phil Costanzo gave generously of his time, bibliography, and advice. From Ontario, Linda Chapman, Rob McKay, Jodie Waisberg, and Christian Keresztes all provided crucial insights from their own expertise in psychology, as well as their nourishing friendship and their unflagging enthusiasm for the project.

Helen Solterer gave this book her steadfast support from start to finish. Her comments on early chapters, our discussions about the workings of role play, her encouragement at tough times, and her invaluable guidance on the mysteries of permission-seeking were all crucial to the outcome. Jehanne Gheith's work on children of the Gulag profoundly resonated with my own, and her support for this kind of work was invaluable, as was her reading of early versions of the manuscript. I will never forget conversations with Harriet Turner as she read early chapters at my dining room table and explained to me the concept of the Velcro effect; she also graciously used her gift of translation to help me provide the best English rendering of difficult phrases. And Roberta Johnson gave of her open heart, her keen critical eye, and her strategic advice throughout this project.

Maite Zubiaurre, Jo Labanyi, Elisa Martí-Lopez, and Kim Curtis also generously read parts of the manuscript in its early stages, and their incisive comments helped me sharpen both my focus and my prose. Mina García Soormally and her mother kindly helped me translate the *andalucismos* in these *coplas.* And at the end, John Tallmadge used his magical combination of enthusiasm, encouragement, and critique to help me bring this project to completion.

I have been very lucky to have many research assistants contribute to the making of this book over the years. I especially want to thank a number of them who made the book possible in special ways. Undergraduate Michael Bannon tracked down a wealth of bibliography on the health benefits of music. Clinical psychology graduate student Alison Papadakis taught me how the field of academic psychology was organized, and helped me research the treatment of bereavement, trauma, and terror. Among my Spanish graduate students at Duke, Rebecca Ingram and Zachary Erwin guided me expertly through the labyrinth of the Biblioteca Nacional, and worked shoulder to shoulder with me there to explore the wealth of invitations to role-play in popular magazines of the 1940s. I will never forget running all over Madrid with Cristina Ruiz in search of permissions to use images, nor her wonderful help in a host of other ways. Leonardo Bacarreza used his technological wizardry to work with images, and Martin Repinecz patiently devoted his elegant computer skills to formatting the manuscript. My very special thanks go to Diego Gaspar Celaya, a History graduate student at the University of Zaragoza, who generously gave of his time and initiative to help me gather permissions for the use of lyrics and images

As this book was being researched and written, I have been very fortunate to have had the support of many other friends and colleagues in the United States, Canada, and Spain.

My dear friends in Madrid and Bilbao sustained me for many summers during the writing of this book. María Jesús San Segundo took pride in my work during thirty years of friendship, until her untimely death in 2010; her wonderful family continues to sustain me with their love. Bubi (Federico Grafe) and Mari Carmen Castells have been true friends through the best and the worst of times; they contributed to this book in countless ways. Federico Grafe and Juan Urrutia kindly shared with me their memories of growing up in postwar Spain. Eva Grande and Paloma Navarro took me into their hearts and their houses as I wrote this book, with unfailing generosity and support for the project. Violeta Demonte offered me her loyal friendship, her intellectual rigour, and her support for me as a scholar. Carmen Ortiz supported this book in many ways, from giving me books on the *copla* to advising me on permission questions and inviting me to try out my ideas at a lecture at the CSIC. (I will never forget how we ended the discussion with a collective singing of "Tatuaje," led by Antonio Cea.) Pilar Martínez, librarian at the CSIC, offered valuable advice on the thorny question of rights to magazines from the 1940s. Many thanks to Manuel Rey for sharing his vast knowledge of the *copla*, for keeping the genre alive through marvellous performances at La Fídula, and for dedicating his rendition of "En tierra extraña" to me. Marina Mayoral and Carmen Sainz de Aja offered support and valuable insights during the writing. And Angel de la Llave and Carmen Peral organized many memorable evenings of *tortilla española* on the Plaza de Olavide.

I am extremely fortunate to have many friends and colleagues at the University of Zaragoza, where I tried out ideas from this book as a Visiting Professor in the doctoral program, "La España del Siglo XX: Literatura, Historia, Sociedad." Both students and faculty offered me insights, sources, and advice over the years, as well as much loving support. María Angeles Naval shared not only her course with me, but her house, her family, and above all, her friendship. Luis Beltrán was always ready with gracious hospitality and iconoclasm. Carmen Peña generously helped me think about *coplas* in cinema and took time out from her own research to advise me on Piquer's films; our conversations over the years have been a major source of sustenance. Carlos Forcadell sent me books, invited me to cultural events, and made sure I went to El Plata. Antonio Ansón sent me music, books, and articles. Julián Casanova offered me books and encouragement. Angela Cenarro shared insights on the Sección Femenina and offered helpful advice to guide me in the archives. Javier Barreiro generously welcomed me into his home archive of materials on the *cuplé* and the *copla,* a treasure trove that I recommend to other scholars. José Luis Calvo Carrilla generously shared his office with me. Angeles Ezama gave me her steadfast support and help with sources. I especially thank Leonardo Romero, who shared his memories of growing up in Burgos in the 1940s and 1950s and hearing *coplas* in a variety of venues. And I will never forget my conversations with the late Juan José Carreras. In Valencia, Antonio Méndez Rubio was a gracious host, and this project benefited greatly from his insights.

In Toronto, Linda Hutcheon offered me her unfailing encouragement and crucial advice at key points in the project, and engaged me in dialogue about music and bereavement. Bob Davidson gave me his support and helpful suggestions, and Steven Rupp and Alison Keith spurred me on to finish. Words cannot express my gratitude to the many dear friends I share with my mother. They have followed the development of this book from its inception and have encouraged and sustained me over wonderful meals and unforgettable conversations over the years.

In the United States, Kathleen Vernon and Jo Labanyi shared insights with me from their work on cinemagoing in postwar Spain. Luis Fernández Cifuentes asked me the key question of whether *coplas* were *sucedáneos,* ersatz substitutes for what was not available in postwar Spain; this book is my response. Jordi Marí and Elvira Vilches gave me their unfailing friendship and their incisive suggestions throughout the writing. Verónica Feliú shared her experience of leading theatre groups in Pinochet's Chile. Lindsay Waters shared his own ideas about music and feelings; his invitation to participate in an MLA panel on literature and affect helped me situate my work in a broader context of scholarship. In North Carolina, I talked through this project with Donna Giles and Sue Sneddon, who shared with me what music meant in their lives, and who renewed my spirit at their house in Shallotte. June Merlino, Fabienne Worth, Corinne Fox, and Harriet Whitehead were in my corner throughout, and Anna Clark and Anne Carter provided expert advice from Minneapolis. And throughout, Jean O'Barr gave me the gift of her wisdom and her hospitality at 713 Anderson Street.

Ev Machtinger came into my life in the final stages of this project, supported each step towards its completion, and shifted my focus from survival to thriving.

My mother has supported this book in every possible way, reading drafts, encouraging me throughout the process, and sharing her insights about what it means to grieve without a body or a grave. My mother's family lived in hiding in Belgium during the Holocaust; my grandfather was taken by the Nazis toward the end of the war, and never returned. This book grew not only out of my love of Spain, but also out of the ways my mother and maternal grandmother coped with their traumatic experience and their loss. Through their understated dignity, their strong love, their remarkable sense of humour and laughter, and the way they listened to classical music with their souls hanging on every note, they have taught me the most important things I know about what survival means.

Durham, North Carolina, November 2012

SURVIVAL SONGS

Conchita Piquer's *Coplas* and Franco's Regime of Terror

Introduction: Conchita Piquer's *Coplas* as Psychotherapy

After the Spanish Civil War of 1936–9, Spain was a nation under duress. The countryside had been ravaged by battles, and the cities by bombings. People on either side of the conflict found themselves facing chronic hunger, epidemic disease, grinding poverty, housing shortages, and lack of heat, water, and electricity. And the cultural horizons of Spaniards were hardly less bleak than the landscape, as the regime imposed a stultifying curriculum on schools and severe censorship on the media and literature. As well, people on both sides were in mourning for family and friends killed in the conflict. In this context, both the winners and the losers of the war turned with a particular intensity to forms of popular entertainment, seeking both distraction from these hardships and ways to cope with them.

Those who remember the postwar period uniformly single out one performer above all others as the voice to which they clung throughout the period. Her name was Conchita Piquer, and she was unforgettable because of her incomparable ability to act in song; because of her compelling, astringent voice; and because of the tragic stories she told with such emotion. The most famous *coplas* were sad and bitter stories, of fallen women who had lost their true love, or penniless men down on their luck and without social support.

The *copla* was the dominant genre of popular music throughout the 1940s and 1950s. It was part of a larger culture of mass entertainments that all overlapped. *Copla* singers played starring roles in many Francoist films, and Spanish singers and actors appeared in popular magazines that also featured Hollywood films and their stars. Fashion magazines, in turn, made constant reference to film. The culture industry thus constituted a kind of parallel universe to which Spaniards could turn for relief from the harsh realities of daily life.

In her 1995 article, "Popular Culture in the 'Years of Hunger,'" Helen Graham suggested that "the task of ensuring survival in such an atomized and deprived society was as crucially a psychological as a physical struggle" (241). She called for further research on the psychological strategies of survival, particularly with reference to how people used popular songs. This book does indeed explore the mechanisms of psychological survival, but I will be focusing on the predicament of the defeated rather than on the winners of the war because, while Spaniards on both sides had undoubtedly been traumatized by violence, bombings, and bereavements, the defeated also faced a concerted attempt to annihilate them both physically and psychologically long after the war had ended. The threats to their survival were more numerous and more intense than those faced by the winners, and the resources at their disposal to remain psychologically alive were few and far between.

This was the case because, after his victory in 1939, Franco instituted a systematic apparatus of terror that investigated, jailed, and executed those who had not actively supported him in the Civil War.[1] Those who survived were forbidden to bury or to mourn their dead. Most lived in starvation conditions. Insulted and humiliated on the streets by fascist militias, they were excoriated by Franco and his propagandists as the "anti-Spain," supposedly to blame for all of the war's death and destruction. Many were subject to "re-education" programs in an array of institutions created by the regime, programs designed to empty them of their former identity and refill them with Francoist beliefs. The period is known as the "time of silence" and the "years of hunger."

In the 1970s, leading intellectuals in Spain's transition to democracy eloquently recalled the role of songs during the terrifying years of the 1940s. In her memoir-novel *El cuarto de atrás* (*The Back Room*, 1978), Carmen Martín Gaite reflected on their importance:

> En tiempos de escasez hay que hacer durar lo que se tiene, y de la misma manera que nadie tira un juguete ni deja a medio comer un pastel, a nadie se le ocurre tampoco consumir deprisa una canción, porque no es un lujo que se renueva cada día, sino *un enser fundamental para la supervivencia*, la cuida, la rumia, le saca todo su jugo.

> When everything is scarce, you have to make what you have last. So, just as no one would throw away a toy, or leave a cake half-eaten, nobody would even think of consuming a song quickly, because it is not a luxury item that can be replaced each day, but *a fundamental tool for survival.* You care for it, you ruminate on it, you suck all the juice out of it. (179; italics mine)[2]

But not all songs were equal for Martín Gaite. She revered Conchita Piquer as the performer who was able to express in all their bitterness the feelings that many Spaniards were having and that the Franco regime was trying to paper over. Similarly, in Basilio Martín Patino's documentary film *Canciones para después de una guerra* (*Songs for After a War*) (1971/76), the voiceover of an elderly woman links songs and survival during this period:

> Eran canciones para sobrevivir. Canciones con calor. Con ilusiones. Con historia. Canciones para sobreponerse a la oscuridad, al vacío, al miedo. Canciones para tiempos de soledad ... Canciones para ayudarnos en la necesidad de soñar, en el esfuerzo de vivir.

> They were songs for survival. Songs with warmth. With excitement. With a story. Songs to help us overcome the darkness, the void, the fear. Songs for times of loneliness ... Songs to help us in our need to dream, in our effort to stay alive.

The voiceover says these words while Piquer sings the song that dominated the airwaves in postwar Spain, the song that came to epitomize the period, "Tatuaje" ("Tattoo"). Manuel Vázquez Montalbán contends that a handful of the best songs of the postwar period reflected the lived experience of ordinary people as no other social discourse did (*Cancionero* xx). All of the songs he names were sung by Conchita Piquer.

According to Carmen Martín Gaite, one of the most powerful attributes of Piquer's *coplas* was that they were able to lay bare the deep pain of people's losses in the context of what Martín Gaite calls the "anaesthetised" society of the postwar years, during which a forced cheerfulness reigned and the regime resorted to triumphal rhetoric in an effort to cover over the pain and deny its causes. Martín Gaite began to write *El cuarto de atrás* on the day of Franco's funeral in 1975. She and others of her generation felt that Spain could not move forward unless it could link itself to the lived experience and the emotional pain that had been repressed under Franco. The country was emerging from a forty-year dictatorship that had kept Spaniards from knowing the history of their own country, including the experience and feelings of their own parents. To Martín Gaite's generation had fallen the task of conveying to younger Spaniards what the postwar period had really been like and what the defeated had really been feeling in the "time of silence." The leading writers of the 1970s agreed that the songs of Conchita Piquer were one of the main vehicles of access to those silenced feelings and experiences.[3]

Nevertheless, anaesthesia in the form of amnesia continued to characterize Spanish society after Franco's death. The new democracy had been founded on an amnesty law that meant that no one would ever be tried for crimes against humanity that had left more than 100,000 bodies in mass graves. The Francoist elites and the opposition had agreed to leave the past in the past and to move on. It is only in the twenty-first century that the feelings so long repressed by the defeated are coming to the surface. Martín Gaite used the metaphor of the "spade" to describe how *coplas* had functioned in the 1940s: Piquer's *coplas* were excavating tools to lay bare the pain of the war and the postwar years (*El cuarto* 152). Today, in the twenty-first century, real spades are finally digging up the bones of the dead whose relatives had been silenced for so long under the "pact of forgetting." And survivors are finally speaking. Their stories have been recorded by historians and journalists, recalled on camera in recent documentaries, and printed in the press. Through them, we learn that surviving relatives are still trying in the twenty-first century to locate and properly bury their dead family members, executed by the Francoists in the 1930s and 1940s. My readings in this book are founded on this testimony about the 1940s. If we are to gain an understanding of the strategies of psychological survival in the period, we must first become familiar with the emotional threats to survival that the defeated were facing and understand what kinds of factors could exacerbate or alleviate those threats. The work of historians and the testimony of survivors make clear that three of the major psychological threats to survival in the period were chronic terror, blocked mourning, and traumatic stress. These were greatly exacerbated by the regime's treatment of the defeated as subhuman and by the systematic silencing that prevented them from expressing any of their intense feelings. What was special about the form, content, and performance of Conchita Piquer's songs that made them privileged vehicles for surviving such crushing, cumulative threats?

To answer this question, this book uses a new lens: clinical psychotherapy. My goal is to theorize the largely unconscious ways in which people oppressed under Franco could use Piquer's *coplas* to work through intense feelings of terror and grief in ways that were both politically safe and emotionally manageable. I focus on four major operations in which people engaged when they sang along with Piquer: They were *playing the role* of a fictional character, which provided them with a kind of emotional camouflage; they were participating in a deeply felt *ritual* experience, wherein certain *coplas* came to stand in for the mourning rites that had been denied them; they were collaborating with Conchita Piquer in the co-creation of a *narrative*; and they were *making music*. In researching how psychotherapists have treated patients suffering from traumatic stress, chronic fear, and blocked mourning, I discovered that these same operations were widely used.

This study is grounded in familiar Freudian concepts such as repression, projection, and working-through. But it also goes beyond Freud to consider the more recent writings of clinical psychotherapists who use a variety of methods. In particular, I believe that when the defeated sang along with Piquer's *coplas*, they were getting some of the same benefits that creative arts therapies provide to trauma survivors. I argue that in each *copla* studied here, there is an analogy between the predicament and feelings of the protagonist and those of the defeated that allowed the latter to work through their own painful feelings as they sang. The five chapters that form the core of this book analyse how the four elements noted above came into play as the defeated sang six of Piquer's most famous *coplas*, and show how each song enabled them to perform a crucial psychological move to cope with specific repressive measures instituted by the regime. I hypothesize that Piquer, through her voice and performance, played a role somewhere between therapist and ritual high priestess, a role that did much to enable the defeated to work through some of the intense traumatic feelings they carried within as they sang along with her. Thus, just as a patient in psychotherapy works bit by bit through painful feelings related to grief or trauma in successive sessions with the help of a therapist, I believe that those who listened to the radio in postwar Spain used the repeated singing of these songs, which were broadcast regularly on the radio for years and often decades, as a way to carry out the extended process of working-through that such traumatic experiences require. I argue, in sum, that singing along with Conchita Piquer constituted a powerful form of psychotherapy. In addition to reading the work of clinicians, I have consulted with psychotherapists throughout the writing of this book to make sure that what I am proposing about these *coplas* does not contradict anything they have seen in their practice.

Judith Herman's *Trauma and Recovery* is a foundational study of the effects of repeated exposure to helplessness, terror, and atrocities, as well as a blueprint for recovery. In her afterword, Herman recognizes that most of the world's traumatized people never see the inside of a therapist's office and therefore cannot benefit from psychotherapeutic techniques as they come to terms with the trauma. She calls for the study of the methods that untreated survivors use to recover from the trauma to some extent (241). The present book makes the claim that popular music is one of the most potent, and most easily available, mechanisms for ordinary people without access to psychotherapy to work through trauma, blocked mourning, and chronic fear, and that this is why Piquer's *coplas* have been described as survival tools during the Franco dictatorship.

Each *copla* is distinctive in form and content. Taken together, and repeated daily over years on the radio, they enabled the defeated to perform a series of psychological moves that were necessary to their survival. A key implication of the present study is that there is an analogy between the singing of *coplas* in the 1940s and the exhumation of the bodies of Franco's victims today. Today, survivors of the period are reconstituting their personhood, citizenship, and dignity by digging up the remains of their dead, reburying them, grieving for them, and telling their stories. I contend that in the 1940s and 1950s, when they could not dig up their dead, one major vehicle they used to mourn and to reconstitute their personhood was to sing the *coplas* created by León and Quiroga for Conchita Piquer.

But survival is not only emotional, it is also existential. Drawing on Viktor Frankl's theory of the necessary conditions for survival in the Nazi concentration camps, I consider how *coplas* contributed to the survival need that Frankl considered the most basic of all: the need for meaning. At a time when they had given everything to fight for their values and had been defeated, when they were suffering severe material privation, and when they had little hope that they could better their lot in the future, how did the defeated keep from giving in to despair? And what did *coplas* have to do with the recovery of a sense of meaning? I address these questions by exploring the significance of the narrative form of Rafael de León's tragic *coplas*.

These *coplas* are rich, polysemic artistic texts that are open to multiple readings today, as they were in the postwar period. I am not proposing that the songs' creators intended the uses I am postulating, or that those among the defeated who sang along with Piquer interpreted the songs consciously in the way I do here. My reading is one of a panoply of possible interpretations. It focuses primarily on how these *coplas* could be *used* in the enterprise of psychological survival, much of which was necessarily unconscious. Thus, the close readings of the songs aim to show how these stories, the gaps in them, and the nuances of the lyrics, music, and performance could serve as vehicles for the defeated to work through particular psychological predicaments.

It is also important to clarify that although throughout this study I refer to "the defeated" for the sake of brevity, I do not assume that all of the defeated sang *coplas*, or that those who did so necessarily used them in the same way. The defeated were not a homogenous group in any terms, and their feelings about *coplas* reflected this. Some of them associated *coplas* with Francoism and shunned them, while others sang them with all their hearts and were devoted to their favourite *copla* stars. Furthermore, each individual among the defeated would have had personal memories and associations with particular *coplas*. As well, while some of the defeated had other strong ways of making meaning out of their suffering, such as political beliefs, others had ceased to believe in anything at all. Thus, I am not arguing that all of the defeated used the songs in precisely the ways I present in this book. Rather, I assume that people struggling for their psychological survival will seek out and make intense use of any outlet that will promote that survival. These songs were some of the very few outlets available, and they are remembered as especially significant.

The winners of the Spanish Civil War undoubtedly also used these songs to help them mourn and to cope with traumatic stress after the violence of the war. They loved these *coplas* as much as the losers did. Yet this study is not about the winners' relations to the *copla*. The reason is that emotionally, the losers faced a much more serious threat to survival than the winners. This is not only because they faced ongoing terror and cumulative losses in the 1940s that the winners did not. It is because social support is needed if a person is to recover from bereavement or trauma. The winners could speak publicly of their losses and had the explicit support of the authorities to do so. All the social institutions were on their side and were potential sources of comfort. The winners could ritually bury their dead and gather safely with friends and family to mourn. But no social discourse confirmed the experience or the feelings of the defeated, which had to be kept entirely hidden. And their communities had been shattered. Thus, while the winners, too, surely used some of Piquer's *coplas* as vehicles for mourning, the songs were only one of a number of sources of support and possibilities for expression of these losses. For the defeated, the *coplas* were one of very few ways that they could raise their voices and tell a painful story in the first person without putting themselves in danger. The connection between songs and survival was much clearer in a population that, like a character in one of Rafael de León's *coplas*, had "no law to protect [them] and no door to knock on."[4]

Remarkably enough, this book is the first full-length academic study of the *copla,* a genre that dominated the Spanish airwaves for two decades and that has never ceased to be heard since.[5] Most discussion of the *copla* still relies heavily on the perceptive testimonies and theories of Vázquez Montalbán, Martín Gaite, Patino, and Moix. This book takes their work as its foundation but attempts to be more specific in its consideration of how the work of survival took place through singing, and exactly what kinds of emotional and political content were being aired in code when the defeated sang Piquer's *coplas.*

One important context for this book is the recent scholarship on "historical memory" within Spanish cultural studies. This term has been used in two ways relevant to this study. The first has to do with the special power of songs to capture feelings and memories associated with a particular time and place. As José Colmeiro and Annabel Martín have shown, in the 1970s, some of the leading intellectuals of the Spanish transition to democracy found in these songs an important vehicle for recovering how people had really been feeling during the postwar period, as well as a source of coded allusions to what they had been experiencing at the time. These feelings and experiences were diametrically opposed to the content of official, Francoist histories of the period.[6]

In recent years, however, the term "historical memory" in scholarship has referred mainly to the movement founded by the families of the executed to exhume the bodies of their dead; this survivors' organization is called the Asociación para la Recuperación de la Memoria Histórica (Association for the Recovery of Historical Memory). The effect of this movement has been to make visible and subject to public discussion the atrocities of the Francoist repression. Journalists have produced documentaries containing the testimony of surviving family members about what happened to their relatives; historians have documented how the repression worked, and its scale; and scholars of cultural studies have analysed the resulting texts and the political debates now raging in Spain as the right protests that the exhumations and the consequent discussion violate the agreement to leave the past in the past that allowed Spain to move from dictatorship to democracy.[7]

The scholarship on the documentaries that have been produced in the past decade has explored the mediations involved in the construction of such texts, and thus of memories of the period.[8] My own study is not about memory as such; rather, it attempts to identify the unconscious processes that took place in the 1940s when people sang along with Piquer. I draw on the current testimonies not in an attempt to recover an exact account of what happened during the Francoist repression, but rather in order to understand the intensity and specificity of the survivors' feelings of terror, as well as the suffering that blocked mourning compelled them to endure. The intensity of the survivors' feelings even today has led them to fight to be heard even as the major political parties have tried to avoid listening; this suggests what they must have experienced during the "time of silence," which in turn offers us clues as to just what kinds of historical "huellas" – "traces," to use Vázquez Montalbán's term – we may find in the *coplas* (*Cancionero* x). The only specific kind of testimony on which I rely in this study concerns the examples in chapter 1 regarding the roles the Francoists forced the defeated to play, and how important it was that they play them perfectly in order to avoid punishment.

While my study is neither about memory nor about contemporary Spain, it is relevant to the current debate in several ways. First, Jo Labanyi points out that recent documentaries and oral histories tend to construct those who experienced the Francoist repression as victims; this conveys a view of the Spanish Republicans as "helpless objects of historical events beyond their control" ("Testimonies," 199). She notes that in literature on the Holocaust, the emphasis on trauma has similarly constructed survivors as victims. I concur entirely with Labanyi's suspicion of the seductiveness of trauma as a concept in discussions of Holocaust survivors, and with her objection to the construction of survivors of Franco's repression as victims without agency. But I do not see the emphasis on trauma as the problem; rather, the problem is that people who have undergone traumatic experiences are constructed as victims, as damaged and without agency. Having grown up in a family of Holocaust survivors and in a synagogue community in which survivors abounded, I have always been struck by their resilience, their courage, their humour, and their ability to rebuild their lives. This is in stark contrast to the way survivors are often characterized in trauma theory. But a focus on trauma need not emphasize victimhood. Judith Herman's landmark book, *Trauma and Recovery,* refers to those who have experienced trauma as survivors. The present study, which is focused on survival, takes for granted the resourcefulness of the defeated in seeking out and making intense use of the few vehicles for survival at their disposal, such as Piquer's *coplas.* I see them as immensely strong and resilient and as able to use those vehicles of recovery from trauma. I hope this book will help counteract the characterization of the survivors as helpless victims.

Second, Labanyi underscores the therapeutic and ethical significance of the public testimonies of survivors ("Politics" 119). The ability to articulate one's pain and to be heard and supported by the larger society is a key element of recovery from trauma, for it involves the recovery of personhood by those who have been defiled, treated as unworthy, as sub-human. The silencing that occurred in postwar Spain was a major feature of the denial of personhood. In this book, I hypothesize that singing Piquer's songs was an important vehicle for recovering personhood in the 1940s and 1950s, when survivors could not do so directly. Singing along allowed them to raise their voices audibly, to tell their painful stories in code, to tell them collectively, and to assert their own personhood and dignity under cover of the role of the protagonist.

The other important context for this book within Spanish cultural studies is work on Francoist melodramatic films involving *coplas* and *copla* stars, known as *folklóricas*.[9] Such studies are part of a larger endeavour on the part of Spanish film scholars to take account of the effects of the emotions expressed in films on their spectators.[10] Where it had once been assumed that audiences passively accepted the conservative messages about family and morality that were imposed in the films' endings, recent scholarship has focused on the alternative possibilities for interpretation opened up both by the plots of the films and by the excessive emotions acted out by the stars. Two methods have been used in such studies, exemplified by two articles by Eva Woods that have the strongest connection to my own approach. The first, "Excess, Affect, and Emergent Classes," uses close reading to show how, at a time when the defeated had little opportunity to represent themselves, a time when censorship meant that "the ellipsis reigned" – Vázquez Montalbán's phrase – the excesses of desire or anger represented in Francoist melodrama created a space for an interpretation that was antithetical to Francoist morality (*Crónica* 36).[11] For Woods, the relevant categories in thinking about the alternative subject positions opened up by the excessive feelings and ideological contradictions of these films are class and gender. This book adds another category to her analysis: the heavy emotional burdens carried by the defeated. My readings in this study attempt to look more closely at the unconscious emotional processes that were set in motion once the *coplas* had evoked such "excessive" feelings in their listeners who sang along.

The second method used by Woods focuses on reception. Woods is a member of the research group led by Jo Labanyi that has collected oral histories of Spaniards' memories of cinemagoing in the 1940s and 1950s. This research is producing a wealth of new knowledge about the practices of everyday life as they related to cinema.[12] Woods's article,

"Identification and Disconnect through Popular Melodrama," focuses on select interviewees who insisted that the cinema was a sphere separate from their political and social life. Woods makes use of the theories of Slavoj Zizek to analyse this technique of "disconnect," noting how the spectators' desire to see cinema as separate reveals "the need and desire for a dream factory in which a reality parallel to Francoism could survive" (126). Woods's comments about the way this separate, alternative universe allowed the audience to release emotion dovetail with the theories of drama therapists on which I draw in this book to explain what happened when listeners sang along with Conchita Piquer. These theories explore the unconscious therapeutic work that can be done while acting the role of a character in a play. Piquer's *coplas*, too, partake of melodramatic excess and theatricality, although they are also quite different from the *folklórica* films in the way they end.

Both methods used by Woods and other critics in relation to Francoist melodramatic film reach conclusions that complement the ones I have reached about the act of singing along to Piquer's *coplas.* I apply a very different method, however, one that brings together research in clinical psychotherapy, close attention to historical context, and close reading of the songs. This complementarity of results achieved by three quite different methods is exciting and suggests that we are on the track of understanding crucial elements of the psychology of survival through popular culture in the period.[13]

It would be desirable to be able to document my reading of how people used Piquer's *coplas.* However, several factors combine to make this difficult if not impossible. The first is that in the postwar period, it was not safe to document such readings, and today, the oral history of people's memories of *coplas* has not yet been done. The second is that the nature of popular song, and its social uses, are such that people may know every line and nuance of a song, and may sing it individually and in groups over a lifetime, without ever pausing to interpret its content, since the pleasure of singing is usually enough in itself. This is not the case with film, for discussing the film afterwards is integral to filmgoing. But most important, the theories on which I rely in this book suggest that while some people clearly did consciously interpret *coplas,* there were unconscious levels of emotional processing at play, and these are the ones I attempt to explore in this book.

Thus, while I have spoken informally to many Spaniards who remember the period as well as to historians to find out where and how people heard and sang *coplas* in postwar Spain, the emotional processes I aim to explore in this study are not ones that can ever be documented, precisely because some of the levels of their engagement with Piquer's remarkable songs were unconscious – indeed, they had to be so in order for singing the *coplas* to work its therapeutic effect.

Because this is the first academic book on the *copla*, it is important to clarify what this book does *not* do. It is not a sociological overview of the *copla* genre along the lines of Serge Salaün's influential study of the *cuplé*. Nor is it an archival study of Conchita Piquer's career and political connections, or the way she was portrayed in the press. While I briefly describe some aspects of Piquer's visual performance style, I am most concerned with what she could convey through her voice alone to those who heard her exclusively on the radio. This is not a panoramic study of the whole variety of songs grouped under the generic name of *coplas*, nor even of the *coplas* sung by Piquer. It is a close reading of a handful of her most beloved tragic *coplas*, focused on the question of psychological survival. It is important to note, however, that there are many other *coplas* by Piquer and other singers that I could have read in the light of the emotional suffering explored in this book; Miguel de Molina's "La bien pagá" and Juanita Reina's "Yo soy ... ésa" are but two examples.[14]

Survival Songs has eight chapters. Chapter 1 provides the psychological foundations for the study. It outlines the physical, emotional, and existential threats to survival in Franco's Spain, as well as the specifics of the psychological suffering and risks to health involved in each one. It explains the approach I will be taking to trauma in this study, which differs somewhat from the trauma theory in common use in the field of cultural studies. It goes on to explore role play as the most basic strategy that people used to stay physically and psychologically alive, drawing a distinction between the roles imposed by the regime and the roles people chose to play through popular culture in order to express alternative identities under camouflage. Finally, it outlines the psychological concepts that ground my reading in later chapters of the unconscious processes that were at work when the defeated sang the *coplas*.

Chapter 2 focuses on the history, form, and ambiguous ideology of the *copla* genre and on the special characteristics of Conchita Piquer as a performer that made her songs so important to the survival of the defeated. The next five chapters focus on some of the most famous songs written by León and Quiroga and sung by Conchita Piquer.[15] I interpret each song as a tool for coping with a particular emotional burden. The 1940s were years of rationing, investigations, trumped-up military trials, and constant executions. In chapter 3, I read "La Parrala" ("The Wine

Lady") as a compendium of lessons in coping with terror. Chapters 4, 5, and 6 focus on how three of Conchita Piquer's most famous *coplas* addressed the dilemma posed for the defeated by the regime's denial of access to rituals of mourning, and by the danger involved in expressing their grief. I read "Ojos verdes" ("Green Eyes"), "Tatuaje" ("Tattoo"), and "Romance de la otra" ("Ballad of the Other Woman") as clandestine rituals corresponding to the three stages of mourning: separation, transition, and incorporation. Chapter 7 reads two *coplas* from the 1950s, "La Ruiseñora" ("The Nightingale") and "Romance de valentía" ("Ballad of Bravery"), as grappling with the problem of being silenced, denied personhood, and prohibited from using one's talents. Chapter 8 focuses on how singing these *coplas* could facilitate the recovery of a sense of meaning in life. It shows how the narrative form and musical structure of León and Quiroga's *coplas* combined to allow those who sang along to repair some of the damage to their sense of self caused by cumulative traumas and ongoing terror. The Conclusion summarizes my findings, discusses their implications for the study of popular music in other contexts, and suggests further directions for research on the *copla*.

Chapter One

Camouflage: The Psychology of Survival in Franco's Spain

I. Threats to Survival[1]

The physical threats to survival in Franco's Spain are well known. The greatest of these was execution. The Nationalist generals who rose up against the Republic adopted a clear strategy of instilling terror in the civilian population, which was largely hostile to them. General Mola gave secret instructions:

> Hay que sembrar el terror ... hay que dejar sensación de dominio eliminando sin escrúpulos ni vacilación a todos lo que no piensen como nosotros.
>
> We need to spread terror ... we have to give the impression that we are in control by eliminating without scruples all those who do not think as we do. (qtd. in Reig Tapia 146)

General Queipo de Llano terrified southern Spain not only by ordering brutal killings, but also through his regular radio broadcasts, in which he spelled out the Nationalists' philosophy of terror:

> Ya conocerán mi sistema: por cada uno de orden que caiga, yo mataré a diez extremistas por lo menos ...
>
> They'll soon get to know my system: For every person on the side of order that falls, I'll kill at least ten extremists.[2]
>
> Del Diccionario quedarán borradas las palabras de perdón y amnistía. Se les perseguirá [a los rojos] como fieras, hasta hacerlos desaparecer a todos.

> The words pardon and amnesty will be erased from the dictionary. We will persecute [the Reds] like wild beasts, until we have eliminated them all.[3]

In practice, this meant that when the Nationalists entered a town, they would kill local authorities, political party leaders, and military people immediately. But this was only the start; they also executed people simply for carrying the card of a left-wing political party. They hunted down middle-class lawyers, doctors, teachers, and civil servants who were liberals. And masses of common people were victims of what were called *paseos* ("being taken for a ride"): they were taken from their homes or from jail at dawn by Fascist militia, who loaded them into a truck, drove them to the outskirts, and left them in a ditch with a bullet between the eyes (Reig Tapia 101). Often, those murdered were never officially recorded as dead.[4] Then Republican sympathizers were forced to bury the bodies in ditches (Silva 53). These mass executions took place whether the Nationalists encountered resistance in a particular area or not. In Badajoz, where resistance had been fierce, more than 1,000 people were gunned down in the bullring in a massacre that attracted international attention (Jackson 56). In La Rioja, the Nationalists met no resistance when they walked in, but they killed 2,000 anyway (Villarroya i Font and Solé i Sabaté 54). After the war, the regime extended the large-scale killings to all of Spain. Kangaroo military courts convicted of "military rebellion" those who had fought for a democratically elected Republic and condemned them to death. "Unofficial" executions by Falangist militiamen continued as well. Jails were emptied and refilled repeatedly as the killings continued (Reig Tapia 101). By the end of 1939, more than one-quarter of a million people were in jail for political reasons. This often entirely arbitrary slaughter left more than 100,000 dead and achieved its goal of terrifying most of those who survived into silent submission for decades.[5]

Everyone was investigated. The "Ley de Responsabilidades Políticas" ("Law of Political Responsibilities") of 1939 held people responsible for their party membership and political activities and ideas as far back as 1934, two years before the war. Then in 1940, Franco formally involved the civilian population in the regime's apparatus of terror by launching the Causa General ("General Cause"). This required people to denounce their neighbours' political, material, and moral crimes during the war. Those who did so benefited by looking above suspicion themselves. Informants were rewarded with good jobs during a time of desperate hunger. People denounced neighbours whose job or house they coveted. No one could be trusted (Casanova "Una Dictadura" 30–1). The terror thus meant radical isolation for those on the losing side. Many members of their communities had died at the front or by execution, or were in exile or jail. The regime very deliberately broke up social and political networks by condemning Spanish Republicans not considered dangerous enough to execute to internal exile, banishing them to a distant province where they knew no one.

The terror went so deep that it far outlasted the forty years of the Franco regime. But the victors were not content to reduce the vanquished to silence. They constantly humiliated them, treating them as subhuman and denying them personhood, in an attempt to crush their spirit.[6] This treatment included insulting, threatening, and beating them, forcing them to drink castor oil, and shaving women's heads and parading them through town. But it also included more lasting forms of harassment, such as taking away their land. Many committed suicide because they could not stand the constant brutality; Francisco Moreno Gómez indicates that the suicide rate in the first years following the war was 30 per cent higher than in previous years.[7]

The denial of personhood was systematic and pervasive. The regime considered the working class and all others who had fought against Franco to be a "cancer on the body of Spain" that must be extirpated (Richards 44). Richards notes that during the civil war, the Francoist side referred to the enemy as "'inferior to animals' or 'inhuman': 'turbio' (restless, disturbed, as well as 'sediment' or 'sludge'); 'escoria' (scum), 'encenagado' (depraved); 'inmundo' (foul); 'hediondo' (stinking); 'sucio' (dirty, filthy, vile); 'baba' (slime); 'cochambre' (filthy, disgusting); 'detritus' (detritus, waste); 'tiniebla' (dark, 'black ignorance')" (48). In the postwar period, the label "Red" "implied not simply a previous leftist political affiliation but a 'dirtiness' or apartness, to be outcast"[8] (48).

The denial of personhood was part of the regime's effort to eradicate competing ideologies and beliefs from Spanish soil. The intention was to break the spirit of the defeated by humiliating them, to compel them to abandon their most cherished values, and to replace these with Francoist beliefs. The regime realized that it could not kill all dissenters, for it needed a labour force. It began a rhetoric and a practice of "re-educating" Republican prisoners so that they could redeem themselves for what was seen as their collective sin. Historian Javier Tusell put it this way: "El que pensaba diferente era un pecador" (*Rejas en la memoria*) ("Those who thought differently were defined as sinners"). Historian Angela Cenarro Lagunas explained the regime's goal: "El objetivo fundamental es que lo que sale de la cárcel sea sustancialmente diferente de lo que entró.

El precio para formar parte de la Nueva España es haber renunciado a su identidad, a lo más íntimo del ser humano" ("The main objective was that what came out of jail must be substantially different from what went in. The price for being part of the New Spain was to have renounced one's own identity, the most intimate part of being human") (*Rejas en la memoria*). A propaganda film of the time shows a man opening the closed fist of Socialism to form a Fascist salute – a filmic equivalent of what the Francoists aspired to do to the minds of their prisoners (*Rejas*).

This treatment put the defeated at risk emotionally in multiple and cumulative ways. First, they lived in a state of chronic terror. As we know from the work of therapists who risked their lives to help terrorized people under the Pinochet dictatorship in Chile (1973–90), and under the military junta in Argentina (1976–83), collective fear has devastating psychological consequences. People are cumulatively terrorized by the deaths and the torture they have witnessed or heard about. As well, because power is exercised arbitrarily, people are unable to predict the consequences of their own behaviour. They may be arrested for a word or a kiss out of place, or for something they did perfectly legally before the dictatorship began. They never know what is safe and what is not. They lose their ability to cope with or gauge reality, and they begin to apply a generalized anxiety to everyday activities. Lack of reliable information allows terrifying fantasies to add to the torment of the real threats to safety (Salimovich et al. 76). Ongoing fear, experienced over many years, can break people's spirits, reducing them to a numb, hollowed-out state (Lechner 26). Furthermore, when the human fear response, meant to be short-lived, lasts months or years, it undermines the immune function and thus has been linked to diseases such as cancer and heart disease, autoimmune disorders, and anxiety disorders (Gaynor 62).

A second emotional threat to survival was posed by the cumulative, traumatic bereavements experienced throughout the 1940s by many on the war's losing side. Even in times of democracy, bereavement carries its own threat to survival: widows and widowers are significantly more likely to die in the first six months after bereavement than others of their age group, and 75 per cent of these deaths are due to heart disease, which led one group of researchers to call their study "Broken Heart."[9] The sudden, violent executions under Franco made it likely that the bereaved survivors would suffer from a condition called "complicated grief," diagnosed when the bereaved person, more than a year after the loss, continues to have symptoms that are present for a limited time in "normal" grieving. These include uncontrollable memories of the deceased, symptoms of separation distress such as yearning for and searching for the person who died, and a sense of purposelessness and futility. The bereaved survivor's ability to function in daily life is significantly impaired. Complicated grief has been linked to serious physical and mental health problems, such as increased suicidality, heart disease, cancer, and high blood pressure. Sufferers often develop psychiatric disorders such as major depression or panic disorder (Prigerson et al.; Melham et al. 885). The most important factor determining whether an individual's grief will become complicated is his or her support system, and the defeated in Franco's Spain were quite deliberately deprived of such support. The defeated, then, faced a lethal double bind: they were in immediate physical danger if they mourned their dead, so repressing their grief was often essential as a matter of short-term survival; yet not mourning had physical and psychological consequences that threatened their health and ability to function.

A third major emotional threat to survival was traumatic stress syndrome, a result of experiencing terror in conditions in which one is helpless to act to change the situation. The effect of trauma is summarized in the title of Ronnie Janoff-Bulman's book, *Shattered Assumptions.* Traumatic events destroy the ability of survivors to trust others, their basic beliefs in their personal safety, and their assumptions about the world as a benevolent place where events are predictable and have meaning (Ruiz Vargas 307). As psychologist José María Ruiz Vargas notes, the shattering of assumptions was even more devastating in the context of the Spanish Civil War and the ensuing repression, because those perpetrating the atrocities were often not strangers, but neighbours or even family members (316).

Long after safety has been restored, trauma survivors may be subject to uncontrollable, vivid flashbacks in which they relive the traumatic event with all its original, overwhelming intensity. Post-traumatic stress disorder (PTSD) involves changes in brain chemistry so that a person's neural "alarm system" becomes heightened. Traumatized people thus react to ordinary events "as though they were emergencies" (Goleman 204). They are hypervigilant, permanently "on guard" (Ruiz Vargas 310). Trauma survivors tend to constrict their lives so as to avoid people, places, or activities that might trigger intrusive memories of the terror (Herman 46). Those who cannot consciously remember what happened tend to oscillate between being flooded with terrifying emotions, and becoming numb and feeling nothing (47). But even those who remember perfectly what happened to them are tormented by especially vivid memories that do not fade over time (Ruiz Vargas 304–5). PTSD has been shown to increase the likelihood of suicide, as well as of a range of illnesses, including cardiovascular illness and digestive disorders (Friedman and McEwen 172; Green and Kimeling 23).

Psychiatrists have noted differences in symptoms between survivors of a single traumatic event and those who lived under totalitarian control for a prolonged time. The symptoms of what is now known as "complex post-traumatic stress disorder" include alterations in consciousness in the form of flashbacks or rumination on the traumatic events; a sense of helplessness or paralysis of initiative; shame, guilt, and self-blame; persistent distrust, including alterations in intimate relationships; and a loss of sustaining faith (Herman 121). The survivor risks being emotionally paralyzed, stuck at the time of the trauma.

Complex PTSD has as its core feature a kind of "mental death," defined as "the loss of the victim's pretrauma identity ... characterized by loss of core beliefs and values, distrust, and alienation from others, shame and guilt, and a sense of being permanently damaged" (Ebert and Dyck 617). As the authors note, it is the deliberate intention of totalitarian regimes to create such a "living dead, whose brokenness is intended to serve as a deterrent to others" (618).[10]

Trauma is at the foundation of the other two important emotional threats to survival explored in this book: terror and mourning. My approach to trauma throughout this study differs in several respects from those of trauma theories in wide use in cultural studies, such as those of Cathy Caruth.[11] First, I focus less on the philosophical and hermeneutic questions posed by trauma, and more on clinical questions having to do with the psychological work of mourning and recovery. Second, the very name given in European and Anglo-American scholarship to the symptoms resulting from trauma needs modification. As David Becker has noted, the term "post-traumatic stress disorder" is inadequate to describe situations under a dictatorship, in which the terror is ongoing; thus the work of clinicians treating patients during the Chilean and Argentine dictatorships will be especially relevant for this study (Becker 100).

A third distinction is that trauma in Franco's Spain was not just an individual matter; it was also a collective one. It is likely that a significant proportion of the Spanish population suffered from symptoms of traumatic stress during the postwar period.[12] José María Ruiz Vargas, a professor of psychology at Madrid's Autónoma University, who specializes in memory, estimates that, based on what we now know about the prevalence of PTSD among combat veterans, about 40 per cent of those who fought in the Spanish Civil War would have developed such symptoms (Ruiz Vargas 309). In addition, many civilians would have been traumatized by the bombing of their homes and by the horrifying deaths of their loved ones in those bombings. And after the war, many more people were subjected to multiple additional traumatizing events, such as being tortured or beaten; witnessing the execution or torture of their loved ones; hearing the fusillades of the firing squads every night; living with death threats; having their homes broken into; and much more.

Notions of individual trauma do not account for circumstances like these. Ignacio Martín-Baró coined the term "psychosocial trauma" in the context of the civil war in El Salvador to describe traumatic experiences affecting an entire population and its social context (292). Similarly, in Pinochet's Chile, psychotherapists refined the concept of trauma to include different degrees of traumatization, ranging from the person who directly experiences the violence (primary traumatization) through the person who is traumatized by witnessing violence against a loved one (secondary traumatization) to the observer who has no direct emotional ties to the victim of the violence, such as a neighbour or a therapist (tertiary traumatization). The fact that traumatizing events are frequent under dictatorship is also important, for there is no way that a traumatized individual can rebuild trust (Agger and Buus Jensen 68–9).

These findings from Latin American dictatorships have led me to broaden my understanding of who can be considered traumatized. The basic definition of PTSD tends to centre on those individuals who cannot consciously remember the traumatic experience and therefore experience terrifying flashbacks in which the repressed material erupts into consciousness in fragmentary form. Yet it is not the case that those who *do* remember the horrific events they experienced are not traumatized. Even in North America, clinicians paint a more complicated picture of the relationship between trauma and memory than is sometimes done in trauma theory. Art therapist Linda Chapman observes that there is great variation in the degree to which different clients who have undergone traumatic experiences will dissociate. According to her, factors that might explain why a particular trauma survivor does or does not dissociate include the survivor's degree of biological resilience; the presence or absence of prior traumas; and whether the survivor had an adequate support system or a strong religious or political framework for making meaning out of the experience.[13] Clinical psychologist Jodie Waisberg describes the relationship between trauma and dissociation this way: "If someone is dissociating a lot there is a very high chance that he/she has undergone trauma, but the reverse isn't necessarily true. Just because someone has undergone trauma doesn't mean they will necessarily dissociate."[14] What links those who remember the trauma and those who have repressed the memory of it is that the traumatic memory appears to be "engraved" on the brain with a special intensity that makes it indelible (Ruiz Vargas 304–6). Whether remembered consciously, or intruding in the form of uncontrollable flashbacks, it will haunt the survivor and produce a number of the symptoms associated with traumatic stress.

In postwar Spain, the defeated were in a situation that, far from promoting recovery from the symptoms of traumatic stress, compounded those symptoms, thus ensuring they would become chronic. According to psychologist José María Ruiz Vargas, the amount of support received from society and family is directly related to the severity of PTSD symptoms that a survivor will experience and to the speed with which he or she will recover (327). As Ruiz Vargas eloquently expresses it, the key factor is the word:

> La primera ayuda fundamental para cualquier víctima sobreviviente de una situación infernal gira en torno a la palabra ... La víctima necesita saber ... que no está sola, que tiene una familia y unos amigos a su lado para apoyarla y protegerla, que es aceptada por el grupo… No hay vía más rápida y eficaz para ello que las primeras palabras: palabras de bienvenida, palabras de solidaridad con su dolor, palabras de ánimo. (327)

> The first fundamental kind of support for any survivor of an infernal situation has to do with the word ... The victim needs to know ... that he is not alone, that he has family and friends at his side to support and protect him, that he is accepted by the group ... There is no faster or more effective way to convey this than the first words: words of welcome, words of solidarity with his pain, words of encouragement.

The second crucial factor, says Ruiz Vargas, is the opportunity for the victim to tell his story, to turn the trauma into words, thereby modifying the "associative networks of fear" in the brain (331–2). But the Francoist repression made both social support and the telling of one's story impossible for most of the defeated. And those relatives and friends who remained in one place knew better than to talk to one another, for to do so would have been to risk arrest and worse, given Franco's command that all Spaniards inform the authorities of the political activities of their neighbours. Thus, they were often forced to bear their heavy emotional burdens without speaking of them to anyone.

One of the main things being kept quiet was the truth of the many murders of Republicans, and people's grief and anger about them. The silence was so thick that for decades, those whose loved ones lay in ditches did not talk about it even to their own family members. One example among countless others is recounted by survivors in the documentary *Víctimas todavía* (*Still Victims*), made in 2005. Samuel and Antonio grew up together as best friends in the small town of Almansa. They went to camp together, worked together, lived near each other, and saw each other all the time. Yet they never told each other that their fathers had been executed right after the war's end.

Ruiz Vargas asked one survivor, RM, whether he had told his family of his experiences when he returned from a Francoist concentration camp. RM replied that he had told no one, that it was not safe to open one's mouth, not at home because informants were listening at the door, and not in public because everyone was constantly watched. RM characterizes this situation with these chilling words: "Allí no podíamos nosotros abrir la boca ... ni allí ni en ningún sitio. ¡Si las personas estábamos, como quien dice, 'muertos'! ... ¡Si estaba todo el mundo muerto! Si no podías referir nada de nada. Ni juntarnos ni unirnos ni nada" ("We couldn't open our mouths: not there, not anywhere. We were like dead people! ... Everyone was dead! You couldn't tell anything whatsoever. We couldn't get together at all") (Ruiz Vargas 332–3).

As Ruiz Vargas notes, RM's words recall the term "mental death" used by Ebert and Dyck to describe the core feature of complex PTSD. RM was not the only one to describe having experienced psychological death. Unexu Álvarez was only a small boy when he was taken to the orphanage of Auxilio Social after his father was put in jail as a "Red." He summarized the impact of this: "Me lo robaron todo, me robaron el transcurrir de mi vida, que hubiera sido otra. A mí me mataron en el 36. Soy un muerto" ("They stole everything from me, they stole my life history, which would have been different. They killed me in '36. I am a dead man").[15]

Here again, the defeated faced a double bind in their efforts to stay alive. They had to keep quiet to avoid immediate physical harm. Yet, as researchers have discovered, isolation and keeping painful secrets create long-term emotional problems and increase the threat of disease and mortality; this is the case even under democracy. In his book *Emotional Intelligence,* Daniel Goleman reviews scientific research indicating that one of the most dramatic health threats to human beings is isolation, which significantly increases the risk of death. As Goleman reports, "studies done over two decades ... show that social isolation – the sense that you have nobody with whom you can share your private feelings or have close contact – doubles the chances of sickness or death. Isolation itself ... is as significant to mortality rates as smoking, high blood pressure, high cholesterol, obesity, and lack of physical exercise" (178). As experiments by James Pennebaker with other researchers have shown, keeping painful or traumatic experiences secret undermines the immune system and increases the probability of illness.[16]

In his documentary *Canciones para después de una guerra* (*Songs for After a War*), Basilio Martín Patino has the voiceover of an elderly man underscore the oppressive nature of the silence:

> Aquel silencio. Aquel prolongado y aturdido silencio. Aquel terrible silencio ... Un silencio lejano, fuerte, oscuro como las noches sin dormir, o como el hambre, o como tanto callar.
>
> That silence. That prolonged and stunned silence. That terrible silence ... A silence that was distant, thick, dark like nights without sleep, or like hunger, or like so much keeping quiet.

Carmen Martín Gaite, too, refers to "un silencio artificial, un hueco a llenar urgentemente de lo que fuera" ("an artificial silence, a gap that had urgently to be filled with anything at all") (*El cuarto* 153).

The danger, then, was that in the face of daily humiliations, the defeated would internalize the Francoists' vilifying view of them, would regard their own lives and beliefs with shame, and, unable to articulate alternative beliefs due to the enforced silence, would cease to exist psychologically. Faced with these attempts to annihilate their former being and their humanity, leftist prisoners made concerted efforts to retain them. They were living in unspeakable conditions in overcrowded prisons. But they had one advantage that the defeated outside the prison walls did not: one another. María Salvo, who spent sixteen years in prison, recalls: "Por encima de todo, nosotras estábamos imbuidas de que teníamos que mostrar a la prisión que éramos personas que conservábamos en todo momento nuestras ideas y nuestra dignidad" ("Above all, we were determined to show the prison guards that we were people and that we retained our ideas and our dignity at all times") (*Rejas*).

These emotional threats to survival were inseparable from an existential threat: the danger of feeling that life no longer had meaning. The silence of the postwar period left the defeated alone to face what has been described as a terrifying void. In voiceover, an elderly woman in Martín Patino's *Canciones* states that songs were used to "sobreponerse a la oscuridad, el vacío, el miedo" ("overcome the darkness, the void, the fear"). Martín Gaite, too, speaks of songs as keeping at bay "el horror al vacío" ("the terror of the void") ("Cuarto a espadas" 171). The void, for the defeated, meant the loss of their known world, in the form of the absence of their loved ones, the destruction of their physical surroundings, and the elimination of their former way of life. It involved the loss of their ability to live according to their values. And for the many who had been traumatized by the horrors of the war and the atrocities of the postwar years, it also involved the disruption of their ability to compose a narrative of who they were and how they envisaged the future. The triumphal rhetoric of the Franco regime, utterly divorced from what people were actually experiencing, meant that the defeated could not find validation for their own experience, and this made such a narrative all the more difficult to construct. In *Man's Search for Meaning*, psychiatrist Viktor Frankl developed a theory of survival based on his experiences in the Nazi concentration camp of Auschwitz. He argued that meaning was the most basic human survival need. Many in postwar Spain must have found it difficult to find such meaning, and this existential void may have been an even greater threat to the survival of the defeated than the hunger and the material privations they suffered.

II. Camouflage: Playing Imposed Roles for Physical Survival

When the civil war ended in 1939, Pilar Primo de Rivera, head of the Women's Section of the Falange, told her followers that their next task was to teach all the Republican women who were considered redeemable what the values of the Falange were, and to do so in a way that would make them cease to exist in their former identity: "Tenemos que meterles tan dentro de sí ese espíritu nuestro, que lleguen a olvidarse de su procedencia" ("We have to imbue them so deeply with our values, that they come to forget where they came from") (20). Under Franco's regime of terror, the defeated were forced to play the roles the Francoists laid out for them. But as they erased all visible traces of their forbidden beliefs and desires, they risked the erosion of their sense of self. The very obedience in behaviour, dress, gestures, and words that helped keep them physically safe worked psychologically to undermine them.[17]

People play roles under democracy, too. In fact, many psychotherapists view the human personality as a collection of roles. Practitioners of psychodrama (Jacob Moreno, Blatner) and drama therapy (Landy, Jennings) argue that the human personality develops from infancy precisely by playing roles, as children imitate behaviours observed in the outside world. But even in childhood, human beings do not simply reproduce mechanically what they observe in others. They introduce their own personal style and innovations and may even redefine a role altogether. The important thing for emotional health is that the individual have a range of options for which roles to play, as well as room for individual expression in the way he or she plays each one.

Under Franco, however, most of the roles people played were forced on them, with little or no margin for individual variation. Even the most minuscule behaviours were mandated from above, and the tiniest deviation could result in fines, humiliations, beatings, jailing, or worse. People refined their talent for role play, schooling themselves to give a perfect rendition of what the Francoists expected. Their lives often depended on how well they played the imposed roles and how effectively they repressed spontaneous manifestations of other, forbidden aspects of their personality and values.

One set of imposed roles came from the Catholic Church. Because the regime saw Spain as an essentially Catholic country, the largely anticlerical working class and liberal middle class were now forced to appear at mass and to participate in the many religious practices that the regime had placed at the centre of public life:

> El ciudadano se veía impelido a hacer pública ostentación de virtud. La vida social se centró en las prácticas religiosas ... Durante toda la década y buena parte de la siguiente menudearon Santas Misiones, Via Crucis, Adoraciones Nocturnas, manifestaciones eucarísticas, ejercicios espirituales, procesiones ... Peregrinaciones, visitas a los sagrarios ... entronizaciones de vírgenes.

> Citizens found themselves required to show their virtue publicly. Social life was centred around religious practices ... During the entire decade and most of the next one there proliferated a series of Holy Missions, Via Crucis, Nocturnal Adorations, Eucharistic ceremonies, spiritual exercises, processions ... pilgrimages, visits to the shrines ... enthronements of Virgins. (Eslava Galán 71)

Other roles were imposed by the Falange, Spain's Fascist Party, which was the only permitted political organization under Franco. As the Nationalists took control of cities and towns during the civil war, the streets became crammed with people wearing the blue shirt of the Falange, which soon came to be known as a "life preserver." One survivor of the period recalled being arrested in by the Francoist authorities. The man who came to get him was decked out in the cap, blue shirt, and yoke-and-arrows insignia of the Falange. A few days earlier, that man had been a Republican lieutenant with whom the arrested man had often gone out drinking. During the war, this lieutenant had been in charge of disciplining the right-wing prisoners held in the town (*Víctimas todavía*).

Fascist roles were imposed on people both inside and outside jail. One man in the town of Almansa (Albacete) recalls that in jail, prisoners had to sing the Falangist anthem "Cara al sol" ("Face to the Sun") three times a day. Another man adds:

> Eso no se podía evitar, en ningún sitio. Había que confesar, y había que comulgar, y era obligado. O sea que no podías decir que no; te formaban y teniás que ir.
>
> You couldn't avoid that anywhere. And you had to confess, and you had to take communion. It was compulsory. You couldn't say no. They made you line up, and you had to go. (*Víctimas todavía*)

Children were forced to attend Falange summer camps, where they were required to perfect these roles and to memorize the doctrine behind them. Those who lived in the orphanages of the Falange-run social services agency Auxilio Social were forced to play Falangist roles publicly. Unexu Álvarez points to the mental contradictions this entailed for him as a small boy during the war:

> Mi padre en la cárcel condenado a muerte y yo desfilando por las calles vestido como guardia de José Antonio con antorchas en la mano y celebrando invasiones de ciudades.
>
> There was my father in jail, condemned to death, and there I was, parading through the streets dressed up as one of José Antonio's guards, carrying torches, celebrating [the Nationalists'] invasion of cities. (Vinyes 136)

He recalls the attempts to fill his head and his activities with Francoist roles:

> No me enseñaron nada, sólo las cuatro reglas, leer y escribir, pero ni un oficio, nada. Eso sí, yo me sé todos los himnos épicos de Falange: "Cara al sol," "Yo tenía un camarada," "Prietas las filas" ... Y luego todo lo de la Iglesia ... Teníamos que ser como ellos. A mis dos hermanos les mentalizaron de tal manera que se hicieron curas, aunque luego se salieron.
>
> They didn't teach me anything, just the three "R"s, but not a trade or anything. But I do know all the epic anthems of the Falange: "Face to the sun," "I had a comrade," "Perfect ranks," from start to finish. And all the Church stuff ... We had to be like them. My two brothers were so brainwashed they became priests, although later they left the priesthood. (Vinyes et al., *Los niños perdidos,* 135–6)

The psychological cost of this false life was great. Álvarez describes it in terms of not having learned how to play normal social roles because of his incarceration in the orphanage:

> Perdí la infancia, la pubertad y no supe ser joven, no disfruté de la juventud. Tampoco aprendí a formarme como hombre, como esposo, como padre. ¿Cómo podía saber ser padre si nunca supe ser hijo? No tuve ningún rodaje ... Tengo setenta y un años y todavía soy un niño porque estoy sin realizar.
>
> I lost my childhood and puberty. I never learned how to be young, I didn't enjoy my youth. I also never learned how to be a man, a husband, a father. How could I know how to be a father when I never learned how to be a son? I had no script ... I'm 71 years old and I'm still a child because I never developed. (Vinyes 136)

Sometimes role play was quite literally necessary in order to eat. A man from Asturias, Juan Sánchez García, was a child when his Republican father was executed. Afterwards, as an orphan, he was sent to eat meals at the dining halls of Auxilio Social. He recalls: "Salíamos a los comedores, y si no levantabas bien la mano para cantar el 'Cara al sol,' te quedabas sin comer" ("When you entered the dining room, if you didn't raise your hand properly [in the Fascist salute] when singing 'Face to the Sun,' you didn't get to eat"). But hunger wasn't the only incentive to play the Fascist roles correctly. There was also fear. Juan recalls that the building where the children ate had three storeys. The Falange had its headquarters on the top floor, and the dining halls of Auxilio Social were on the bottom floor: "Desde abajo sentíamos los gritos de los que estaban arriba en Falange, de las torturas que hacían con ellos" ("We could hear from below the cries of those being tortured above our heads").[18]

Those lucky enough not to be in prison made the Fascist salute on the streets and sang the Fascist anthem with arm raised at every movie theatre. Hemlines, swear words, and physical contact among unmarried people were obsessively controlled. One man recounts how he spent six months in jail for using the word "Salud" to say goodbye instead of "Adiós." (*Víctimas*). "Salud" had been in use behind the Republican lines during the war in order to eliminate the reference to God in "Adiós." It would have become a habit over three years. But such habits had to be broken instantly to avoid jail.

It was women whose roles the new regime most needed to change if it was to stay in power. To perpetuate its new norms through the family, the Fascist regime derogated the laws of the Spanish Republic that had begun to better the lot of women; as a result, women were in many respects brought back to the nineteenth century. They were once again subject to the Civil Code of 1889, which gave men control over their wives' property and right to work (Scanlon 347). New laws were put in place to ensure that women stopped working once they married (321). Women who had been on the Republican side faced special persecution. They were regarded as immoral and perverse and as needing Catholic regeneration. After 1944, the courts pursued moral crimes such as abortion, prostitution, and adultery (Mir 129). They prosecuted "delitos contra la religión, la moral y las buenas costumbres, así como los delitos sexuales" ("crimes against religion, morality, and proper behaviour, as well as sexual offences") (160). Citizens were called upon to denounce not only the political activities of their neighbours, but also their sexual behaviour and other aspects of their private lives. Thus, through surveillance and indoctrination, the regime came to exert a remarkable degree of control over what people did, even in the privacy of their bedrooms (160). Role play was also required for women who wanted to enter the workforce or hold a passport. They were required to spend years in the "Servicio Social" ("Social Service") courses run by the Women's Section of the Falange. There, in uniform, they were obliged to learn the tiniest details of home management and were indoctrinated in their religious and patriotic mission as obedient wives and mothers.[19]

While the losers were being forced to act out the roles imposed on them, Spain's new rulers enthusiastically enacted roles they had chosen for themselves, roles that would justify their treatment of the enemy. During the war, Church officials such as Cardinal Isidro Gomá, Archbishop of Toledo and Primate of all Spain, had called the Francoist cause a "Crusade" (Preston 222–3). The Francoists themselves described the Spanish Civil War as a "Crusade," a re-enactment of the medieval "Reconquest" of Spain by the Christians from the infidel Moors. Medieval codes of conduct, according to which it was permissible to kill in the name of God, were invoked, and this justified the extermination of the Republicans. When Franco won the war, a solemn ceremony was held in the church of Santa Bárbara in which the Church bestowed upon him the Sword of Victory, as if he were a medieval warrior (*Rejas*). School textbooks compared Franco to the medieval warrior and epic hero El Cid, as did writings by Francoist intellectuals like Alvaro Cunqueiro and Eduardo Marquina.[20] In 1940, with Spain in ruins and most people hungry, the regime's intellectuals published a multivolume *Historia de la Cruzada Española* in huge, leather-bound tomes.[21] On the frontispiece was an engraving of a medieval warrior on horseback brandishing a flag.[22] The common people were encouraged to see themselves as part of Spain's glorious epic and imperial tradition through the regime's film industry, which made historical films about these periods. The public, by and large, preferred Hollywood.

The harshly imposed roles meant that the defeated had to repress their intense fear, grief, and anger, keeping their deepest feelings from showing through. They were being forced to act out feelings, words, and gestures that were antithetical to their actual beliefs and emotions. All of this would have been enormously draining. The regime's propagandists spoke constantly of cheerfulness, yet their rhetoric rang false. Carmen Martín Gaite recalls that in the obligatory Social Service classes, students were constantly being told to imitate Isabella, the Catholic queen, in her cheerfulness and incessant activity:

> Yo miraba aquel rostro severo ... que venía en los libros de texto, y lo único que no entendía era lo de la alegría, tal vez es que hubiera salido mal en aquel retrato, pero, desde luego, no daban muchas ganas de tener aquella imagen como espejo, claro que algunas de las monitoras que nos instaban a imitarla también tenían aquel rictus seco en la boca y aquella luz fría en los ojos, aunque hablaran continuamente de la alegría.

> I looked at that severe face ... in the textbook, and the only thing I didn't understand was the part about cheerfulness; maybe the picture just didn't come out well, but one sure didn't want to take that image as a model. Of course, some of the Monitors who urged us to imitate Isabella also had

> those same tight lips and that cold light in their eyes, even if they were constantly talking about happiness. (*El cuarto* 95–6)

On top of this, as the defeated acted out these false feelings, they would have experienced the shame and contamination of collaborating in their own execution, to use Azar Nafisi's term (Nafisi 76).

III. From Imposed Roles to Chosen Roles: Popular Culture as Camouflage

If the defeated were to survive psychologically in postwar Spain, they had to find a way to grapple with their real feelings of terror, grief, and trauma, the very experiences that the regime was denying and covering up. They needed to find a way to articulate their own experience in the absence of almost any external validation and despite the danger of speaking. And they also needed a reason to stay alive. I believe that the defeated met these challenges by using a different kind of role play, in which they took on chosen roles from Hollywood film and popular songs to help them maintain a distinct and dissident sense of self without putting themselves in further danger. Thus, of the four operations in which the defeated engaged when singing along with Conchita Piquer (role play, ritual, narrative, and music making), I believe that role play was the foundational mechanism, the one that permitted psychological survival and that allowed the other three operations to exist.

As is well known, the Franco regime viewed public entertainment as privileged ground for indoctrinating the masses. Many popular films and songs exalted all things Spanish, and historical films glorified Spain's imperial past. For the regime, an equally important function of mass cultural forms such as soccer, bullfighting, Hollywood film, radio serials, and popular music (both on the radio and live in travelling shows) was, as Vázquez Montalbán put it, to "despolitizar la conciencia social" ("depoliticize social consciousness") (*Crónica* 35). This undoubtedly worked to an extent. Although Spain was an extremely divided society after the civil war, it was not quite as starkly divided as has long been thought. Especially in cities, where greater anonymity was possible, friendships existed across political lines.[23] These might involve going to the movies together, or opening a door to make the radio available for the neighbours, regardless of political affiliation.[24] Spaniards on both sides loved the same songs.

Yet as writers such as Vázquez Montalbán, Martín Gaite, and Moix recall, not only did people exercise agency by choosing Hollywood films over Francoist historical propaganda films, but they also often used popular texts in ways the state did not anticipate.[25] Vázquez Montalbán makes clear that those on the left often used a line of a song as a coded way of expressing resistance: "qué agresivo puede ser el verso, 'del por qué de este por qué la gente quiere enterarse.' ... Había que oírlo cantado por las mujeres de la posguerra" ("The line, 'People want to know the reason for this enigma' could be very aggressive. You had to hear it sung by the women of postwar Spain") (36). This indicates that even if people on both sides sang the same songs, it did not necessarily mean they were using the songs in the same way. Vázquez Montalbán writes that however hard the Franco regime tried to manipulate the common people through popular texts, if those texts did not help satisfy the people's real needs, they simply were not accepted. He points out that the ultimate meaning of a popular text lies in the use to which it is put by those who consume it, and that the people often used songs in ways antithetical to what the Franco regime intended (*Cancionero* xvii).

Vázquez Montalbán's theory, published in the early 1970s, is founded on the same principles as that of Antonio Gramsci, whose theory of hegemony would be foundational in the British school of cultural studies. Both Vázquez Montalbán and Gramsci recognized that the dominant classes manipulated popular culture. But both also conceived of the receiver of the messages as active, critical, creative, and able to use the texts in ways their creators would never have intended.

When the defeated appropriated certain forms of popular culture for their own ends, the ways they used them involved a kind of role play that, rather than erasing the dissident self, functioned to ensure its survival. This use of role play involved agency, with the defeated choosing a role from popular culture that was at odds with the roles imposed on them by the regime. The defeated still used role play as camouflage, but in a new way: instead of concealing their real feelings, as they did when they played out the Francoist roles imposed on them, they used their chosen roles to express their true feelings, but under the pretence that they were simply expressing the feelings of the fictional character they were playing.

Engaging with popular culture afforded them opportunities for subversive declarations of individuality even before they actively imagined themselves in the role of a particular film star or song performer. The oral history project on filmgoing conducted by Jo Labanyi and other researchers has revealed the many small subversions people practised as part of their engagement with the cinema. The Fascist salute was obligatory in the cinema until 1945, and viewers were forced to view the regime's official newsreel (the NODO) before every film throughout the forty years of the dictatorship. Says Susan Martin-Márquez:

> Many leftist interviewees gleefully detail their efforts to avoid the fascist salute and the newsreel by choosing theatres with nooks and crannies for hiding, or strategizing to sit in an aisle seat and sneak off to the toilet at the opportune moment; others simply sought to arrive late or leave early (R.G., I.M., and A.L.) ... Officials quickly recognized and countered these tactics by posting party representatives near exits and toilets, or by playing the NODO at an unpredictable moment midway through a feature film, instead of at the beginning or the end. (F.B.) (118)

Sexual behaviour, severely punished under Franco, was also practised at the cinema despite significant risks; this forbidden behaviour was also politically charged.[26] The cinema became a space of contestation, the site of a struggle for control between Francoist officials shining their flashlights on offending couples and arresting them, and moviegoers paying off sympathetic ushers to turn a blind eye (Martin-Márquez 119).

Since reality was unremittingly oppressive, this intense engagement with a fictional world through mass entertainment became a way to affirm the clandestine self, to survive psychologically, without putting oneself in danger. The world of fiction provided alternative roles to those of the dictatorship. In the stories told in films, novels, and songs, the defeated could watch a protagonist struggle against society's strictures in ways that they themselves could not. They could remember, or learn for the first time, what possibilities existed for personal identity outside the oppressor's definitions. Only through the alternative reality of fiction could they get an idea of who they were capable of being.[27] There was a great degree of continuity among the various mass cultural forms, with singers starring in movies, fashion magazines using film stars to sell the latest clothing, and the radio playing songs people had first heard in a movie. This continuity worked to create an alternative reality, as mass culture offered Spanish consumers a repository of stories, icons, images, and models of behaviour that were clearly inconsistent with the official values of the regime.

Eva Woods has emphasized how important it was to some spectators to keep the sphere of the cinema completely separate from their everyday reality under Franco. This technique of "disconnect" allowed select interviewees in the oral history of cinemagoing project to "disavow any links between their identification with characters projected on screen ... and the socio-political climate of the 1940s and 1950s." Thus when they cried at the cinema, expending intense emotions in melodramatic films in a way that was generally impossible elsewhere, they did not have to recognize that they were crying about themselves, about the injustices and humiliations they were suffering outside the theatre ("Identification" 130). Woods also contends that denying the connection between the screen and their own lives gave spectators the freedom to identify with characters or plots that did not conform to their expected ideological, cultural, or gender roles. This freedom was crucial for the release of "latent emotions that could not be spent under dictatorship" (132). For example, a left-winger could identify with a Francoist character at the cinema and cry over the character's predicament.

Thus, in these times of terror, this small act of agency – choosing a fictional character to imitate or to identify with – became a way to affirm and develop the self. At a time when the defeated had no power to make even the smallest decisions (what to wear, what time to come home), the act of choosing to imitate a character who did not conform to the roles the regime imposed became a way for the defeated to keep on existing, and to keep alive the idea of freedom.

The difference between official and unofficial roles was obvious in the popular magazines of the period. Both men and women imitated Hollywood stars, but my examples here focus on women's roles. The sexless uniforms and the stultifying activities imposed by the Women's Section of the Falange could not have been more different from the glamorous images women found in film and fashion magazines.[28] The regime pressed women to emulate Pilar Primo de Rivera, founder of the Women's Section and sister of the founder of the Falange, José Antonio Primo de Rivera. Pilar stares out at us from the pages of the magazine *Y* "with her severe, plain hair and a sexless blazer" ("Pilar Primo de Rivera"). Under the direction of her *monitoras,* Spanish women wore uniforms with the yoke and arrows of the Falange; made the Fascist salute; recited the prescribed prayers; prayed for the fallen on the Francoist side; and learned the activities associated with being a good wife and mother: sewing, embroidery, weaving, and cooking.[29] Their future lives (if they can be called that) were mapped out in a calendar that described household duties that were to be carried out from seven a.m. to ten p.m. daily ("Calendario del ama de casa 1941"). The calendar outlined what they were to do each day, each week, and each month of the year. Thus middle-class women who under the Republic had considered a career, and working-class women who had been politically militant, were emphatically redirected toward making a home, which was presented as a never-ending job. The mournful expressions on the faces of women forced to take the Social Service courses in order to become teachers give an idea of their feelings about what they were being taught. ("Camaradas que asisten a este curso, en una de las clases"; "Algunas de las maestras opositoras que toman parte en este curso").

Meanwhile, Hollywood offered Spanish women the possibility of looking like Veronica Lake, who, with her cascading, shoulder-length "peekaboo" curls and sultry expression, flirted with the reader from the cover of the magazine *Semana* ("Veronica Lake"), or the glamorous Lana Turner doing the same in *Vestuario* ("Lana Turner"). Or, still more scandalously, they could imitate femme fatale Rita Hayworth in *Gilda* ("'Gilda,' la mujer que despertó la admiración del mundo entero"), a film that took Spain by storm in 1947 despite the protests of the Church. In that year, according to Francisco Umbral, women stopped doing their hair like the more innocent Deanna Durbin and started imitating Gilda's hairstyle; they also adopted her sexy, high-heeled shoes (Umbral, *Memorias de un niño de derechas* 128–9).[30]

Smoking was considered scandalous for women outside the major cities, yet the movies made it possible for them to see themselves as the glamorous smoking star ("El cigarillo, personaje del cinema"). And, in case the distance between themselves and the stars seemed too great, the magazines taught them how to make themselves up to look like them ("Las estrellas nos muestran el camino de la naturalidad"). One magazine, *Cámara,* offered detailed lessons: if your face was square, you could look like one star, if it was oval, like another, and so on. You just had to follow the steps provided for making yourself up ("Para ser bella ante el lienzo de plata"). And if women thought their lives were over as they listened to the never-ending propaganda and prescriptions of the Church and the "Movement," Joan Crawford was available to console them, declaring that "La vida empieza a los 40" ("Life begins at 40").

Hollywood, then, gave people hope that life could some day be both different and better. It did so by encouraging them to imagine themselves as film stars, outside Franco's Spain and subject to different codes of conduct. Carmen Martín Gaite recalls being inspired as a child by hearing that Deanna Durbin had gone to school on roller skates eating a lemon ice cream. This spontaneous conduct, so alien to the stiff, prescribed way of behaving for children in 1940s Spain, became her model of rebellion and freedom (*El cuarto* 59).

The invitation to role play through the cinema was omnipresent; in 1947, Spain had more movie theatres per capita than any other country except the United States (Marsh 114–15). It is no wonder that, as one magazine article reported, 40,000 people dreamed of being in the movies ("40,00 españoles…"). And people took up the invitation enthusiastically. In the oral history of cinemagoing directed by Jo Labanyi, interviewees recalled how children invented "guessing games based on acting out sequences from movies." A half-century later, the adults that Labanyi and her colleagues interviewed still had "an extraordinarily detailed recall of the films they watched – often slipping into an animated reenactment" ("Mediation" 106).[31]

III. Role Play through Songs

Hollywood's influence was massive. However, it had its limits as a source of socially acceptable adult role play. Adults were not socially permitted to play out the whole plot of a movie. They might borrow a line, a gesture, a hairdo, or a style of clothing. But the only acceptable way of playing out the story of a chosen character from beginning to end, in the first person, was by singing and acting out a radio song. This, I argue, was the only way to play the role of the other in a way sustained enough, and repeated enough, to do deep emotional work. It was also the only safe way to express feelings audibly, to break the silence that was so thick with fear. Both Basilio Martín Patino and Carmen Martín Gaite see postwar songs as intimately linked to this thick silence. Says Patino's male voiceover: "Sólo consigo recordar aquellas canciones acordándome del silencio" ("I can only remember those songs if I recall the silence") (*Canciones*). Later in the film, a female voiceover refers to songs as a balm for loneliness ("[Eran] canciones para tiempos de soledad"). Martín Gaite writes that the silence urgently needed to be filled with whatever came to hand, and concludes: "Y ese papel lo cumplieron las canciones" ("And that was the function of songs") ("Cuarto a espadas" 171).

When the defeated broke the silence in song, they did not have to forego imitating a glamorous film star with a cigarette, for on the cover of *Espectáculos* they could see the mesmerizing Conchita Piquer, in a wonderful portrait by the photographer Campúa, staring dreamily off into the distance as she holds a cigarette in the hand on which her chin is propped. ("Conchita Piquer"). For the popular music performers of the day not only performed live on stage, but also starred in films in which they sang their most famous songs. In Spain, *coplas* thus had some of the cachet of the cinema, while providing closer analogues to people's actual lives in postwar Spain than most Hollywood films.

Needless to say, the Franco regime tried to impose roles on people in the realm of song as well. It declared a "Día de la Canción" ("Day of the Song"), to be celebrated by the "Frente de Juventudes" ("Youth Front"), no doubt by singing Fascist favourites like "El novio de la muerte" ("Death's Fiancé") ("El 'Día de la Canción' y el Frente de Juventudes."). Women at university, organized through the government-directed University Students' Union, were compelled to attend camps where they sang the regime's songs ("Mujeres cantando"). And contests were sponsored for the best songs about the love of Mother or of Fatherland ("Los concursos de *Espectáculos*").

What people were really listening to, however, were the quintessentially Spanish *coplas,* as well as *boleros* from all over the Hispanic world. Both had their uses as survival tools. Vázquez Montalbán points out that the *bolero* "Amar y vivir," sung by the wildly popular Cuban Antonio Machín, contained a homespun philosophy ("Se vive solamente una vez") that was more useful than any philosophical treatise for the common people trying to get through the day in postwar Spain (*Crónica* 42). Even so, Carmen Martín Gaite singles out Piquer's *coplas* as the songs that broke through the "anaesthesia" of postwar Spain; in her view, *boleros* reinforced the regime's control. Piquer's heart-rending songs were unique, according to Martín Gaite, because they broke through the fake foundations for happiness that the regime was trying to lay down, to reveal the void they were trying to cover up and the real emotional pain that went with it (*El cuarto* 151–3). Vázquez Montalbán singles out five or six songs of the four hundred he includes in his *Cancionero general del franquismo* as "las más históricamente veraces y estéticamente mejores ... que traducen, como no lo consiguen todas las demás, las realidades de unas gentes" ("those which were truest to history and best aesthetically ... which convey, as none of the other songs manage to do, the lived reality of a people") (*Cancionero* xx). All of the songs he names were *coplas* written for Conchita Piquer.

IV. Piquer's Coplas as Survival Mechanisms: Unconscious Processes

Journalist Elvira Daudet described how the public responded to one of Piquer's first concerts after the war, in January 1940:

> El Teatro Calderón se viene abajo. El público (nunca un público ha sido tan homogéneo como en aquel estreno) demacrado, enfebrecido, aclama a su nuevo ídolo. Hace frío en Madrid, un frío penetrante que cala los huesos. Al salir del teatro, todos tararean dos de los estrenos de la noche, que se harían rápidamente populares, La Parrala y La Petenera. El sentimentalismo es un buen sucedáneo para acallar el propio dolor, como el recuelo de cebada tostada lo es del café.
>
> She brought down the Calderón Theatre. The emaciated, feverish audience (and never was there such a homogeneous audience as on that opening night), hails its new idol. It is cold in Madrid, a penetrating cold that goes right through to the bone. As they leave the theatre, everyone is humming two of the new songs performed that evening, which would rapidly become popular: "La Parrala" and "La Petenera." Sentimentality is a good substitute to keep one's own pain quiet, just as toasted barley, percolated, is a good ersatz coffee. (Plaza, *Conchita Piquer* 76)

Daudet was describing how this gaunt public, suffering from hunger, cold, and mental anguish, learned two new songs at Piquer's show that would help them deal with those physical and emotional difficulties. But her assertion that people used the sentimentality of these fictional stories to keep their own pain quiet is, I believe, only part of the story.

My own approach to what was happening when people sang along with Piquer is grounded in Freud's theory of the unconscious, particularly in his concepts of repression, projection, and working-through. Repression refers to the process "by which an unacceptable impulse or idea is rendered unconscious" (Rycroft 142). Even in democratic societies, people often repress painful feelings. This may be due to their particular personality, or to messages they receive in their family, workplace, or general culture regarding which emotions are permissible to express. However, as Freud and others have demonstrated, repressing feelings not only takes energy but can also lead eventually to physical illness and emotional problems (Pennebaker, Kiecolt-Glaser and Glaser; Pennebaker and Sussman; Goleman; Kemeny). Psychotherapists believe that people will seek an outlet for their repressed feelings to avoid this damage.[32] However, people also put up psychological defences against their own pain; thus they will resist talking directly about their own situation. The mechanism of projection comes into play to resolve the conflict. Projection is defined as "the process by which specific impulses, wishes, aspects of the self ... are imagined to be located in some object external to oneself" (Rycroft 126–7). Rycroft notes: "Projection of aspects of oneself is preceded by denial, i.e. one denies that one feels such and such an emotion ... but asserts that someone else does" (127). When we play the role of a character or engage with a character in a movie, the mechanism at work is projective identification, "the process by which a person imagines himself to be inside some object external to himself." We experience emotions vicariously through the character, while disavowing that those emotions are our own (67–8). According to Madeline Andersen-Warren and Roger Grainger, this is why drama therapy is so effective. When people act out the role of a fictional character, their defences against their own pain are bypassed. They project their own feelings onto the character, and this allows them to explore the feelings of the character much more deeply than they would ever dare to explore their own directly. Drawing on the work of drama therapist Robert Landy, Andersen-Warren and Grainger explain that the distance between a person and the character he plays acts as a kind of alibi that allows him to express his own feelings "in an undercover way. If I am this (the personage in the play) I cannot be accused of being that (the vulnerable person I feel myself to be). Thus the roles we take on in plays act like masks, encouraging us to take risks with ourselves" (Andersen-Warren and Grainger 87).

It is not necessary to act out the role of a fictional character in order to bypass our defences in this way. People often experience their own pain indirectly by crying for a character in a movie, onto whom that pain is projected. The character may have a very different biography from their own, yet may be grappling with similar issues or experiences. Those in the audience make the connection and become emotional. Yet they are not always aware of why they are crying. This unconscious projection is at the root of our engagement with the arts in general.

The defeated in the Franco dictatorship had additional reasons for taking an indirect approach to their painful feelings. First, it was not politically safe to express those feelings, so the oppressed person had to keep them hidden in order to stay safe from immediate physical harm. The second reason related to emotions. Under Franco's regime of terror, individuals were powerless to do anything to change their situation.

They could not solve the problem of the ongoing repression, nor could they do anything to prevent their loved ones from being murdered. According to psychologist Terry Vance, in such circumstances, for the defeated to experience the full brunt of their terror or grief directly would have been psychologically overwhelming in a way that might not be the case for an individual in circumstances that he or she did have the power to change.[33] Yet keeping these intense feelings repressed would have taken a heavy emotional toll. In such a context, indirect means of expression – the only ones possible in the circumstances – would have become even more crucial to avoid the threats to mental and physical health involved in repressing the feelings. This may explain Eva Woods' finding that a number of interviewees in the oral history of cinemagoing project categorically denied any connection between their real lives and those of the characters on the screen ("Identification and Disconnect").

People repress their own pain in part because they are afraid that if they were to feel the pain, it would be inexhaustible, a bottomless pit from which they would never emerge. The final Freudian concept central to this study is that of working-through, the process of coming to terms with painful feelings piecemeal, bit by bit, in successive psychotherapy sessions with time limits built in. Freud describes this process in relation to the work of mourning, which is "carried out bit by bit, at great expense of time and cathectic energy… Each single one of the memories and expectations in which the libido is bound to the object is brought up and hypercathected, and detachment of the libido is accomplished in respect of it." Once this long process is completed, the person is freed up to form new attachments and to move on from the loss (Freud "Mourning and Melancholia" 244–5).

Freudian ideas about the workings of the unconscious have been taken up in a variety of kinds of psychotherapy that draw on the four operations central to this study. For example, rituals play a central role in bereavement therapies designed to help people work through the mourning process. And the creative arts therapies play a key role in treating individuals suffering from traumatic stress. Here, the indirect approach to repressed feelings is especially important. Conventional "talk" therapy entails the risk that as survivors begin to recall the traumatic events directly, they may be retraumatized. Yet if they are to recover, these traumatic memories must be activated. Cognitive-behavioural therapists suggest that the terrifying memories must be evoked in a context in which new information is provided that is incompatible with some of the elements that exist in the feared memory, so that a new memory can be formed (Foa, Steketee, and Rothbaum 167). This concept is called reformulation (Littrell).

The creative arts therapies allow the trauma survivor to approach the memories less directly, through art, fictional stories, theatre, or music. This allows the brain to create new associative networks for the feelings. Psychologist David Read Johnson, co-director of the Post Traumatic Stress Center in New Haven, Connecticut, has used the creative arts in therapy with Vietnam War veterans, among other populations. He asserts that the creative arts therapies are helpful during all three stages of recovery from trauma: accessing the traumatic memories; working through or reconceptualizing the trauma; and reintegrating into the larger society (8). Using art, music, theatre, or dance allows the patient to "play out at arm's length" the feelings associated with the trauma. This allows survivors both to deny that the feelings are their own, and to remain in control of the feelings as they are played out. Johnson also notes that the creative arts therapies allow for repetition: "each allows a re-working of traumatic experience, over and over again, at times indirectly, at times directly" (11).[34]

I will be approaching Piquer's tragic *coplas* as key vehicles for releasing emotions that otherwise would have been too painful and too dangerous to express. I believe that many among the defeated, by identifying with the characters in these *coplas* and projecting their own feelings onto them, were able to work through some of their fear and grief as they sang them over and over again through the years, breaking the stifling silence. As they co-created the fictional stories of the protagonists along with Piquer, they addressed their own traumatic stories and began to repair them.

We have seen in this chapter that the defeated faced a well-coordinated apparatus whose goal was to annihilate them physically and psychologically. The repression had devastating, cumulative emotional consequences, including chronic terror, blocked mourning, and traumatic stress syndrome. All three of these emotional burdens threatened the physical and mental health of the defeated. At their extreme, they could produce a kind of "mental death." The most important factor in recovery from such experiences, social support, was also absent; the silence in itself constituted a powerful emotional threat, for the defeated could neither tell anyone what had happened to them nor receive words of support from others. Role play became a central mechanism in the effort to stay alive amidst the persecution and the silence. To stay alive physically, the defeated said the words and made the gestures of the oppressor, concealing their real ideas and feelings; to stay alive psychologically, they expressed their dissident feelings and desires indirectly, by playing chosen roles from popular culture. While they identified strongly with the cinema, especially Hollywood film, it was songs that allowed them not just to enter an alternative world but to break the thick silence as they did so. Conchita Piquer's *coplas* offered them the chance to play out the tragic story of a character in role from beginning to end, to project their own feelings onto the character and work them through. Now it is time to explore where these *coplas* came from and what it was about their form, content, and performance that made people single them out as especially important in the effort to survive psychologically.

Chapter Two

An Introduction to the *Copla* and Its Star Performer

In Franco's Spain, the composers and performers of *coplas* were on the winning side. The songs were broadcast on the regime's radio. Yet the defeated were nevertheless able to use many *coplas* of the 1940s to meet their own desperate emotional needs. What exactly were *coplas,* and how could both winners and losers love them when they agreed on almost nothing else? How did these songs lend themselves to a double reading that might make them useful to both sides? What features of the form and content of certain famous *coplas* authored by Rafael de León made them especially powerful and especially safe vehicles for working through feelings that otherwise could not be expressed? And what was it about Conchita Piquer and her performances that made them so memorable, as well as so crucial to the effort of emotional survival?

North American readers can understand the *copla* in terms of its analogies to two important American genres: country music, and the jazz standards of the American songbook. The *coplas* of Rafael de León are like country music in that they are narratives, telling a story from beginning to end (Tichi 7). Both genres tell of people down on their luck and in emotional pain. Both are associated with a certain region – the American South for country music, southern Spain (Andalucía) for *coplas;* yet each genre is popular all over the country.

But it is American jazz standards that are perhaps the closest equivalent of Spanish *coplas.* For despite the relentless succession of fashions in the pop music industry, both jazz standards and *coplas* have never ceased to be listened to since they appeared, well over half a century ago. People still love the classic performers of each genre (Ella, Louis, Billie Holiday ..., and Conchita Piquer, Juanita Reina, Miguel de Molina ...), and in each case, new artists have arisen who record the old standards with new inflections or accompaniments.

Coplas and jazz occupy analogous positions in the history of the popular music of their respective countries. Jazz, conveyed to millions on the radio, made popular a kind of music that had originated in work songs sung by blacks in the fields, which later became the blues. Whites began to listen to jazz on the radio in the 1920s, when radio listening swept the United States. Black jazz music was then "co-opted, domesticated, and often bastardized" by white bands (Douglas 85). The jazz standards we know and love were sung in their classic renditions by black performers who usually had grown up dirt-poor and who were subject to the demeaning segregation of Jim Crow no matter how famous they became. The songs were written by whites who were privileged in some ways, yet members of oppressed and marginalized groups themselves: the Jewish Irving Berlin and George and Ira Gershwin, the gay Cole Porter. In the classic recordings of the American songbook, orchestras replaced the original instruments of jazz. The music went from South to North, from rural to urban, from oppressed blacks to privileged whites, being transformed all the while. These songs became America's first pop music.[1]

Coplas were Spain's first pop music. They exist in the same relation to flamenco that the jazz standards do to the blues.[2] Flamenco began as *cante jondo* ("deep song"), a deeply emotional, guttural kind of song that began to be performed in southern Spain in the mid-nineteenth century by persecuted gypsies and non-gypsy peasants.[3] Andalucía was a region of hunger and suffering for landless peasants with no political voice, and these songs expressed the anguish of oppression.[4] Beginning about 1850, the music became commercialized in *cafés cantantes,* where performers could be paid for their singing and dancing and where a broader audience discovered flamenco.[5] Eventually, in a more domesticated form, it made its way onto large, urban stages. And its characteristic rhythms and styles (such as *siguiriya* and *soleare*) were appropriated by privileged Andalusian composers like Rafael de León and Manuel Quiroga, who based themselves in Madrid in the 1930s and who merged these flamenco forms with other musical and poetic traditions to create *coplas.*[6] The guitar accompaniment of flamenco was replaced by an orchestra. The fact that the greatest of the *copla* songwriters, Rafael de León, was gay, again suggests parallels to the privileged-yet-marginalized status of those who created the American songbook. *Coplas* would become wildly popular in the 1930s as the radio began to enter homes across the country; they had their golden age in the 1940s.

The Development of the *Copla* Form

The *copla,* or *canción española,* which had its heyday in the 1940s, was an amalgam of popular, mass, and high-cultural genres that united new forms with traditional ones. *Coplas* were simultaneously poetry, narrative, music, theatre, and sometimes dance. They drew on traditional folklore but also on the highbrow poetry and classical music of the twentieth century, which themselves had appropriated popular forms. Thus the postwar *copla* was an exceptionally rich middlebrow compendium of traditions dating back many centuries in several genres.

Coplas were performed in urban theatres by an orchestra, with one singer and a few props on the stage. Their deepest roots, however, were in the oral tradition of popular poetry and song that had been the means of expression and historical memory of the common people of Spain since the Middle Ages (Vázquez Montalbán *Cancionero* xii–xv). Indeed, the word *copla* refers to a particular form of popular poetry: four-line stanzas with assonant rhyme in the even-numbered lines, with eight syllables per line. This form, which is as old as Spanish literature itself, has many variants. The Andalusian flamenco tradition of *cante jondo,* which so influenced the *copla,* is an example of this poetic tradition. A *cante jondo* has four-line verses and is typically sung in taverns to the accompaniment of the guitar (Acosta Díaz et al. 37). In his songs, Rafael de León made use of popular medieval poetic forms such as the *copla,* the ballad (a narrative told in eight-syllable lines of verse), and medieval love poetry from the *cancioneros.*[7]

The highbrow poetic genre from which the *copla* drew was the lyric poetry of the Generation of 1927, which included Federico García Lorca and Rafael Alberti, both from Andalucía. Many of these poets were fascinated by popular poetry, by Andalusian folklore and *cante jondo.*[8] They collected popular ballads and transcribed Andalusian songs, perhaps in reaction against the modern international influences of *cuplé,* tango, and jazz. They fused the popular forms with highbrow poetic forms such as Surrealism to create something entirely new. Rafael de León and other composers of *copla* lyrics in the 1940s were also minor poets. They had known García Lorca in their youth, and his poetry had a strong influence on their own lyrics. Indeed, Francisco Umbral would later write that the *copla* had kept Lorca alive long after his execution by the Nationalists in 1936.[9]

León, then, developed the *copla* as an ingenious hybrid of high and low poetic forms. His characters were familiar types from the Romantic period: flamenco singers, bullfighters, bandits, aristocrats. His *coplas* were set in spaces that would become his trademark: *cafés cantantes,* ports, palaces. He incorporated popular sayings and expressions into his songs, melding them seamlessly with images that sometimes came from Surrealist poetry. The world he thereby created seemed remarkably familiar, typically Spanish, as though it had always existed (Acosta Díaz et al. 45). It was a predominantly rural world, transported to the theatres and radios of the cities for consumption by urban audiences.

But the *copla* also has its roots in the Spanish theatre. In the eighteenth century, between the acts of plays, a singer, usually female, would perform a miniature musical comedy called a *tonadilla* (Salaün 19–22).[10] By the late nineteenth century, these songs had become independent of the theatre. They were sung in variety shows, and they began to register the influence of French cabaret songs called *couplets* (*cuplés* in Spanish). These were erotic songs performed by women in cabarets to please male audiences, especially working-class men who had come to the cities in search of work and who needed new forms of mass entertainment to replace the traditional forms they had left behind in their towns (Salaün 68–78).

The erotic *cuplé* was wildly popular in the 1910s and 1920s, gradually giving way to more respectable variety shows that the whole family could attend. Singers began to incorporate Andalusian themes into the repertoire, and the *copla* began its rise.[11] The *copla* is also referred to as the *canción española* (Spanish song). This is because it arose partly in reaction to the foreign music that had predominated in earlier decades: jazz, tangos, and the French *couplets.* I will use the term *copla,* since it is the most commonly used term for the genre and the one that its foremost creator, León, himself used to describe his songs.[12]

If León was melding highbrow poetic forms with traditional popular ones in the lyrics of the *copla,* Manuel Quiroga was doing the same with the music. His songs drew on Spanish light opera (the *zarzuela*), on flamenco rhythms and tunes, and on Spanish classical music from the early twentieth century, by composers like Manuel de Falla, Enrique Granados, and Isaac Albéniz (Acosta Díaz et al. 40–1). The result was "una síntesis en la que toda una generación se reconoció y se reconoce" ("a synthesis with which a whole generation identified, and still does") (41).[13]

A *copla* is a miniature play acted out in song on a stage. It is sung by one singer, accompanied by an orchestra. In the 1940s, most of the great *copla* singers were women. The structure of the *copla* is usually as follows:

first stanza, refrain, orchestral bridge, second stanza, refrain. Each song presents an initial situation, a conflict, and an ending that does not necessarily solve the problem. In their heyday, *coplas* were created by teams of three: a lyricist, a composer, and a choreographer. The performer, too, contributed to all three aspects, in a close collaborative relationship. Many songs, and all *copla* shows, were written for specific performers, although the songs were often later recorded by other artists.

The Performance, Transmission, and Reception of the *Copla*

In the heyday of the *copla*'s predecessor, the *cuplé*, singers like Raquel Meller were already performing regional folkloric songs. But the formula for the *copla* shows was invented by none other than the great poet, Federico García Lorca. In 1931, the first year of the Spanish Republic, Lorca made a record of traditional Andalusian songs that he had collected in small towns. He played the piano, and the famous performer La Argentinita sang the songs.[14] In 1932, Lorca and La Argentinita developed a show, a series of folkloric *estampas*, or scenes, in which La Argentinita danced and sang these songs. One of the numbers, "Las calles de Cádiz" ("The Streets of Cádiz") inspired the formula for *copla* performances that would be developed after the war by León, Quintero, Quiroga, and Piquer.

Coplas were sung live in musical revues. These shows were loosely constructed around a theme, and the songs were separated by dance ensembles, comic routines, flamenco guitar playing, and poetry recitals. The songs, however, were the main attraction, and people flocked to the shows to hear their favourite stars. The company would open the show in Madrid or Barcelona, then tour around Spain for months performing in the major provincial capitals:

> Eran grandes espectáculos escritos para ser representados durante varios meses, incluso años, con complicados y costosos montajes escénicos y con una gran compañía entre elenco técnico y artístico. Una forma única de entretenimiento, casi imposible de hacer hoy por los costes actuales.

> They were big shows written to be performed for several months, sometimes even years, with complicated and costly sets, and with a large company of both artists and technicians. A unique form of entertainment, almost impossible to do today because of current costs. (Plaza *Maestro Quiroga* 213)

Conchita Piquer herself toured so much that even today, more than fifty years after her retirement from the stage, there is a popular expression used in Spain to tell someone they travel too much: "Viajas más que el baúl de la Piquer" ("You travel more than Piquer's trunk").[15]

The *coplas*, first performed live as part of a tightly knit variety show, were then broadcast on the radio to audiences in cities and large towns. The genre flourished at a time of transition between the long oral tradition of song in Spain and the advent of the mass media; it retained the live aspect of traditional oral transmission while also bringing songs to the radio. As Vázquez Montalbán reminds us, rural Spain still lacked electricity in the 1940s. Thus, in small towns and even in large cities, there were still people who sang the new songs from the latest shows in streets on town squares, teaching them to the townspeople (*Cancionero general* xiii). The lyrics to *coplas* were sold on the streets; one friend of mine remembers that in rural Galicia in the 1950s one could purchase such lyrics, even though there was still no radio in private homes.[16]

Not every home had a radio in postwar Spain; even so, the radio was an important vehicle for transmitting *coplas*. As Armand Balsebre has noted, in 1923, Spaniards learned of General Primo de Rivera's coup in the press or on posters (39); in 1936, they learned of the coup that would lead to the Spanish Civil War on the radio.[17] By 1936, 300,000 homes had declared their radios for tax purposes, but many more radios were undeclared. By 1943, 1,000,000 radio receivers had been officially declared. Crucially, the radio was used both privately and collectively; radio receivers did not spread to the individual homes of the masses until the 1950s. As Lorenzo Díaz notes, already during the years of the Republic, it was common to listen to the radio in bars, casinos, and *ateneos* (cultural centres) and in the headquarters of parties and unions; it was also common to listen to the radio in the courtyards of apartment buildings (43). There was much communal life in these courtyards, where women gathered to sew, hang laundry, gossip, sing, and get some shade on hot days.[18] This meant that people learned the songs from one another as well as from the radio. So popular did some of León's hits become among domestic servants, even before the war, that one advertisement for domestic help stipulated that candidates must not be familiar with his song "Rocío" (Acosta Díaz et al. 24). Piquer herself became annoyed when her maid sang her songs while doing the housework. And Vázquez Montalbán remembers the women of postwar Spain singing "Romance de la otra" or "Tatuaje" with all their hearts through their open windows (*Crónica* 36, 43).

According to historian Julián Casanova, even in smaller towns where ordinary citizens did not have electricity, there would be a radio in the local bar, as well as in the homes of the few wealthy inhabitants.[19] When wealthier families bought a radio, they often opened their doors so that their neighbours could listen as well.[20] The audience was actively involved in some of the programs; every afternoon between three and four o'clock there was a request program during which callers could dedicate songs to loved ones. As well, films were brought to small towns on Sundays, and since many films featured *folklóricas* and their *coplas,* people learned the songs at the movies as well. And while famous stars like Piquer would not have toured the smaller towns in a province, second- and third-rate companies would have done so, providing more opportunities for rural audiences to learn these songs.

Coplas were broadcast on the radio for years or even decades, becoming the soundtrack of everyday life. As Vázquez Montalbán points out, songs were not yet consumer objects at the time. Hardly anyone owned a record player, and in any case most people were struggling to get enough food to eat, so buying records was not a possibility. Thus there was no incentive for radio stations to replace older songs quickly with newer ones (Vázquez Montalbán *Cancionero* xiv).

The Dream Team of *Copla* Creators: León, Quiroga, and Quintero

Lyricist Rafael de León and composer Manuel Quiroga had been writing hit songs together since the 1930s. Thanks to Conchita Piquer, the choreographer Antonio Quintero joined them in the early 1940s and they began to write songs for the stage. Piquer's lover and manager, Antonio Márquez, brought León, Quiroga, and Quintero together and asked them to create a theatrical show for Conchita, mentioning the example of Lorca's "Las calles de Cádiz." Thus was born Piquer's show, *Ropa tendida* ("Clothes on the Line") (1942), which would set the pattern for the genre: a mixture of Andalusian sketches and popular songs, featuring one star who performed about eight *coplas,* alternating with flamenco singers, comedians, and so on (Manuel Román 16–19).

León, Quiroga, and Quintero created the most memorable *coplas;* they were also the most prolific team in the country, writing songs and creating shows for all the major stars of the 1940s and 1950s, and they would continue writing and composing well after the heyday of the *copla* was over. This trio established the formula for the Spanish pop song. They also managed to get their shows recognized financially, persuading the Sociedad General de Autores, which handles copyright and royalties in Spain, to categorize their shows as highbrow theatre rather than as mere entertainments (Acosta Díaz et al. 11).

There were, of course, other excellent trios of *copla* composers, most notably the trio of Ochaíta, Valerio, and Solano, who also worked for a time with Conchita Piquer.[21] But it was León, Quiroga, and Quintero who created the songs that have become the standards not just for their generation, but for *copla* performers ever since.

The Ideology of the Copla

> La copla ... es la crónica sentimental de aquellos cuarenta años de Dictadura. Llegó a decirse que era fascista; vamos, de derechas como mínimo. ¿Y cómo podía ser de derechas, y menos aún fascista, una cosa tan de pueblo, tan de la gente sencilla, que la hizo suya precisamente para olvidar la pena y el dolor de unos años difíciles, que dejaron en los dos bandos cicatrices y pérdidas irreparables?

> The copla ... is the sentimental history of the forty years of the dictatorship. It came to be said that it was fascist, or right-wing at the very least. But how could it be right-wing, let alone fascist, when it was something that belonged so profoundly to the people, the common people, who made it theirs precisely to forget the sorrow and the pain of those difficult years, which left scars and irreparable losses on both sides? (Ignacio Román 139)

Because the *copla* had its glory years in the 1940s, and because its emphasis on things distinctively Spanish suited the needs of the Franco regime, the entire genre was once dismissed by the intellectual left as Francoist drivel. It is not hard to see why they thought so. Most *coplas* drew on Andalusian folklore: flamenco, bullfighters, and the like. The Franco regime used regional folklore as a tool to legitimate the new state, much as Hitler did in Germany. The Francoists presented the Spanish peasant and rural culture as the expression of the eternal soul of the Spanish "people," as an "essence" that had supposedly been adulterated in urban centres by foreign influences like liberalism, bourgeois materialism, and class struggle.[22] Glorifying Andalusian folklore in particular was an important Francoist strategy; as Terenci Moix has pointed out, under Franco, the gypsy character represented Andalucía, and Andalucía represented Spain (*Suspiros* 19). This was also a way of erasing the Catalan and Basque cultures, which had their own languages and represented a threat to the unified Spain that the Francoists were trying to impose.

The *copla* was also seen as Francoist because it was broadcast on the regime's radio and performed by stars on the winning side. As well, in their content, many typical *coplas* were indeed relatively straightforward celebrations of all things Spanish; as such, they did in fact buttress Francoist ideology.[23] Nevertheless, the ideology of many of the most famous *coplas* is not at all clear-cut. The *copla* crystallized as a form during the Spanish Republic, which was a time of democratization and progressive thinking. Rafael de León wrote his first hits at this time, influenced by his friend García Lorca. Then, during the Civil War, people's aesthetic tastes didn't necessarily adhere to ideological divisions. León was from an aristocratic family, yet he was most comfortable in the world of the cabarets and never mentioned his lineage (Manuel Román 28). During the war, he was jailed by the left in Barcelona, probably along with other members of the theatre world suspected of rightist sympathies. One man who was in jail with him remembers that the favourite poets of León and the other right-wingers who were incarcerated with him were León Felipe, Federico García Lorca, and Antonio Machado; all three were poets whose names were synonymous with the cause of the Spanish Republic. Meanwhile, the *copla* hits written by León were being listened to and sung by both sides in the war, and in 1937, a play based on one of his songs, *María Magdalena*, was performed at the Republican front in Madrid. So, ironically, León's left-wing jailers were probably singing the most popular songs written by their own rightist prisoner (Acosta 25).

The *copla*'s ideological ambiguity extended to the irregular love lives of its creators as well. By all accounts, León was gay.[24] He understood what forbidden love and marginalization meant, and these would recur as themes throughout his songwriting career. He also knew that his friend and one of his poetic models, García Lorca, had been killed, and he would have suspected that one reason for the hatred of Lorca in his native Granada was his sexual orientation.[25] He would have known about the beating and exile of the gay *copla* star, Miguel de Molina, whom he had known in prewar Madrid. And he would have been aware of the intense persecution of gay men in general under Franco, even if his noble blood granted him some immunity. It is hard to believe that this situation would not have created a conscious ideological ambivalence in León; in any case, his lyrics indicate a consistent identification with those who are marginal, oppressed, and suffering.[26]

Heterosexual *copla* artists had their love problems too. Conchita Piquer and her partner, Antonio Márquez, made a choice at the beginning of the war to cross into the Nationalist zone. Piquer's right-wing sympathies seem clear-cut. But she was also a modern woman who had lived in New York during the 1920s and who had performed topless. She had returned to Spain a rich woman, managed her own money, and was always modern in outlook; in 1927 she had been the first female actress in Spain to drive her own car (Plaza 111). She was not about to be railroaded by the stifling nineteenth-century sexual mores imposed by Franco. Piquer could not marry Antonio Márquez because he was legally married to another woman and Franco had prohibited divorce. Because her relationship was not legally or morally sanctioned, when Piquer became pregnant, she was forced to leave Spain for several years in order to have Márquez's child away from the Francoist public eye. They went to Argentina, where Márquez could legally recognize the child. As we will see, her performances often created bridges between herself and the defeated in her audience, regardless of her own political views.

After the war, the gay *copla* star Miguel de Molina had been driven into exile, but his heart-rending performance of "La bien pagá" continued to be heard on the Francoist radio. As for León and Quiroga, they had already composed many hits before the war ("María de la O," "Ojos verdes," and many others), and there was continuity between their prewar and postwar songs. In certain ways, in the 1940s León and Quiroga carried on in the realm of mass culture the work of the highbrow poets of the Generation of 27, of whom some, like Lorca, had been killed, and others, like Alberti, driven into exile. Some of their *coplas* could be described as remnants of the culture of the Spanish Republic. A key example of ideological struggle around a *copla* was "Ojos verdes," one of the most famous *coplas* of all time. Written before the war, it mentioned a brothel in its first line. That line was censored and rewritten under Franco, and the entire *copla* was eventually banned from the radio waves, although it could still be heard live or on disc and was familiar to everyone (Rodríguez 43–4). Conchita Piquer sang the uncensored version and paid fines for doing so. As Jo Labanyi points out, the ideological ambivalence of many songs carried over into film; many of the folkloric musical films of the early Franco era were "built around a song that had enjoyed previous popularity, often under the Republic, thus carrying over considerable cultural ambivalence" (Labanyi "Musical Battles" 210).

After the war, León's *coplas* were ideologically varied. Some were sentimental elegies to the Spanish monarchy of the early twentieth century, which fit well with the values of the right. But many of his *coplas* – the ones that would last the longest and be remembered with the most passion – espoused values that were diametrically opposed to those of the dictatorship. They defended protagonists who were sexually promiscuous, had no family, drowned their sorrows in hard liquor, and stayed out all night. The *copla* genre would later become devalued and clichéd, but in the 1940s many songs still contained something undomesticated, bitter, and raw, "una rebeldía a veces feroz contra las normas, aunque sea una rebeldía sometida y mal resuelta" ("a sometimes ferocious rebellion against the rules, even if it was a rebellion which would be put down and remain unresolved" (Vázquez Montalbán *Cancionero* xx).[27]

It is important to note that flamenco, one of the strongest influences on the *copla,* was itself ideologically ambivalent. It was the voice of some of the most oppressed people in Spain, the landless poor of Andalucía. A genre of emotional excess, it expressed the deep suffering and the passions of those whose experience was otherwise invisible. This emotional excess lent itself to special uses during the "time of silence," when the expression of all painful feelings was prohibited. Thus it was an ideal vehicle for the downtrodden and oppressed of the Franco era, the Spanish Republicans. Yet flamenco was also heavily instrumentalized by the Franco regime, to such an extent that it came to be seen as emblematic of right-wing sentiment.

Coplas as Camouflage: The Song with the Double Reading

While many song genres could help express the hidden feelings of the defeated to some degree, they needed extra forms of protection to do the deep emotional work necessary for survival. The best genres of camouflage songs were those with a double reading: one reading easily perceived and usable by the oppressor, and another, antithetical reading available to be used by the oppressed. Texts with a double reading must appear innocuous to the oppressors. When the oppressed sing them, the oppressors believe they are accepting the ruling values and the roles imposed on them. In fact, they are using the songs to articulate opposite values. It is a type of mimicry in which the oppressed can look obedient, while actually developing alternative values and even an alternative political consciousness.

James Cone has shown how black slaves in the American South used biblical texts in this way. The lyrics of their spirituals often appeared to speak of resignation and of waiting for one's reward in heaven – a reading that buttressed the ideology of the white slave masters. But when slaves sang those Christian lyrics, they were actually affirming themselves as children of God in a society that denied their humanity and was trying to break their spirit.[28] Also, the lyrics were sometimes used as codes for transmitting escape plots; thus, heaven might be a code word for the northern United States or Canada. In this way the spirituals, which at times seemed to advocate resignation, actually helped carve out a new political consciousness for black slaves, under cover of words that white people could also use and accept. These religious songs, says Cone, were "permeated with the affirmation of freedom from bondage and freedom-in-bondage" (Cone 28).

The defeated Republicans in Spain had a similar need to express their own humanity in the face of vilification. But in their case, the discourse of the Catholic Church could not help them do this, for the Church had taken Franco's side during the war and was participating actively in the regime's postwar apparatus of denunciation and persecution. My contention is that the tragic *coplas* of Conchita Piquer functioned as secular spirituals for many on the losing side and that some of her songs acted as substitutes for religious rituals. This was true even though the *coplas* of the 1940s were being composed and performed by those on the winning side.

Coplas presented easy possibilities for a double reading. Since the Franco regime fostered flamenco and bullfighting as emblematic of a united Spain, the winners of the war may have felt at ease with the *copla*'s characteristic Andalusian characters, rhythms, and music as representations of Spain's uniqueness. The winners, then, could read the *copla*'s insistence on the excellence of all things Spanish as a defence of Franco and his form of government – an explanation, as Vázquez Montalbán says, of why Spain was different and could be neither democratic nor Marxist (*Cancionero* xix). Yet the defeated, too, could find in the *copla* ingredients that affirmed their Spanishness. Because *coplas* drew on the most popular form of traditional Spanish oral poetry and on the flamenco music that had arisen among some of the nation's most oppressed people, the defeated could use them as an affirmation that they too were Spanish, that they too were the inheritors of these poetic and musical traditions, even though their country was in the grip of a dictatorship that defined them as the "anti-Spain."

Even the tragic *coplas* sung by Piquer, the ones about people on the wrong side of both the legal system and the Church, were beloved by both sides. The marginalized protagonists of these songs were often gypsies or at least from Andalucía. They are victims of a surrounding society that does not understand their unique characteristics or their value. The winners could identify with these characters as allegories of a Spain that was poor, hungry, ostracized, and misunderstood by the Western democracies, but that was defending its values and its dignity despite its poverty and marginalization. The losers, for their part, could read in the sufferings and the forbidden desires of León's marginalized gypsies and flamenco singers symbolic representations of their own predicament as pariahs who received no understanding or compassion from the surrounding society. They could identify with the characters' rebellion against the surrounding moral values and legal rules, and, above all, with their deep suffering, with their status as victims of a societal injustice that had no possible solution.

For both winners and losers, the tragic stories told by Piquer's *coplas* undoubtedly provided an outlet for their own suffering, in that people on both sides had lost loved ones and been traumatized by the war. The fact that León and Quiroga's *coplas* met many of the winners' needs provided crucial protection for the losers, who could safely use them as a means to maintain their humanity in the face of the regime's attempts to annihilate it. Thus both winners and losers could sing the same songs with all their hearts even while affirming very different values as they did so. In this way, these *coplas* are a perfect illustration of Antonio Gramsci's argument about popular culture: the dominant classes may create texts and interpret them in ways that serve their interests, but this does not stop the subaltern classes from generating contesting interpretations of those same texts (*Selections* 326–7). The use of certain *coplas* by the defeated was thus an example of what Eve Sedgwick calls "reparative reading": how oppressed people can nourish themselves on the cultural products of the very culture that is trying to eliminate them (35).

Playing the Character and the Performer: *Coplas* as Double Camouflage

To those who sang along with them, *coplas* offered more layers of camouflage than other song genres. People play the role of the performer when they sing along to just about any radio song (Vázquez Montalbán *Cancionero* xii). However, *coplas* were more than songs; they were theatre. Rafael de León stated that each song must have the structure of a play (Manuel Román 27). *Coplas* had a lyricist and a composer and a choreographer. Antonio Quintero worked alongside León and Quiroga and the singer herself to create Piquer's shows and choreograph the songs in them. And Piquer wore a different costume for each character, thus making each song distinctive. As a consequence, the audience could choose between two levels of role play as they sang along with her. They could play the role of the colourful protagonist: La Parrala, La Ruiseñora, La Lirio, and many others. Or they could play the role of Piquer playing the role of the character. Indeed, they could do both. *Coplas* thus offered two levels of role play to protect the defeated against accusations that the feelings they were expressing were actually their own.

Furthermore, *coplas* expressed powerful feelings in a dramatic, theatrical way. Their exaggerated quality, what appeared to some later on as excessive or melodramatic, served the defeated as an additional form of camouflage. It was a case of placing something in plain sight and then exaggerating it as a means to hide it (Rogin 499). In the 1940s, half of Spain was hiding intense feelings that had arisen in horrific circumstances. As Martín Gaite tells us, an atmosphere of anaesthesia reigned in postwar Spain, an atmosphere in which conversations were muted so that none was louder than the others and in which people avoided discussing anything that would trigger their pain.[29] In this atmosphere, the best *coplas* sang of emotional pain in a heart-rending way that is referred to as *desgarro* in Spanish. The pain came straight from the throat, from the soul, from the gut. Like the blues for black Americans, the *coplas* that most marked the era were extreme expressions of emotional pain, which was acted out on stage in gestures as well as in song.

I believe that for the defeated, the deep pain expressed in the *coplas* was not excessive at all, but appropriate to their desperate circumstances. In the context of the emotional repression that passed for "normalcy" under Franco, the theatrical excesses of *copla* would have constituted a kind of alibi. The more dramatically one threw oneself into the words and gestures of the *copla*, and the more differently one behaved from the restrained behaviour of everyday life, the less one could be accused of expressing one's own feelings. Thus, paradoxically, the more "over the top" one could make it look, the more exaggeratedly one played the role, the more sincere it would allow one to be.[30]

Transported into the Roles: The Art of Conchita Piquer

Conchita Piquer is always singled out as the supreme representative of the *copla* genre.[31] She was born in Valencia, on the eastern coast of Spain. She was taken to the United States as an adolescent, where she became famous as a teenage star on Broadway in the early 1920s. On her return to Spain in 1927, she triumphed as a singer of risqué cabaret songs. In the 1930s she began to perform the more respectable *canción española,* and in the 1940s, she brought the *copla* to its glory years through her high standards of performance, her enormous talent as an actress, and the deep emotion she brought to each song. Yet she did not have the most beautiful singing voice of the period. Piquer has an effect like that of Billie Holiday: once you have listened to her, you never forget her, though you may forget other artists with greater ranges and smoother voices. While she worked mainly with León, Quintero, and Quiroga, she also worked briefly with the other top trio of *copla* creators, Ochaíta, Valerio, and Solano, in her 1947 show *El puñal y la rosa.* She toured nationally and internationally until 1958, when her voice broke during a concert. She immediately dissolved her company and almost never sang publicly again, although she continued to record until 1961, and her records continue to sell to this day. She died in 1990.

Piquer competed with a number of other giants of the genre. The *copla* performers enjoyed the same celebrity status as film stars, and the best of them regularly appeared in movies to sing their famous hits. Constantly written about in the press, and omnipresent on the radio, they were larger than life. And there were many of them in the 1940s. Imperio Argentina was Spain's most important film star; she sang *coplas* on screen and captivated audiences with her unforgettable smile and her accessible charm. Estrellita Castro starred in variety shows, theatre, and film. Moix credits her with being the first to exploit stereotypes of gypsies in popular culture, and she portrayed gypsy and flamenco characters throughout her career (*Suspiros* 82). Both of these performers were already famous as film and stage stars before the war. They were joined in the 1940s by such giants as Juanita Reina, the singer who performed even more songs by Quiroga, León, and Quintero than Piquer. Reina had a romantic beauty and a velvet singing voice that captivated audiences. Like Piquer, she was most important as a stage performer, although she did make films as well, both *folklóricas* and Francoist historical films (*Suspiros* 96–113). Last but not least, there was Lola Flores, Spain's "prototipo de la folklórica," who cultivated both the stage and film (114). If Piquer maintained perfect control even when she acted out the most intense passions (so it was said), Flores was known and loved for being *out* of control, both on and off the stage. Irrepressibly passionate, she had numerous scandalous affairs that provided fodder for gossip in the sexually repressed postwar period. As a performer, she represented what Moix calls "la insolencia popular en su mejor acepción" ("popular insolence in the best sense of the word") and captivated audiences with her "incandescent" performances (116). There were also male performers, although in the 1940s women dominated the *copla* scene. Miguel de Molina, one of the greatest *copla* stars before the war, was targeted after the war by the Francoists for being gay. He was beaten to a pulp by Falangists in November 1939 and soon after that left for exile in Argentina, although his most famous songs continued to be heard on Spanish radio. In the 1940s, male performers such as Antonio Molina, Manolo Caracol, and Juanito Valderrama were household names.

Why was Piquer singled out, both in overviews of the *copla* genre and in texts dealing with the role of songs in survival in postwar Spain?[32] What made her special, and how were those special characteristics relevant to the emotional survival of the defeated? I contend that the answers to these questions have to do with the talent she had for role play. Piquer was an actress in song in a way that none of her rivals could match. This enabled her to create an alternative world in each song that was so convincing that it seemed more real to listeners than their everyday lives under Franco. The theatrical illusion was firmly in place and utterly complete. Secure in the stability of the world she created for them, the audience could use the compelling characters she created as masks to keep them safe as they painfully worked through their own terror, grief, and anger. Several features of Piquer's way of performing created ideal conditions for them to do so.

First and foremost was what Piquer could do with her voice. Not everyone could go see her perform live. Many depended on the radio to hear her songs. So she had to be able to convey with her voice alone all the roles and all the feelings in each song. And in that, she was unequalled, for she could act a song with her voice even as she sang it, clearly distinguishing the narrator from each of the other characters, without any pauses in the music. All reviewers agreed that her diction was unparalleled – clean and clear. Her biographer, Martín de la Plaza, describes her voice in the 1940s as "una voz más grave y redonda, llena de expresión, inflexión y plagada de susurros y matices" ("a deeper and fuller voice, full of expression, inflection, and full of whispers and nuances") (95). According to one reviewer, she nuanced each song in a different way, "y en todos se mostró dueña de unos registros inigualables que van del dramatismo a la ingenuidad, pasando por el garbo, la dulzura y aun la simpática picardía" ("and in all of them she proved her mastery of an unequalled variety of tones which go from dramatic to naive, passing through graciousness, sweetness, and even playfulness") (100). Her voice was capable of "caricias aterciopeladas" ("velvet caresses"), "quejas" ("complaints"), and sobs.[33]

This ability to convey any emotion, tone, or nuance with her voice is part of her legacy, and every *copla* singer since has tried to imitate her. One of today's best *copla* performers is Martirio, who, like Piquer, is as much an actress as a singer. She says of Piquer:

> Concha Piquer ha sido y es una escuela vocal. La manera, la elegancia, el contenimiento, la ironía, el titubeo, el desgarro, la entrega, la desazón. Si quieres aprender a colocar la voz, oye a Concha Piquer, después canta lo que quieras.
>
> Concha Piquer was and is a singing school. It's her manner: the elegance, the containment, the irony, the pauses, the heartrending quality, the commitment, the disappointment. If you want to learn what to do with your voice, listen to Concha Piquer, then sing whatever you like. (Plaza 235)

We can get an idea of just a fraction of Piquer's versatility in a series of eleven photographs taken of her while she performed one of her songs on stage, published in *Cámara* ("Fotoreportaje: Conchita Piquer"). She begins with earnest intensity, arms and hands opened out to the audience to convey a desire to communicate. Over the successive photos, she conveys deep passion, modesty, comedy, coquettishness, and a talent for slapstick humour, using her facial expression, head positioning, and hand movements to do so.

Because *coplas* rely on Andalusian musical rhythms and stock characters such as flamenco singers and gypsies, in the hands of second-rate performers they can easily degenerate into cheap folklore and patriotic drivel. For listeners to do deep emotional work as they sang along with a *copla*, they would have had to perceive it as a song of the utmost dignity, taste, and seriousness. Piquer brought what Ángel Álvarez Caballero called "un marchamo de clasicismo" ("a stamp of classicism") to every song she performed (qtd in Plaza 226). Reviewers always praised the "good taste" of her performances. She was an absolute perfectionist, preparing every detail of every show. Thus, her *copla* performances became the equivalent of "high" art in the pauperized world of postwar Spain. In a photograph from the private collection of Piquer's daughter, we see Piquer's head and shoulders, in profile, alongside the body of a guitar. The flamboyance of the flouncy flamenco dresses of other performers is replaced here with simplicity: a narrow black necklace standing out against her bare neck, and black lacework connoting solemn reserve. We see her profile, her head erect, eyes intense, and lips parted. The silhouette of the guitar against a lighter background enhances the effect of stark seriousness ("Conchita Piquer with guitar").[34]

Piquer understood the importance of what she was doing when she walked on stage, and her audience sensed it. She had deep respect for the public and for the songs she sang, which she described as "canción española con letras muy importantes, con letras que dicen cosas muy profundas y muy bien" ("Spanish songs with very important lyrics, songs that say very profound things and say them very well") (Plaza 132). Martín Gaite, who saw Piquer perform on stage, would later emphasize Piquer's awareness that the flow of the story must never be broken, even during orchestral bridges between stanzas:

> [Piquer era] consciente de su misión ... Sabía muy bien a lo que salía al escenario, sabía que a aquellas historias no se les podía quebrar el hilo, y así, como buscando enhebrarlas, se quedaba hierática en las pausas, en aquella especie de entreacto solemne entre el preámbulo y el final de la historia, con la mirada perdida en el vacío, donde tal vez leía las palabras, casi siempre trágicas, de aquel desenlace.
>
> [Piquer was] conscious of her mission. She knew very well what her purpose was in going on stage. She knew you couldn't break the thread of those stories, and so, as if she were seeking to keep that thread going, she remained erect and grave in the pauses, in that solemn orchestral bridge between the preamble and the end of the story. Her gaze was lost in the void, where perhaps she was reading the words, almost always tragic, of the ending. ("Cuarto a espadas" 169–70)

In figure 2.1, we get an idea of how Piquer appeared during those pauses: looking straight ahead, her head slightly raised, her neck proud and elongated, her lips together in confident silence. Elsewhere, Martín Gaite describes Piquer as "inhabiting" the pause between the stanzas (*El cuarto* 104). She wasn't the only one to notice what Piquer could do with a silence. Reviewer Santiago Castelo put it this way:

> Concha Piquer no sólo era la voz. Era el empaque, aquellos silencios suyos, aquellas quejas, los quiebros de su voz. Recorría la escena como si el aire se hubiera detenido y sabía llorar y recitar como nadie.

2.1 Conchita Piquer, majestic and proud, in a costume from her show, *Salero de España.* Photograph from the private collection of Manuel López-Quiroga y Clavero.

> Concha Piquer was much more than just her voice. It was her presence, those silences of hers, those laments, the breaks in her voice. She moved across the stage as though the very air stood still, and she knew how to cry and to recite like nobody else. (qtd in Plaza 118)

Máximo Díaz de Quijano declared that she "iluminaba los silencios" ("lit up the silences") (qtd in Plaza 230). Her rivals moved uncomfortably around the stage during orchestral bridges, wanting the second stanza to begin; but Piquer was at home in the silences. Said Quijano: "Semeja que es ella la que ha de volver a cantar cuando le plazca y no cuando se lo apunte el director" ("It seems as if she is going to start singing again when she decides the time is right, rather than when the conductor tells her to do so") (qtd in Plaza 230).

This ability to "inhabit" silence was crucial to maintaining the stability of the theatrical illusion. By filling the silence with the role, Piquer ensured that spectators were in no danger of being reminded of their own everyday lives, their troubles, their own pain, in between stanzas. Instead, the spectators remained on the edge of their seats, waiting for the ending. In this way, Piquer made it safe for her audience to experience the characters' emotional pain; she ensured they wouldn't suddenly be forced to come back to earth and recognize that pain as their own in a way that would overwhelm them. We can see this process at work in figure 2.2, which catches Piquer in the middle of her performance of "Tatuaje," her head raised, not looking at the audience, but fully immersed in her character between stanzas. She is using her hands to full advantage, turning the curtain into a prop with one hand even as she puffs on a cigarette with the other, thus placing the song's female protagonist outside of respectable society.

That Conchita Piquer was by far the best at creating and maintaining the theatrical illusion is all the more remarkable when we consider that she was singing in Spanish, her third language, and that she was usually playing the role of someone from Andalucía, which was not her place of birth.[35] Almost all the other important *copla* singers (including Juanita Reina, Miguel de Molina, Estrellita Castro, and Lola Flores) actually were from southern Spain, as were León, Quiroga, and Quintero. Yet Conchita Piquer became the queen and the undisputed champion of a genre whose language and region were not her own.

The other key feature of Piquer's art was that she was herself completely transported into the characters she played, to the point that, as Díaz de Quijano put it, "Daba la impresión de que Conchita no se había aprendido las canciones. Nacían de ella" ("You got the impression that the songs were born from Conchita, rather than her having learned them") (qtd in Plaza 230). Her principal lyricist, León, declared that "cantaba con las tripas, era una manera de sentir, una forma de vivir" ("she sang with her guts, it was a special way of feeling, a way of living") (qtd in Plaza 230). A fellow *copla* singer, Carmen Sevilla, recalled: "Tenía una voz prodigiosa, pero más que cantar decía ... Hacía de cada canción su historia particular, viviendo el argumento del tema" ("She had a prodigious voice, but more than singing she acted ... She made of every song her own story, living out the plot") (qtd in Plaza 237–8). And Moix declared: "nunca fue igualada ... su sinceridad para convertir un sentimiento en verdad absoluta. En tres minutos, Concha Piquer era capaz de crear todo un mundo" ("The way she could make a feeling into an absolute

2.2 Piquer, immersed in her role, in a pause between the stanzas of "Tatuaje." Photograph from the private collection of Manuel López-Quiroga y Clavero.

truth has never been equalled. In three minutes, Concha Piquer could create an entire world") (*Suspiros* 42) (figure 2.3).

Piquer was revered much more for her live performances than for her films, which only hint at the impact of her actual performances, since the camera often leaves her to focus on other characters, or a landscape. One of her films, though, opens with a simulation of a stage performance that suggests what it must have been like to see her perform live. Luis Marquina's *Filigrana* (1949) opens with her on stage singing a *copla* by León, Quintero, and Quiroga called "Como si fuera verdad." The story and the theme are typical of León's lyrics: the female protagonist knows that her lover has another woman and that he no longer cares for her, but she begs him to tell her he is madly in love with her, "as if it were the truth." We see Piquer in role, looking sorrowfully after her lover as he leaves the stage. We see her use her hands artfully to intensify the passion that the words, the music, and her facial expression are conveying. At times, she places her hand near her mouth, fingers closed against her thumb, then opens out her hand like a flower, as if sending the words physically out into the world. She opens her arms out to declare her sorrow to the audience, then closes both hands against her chest as the lyrics beg her lover to lie to her. In figure 2.4, a still from *Filigrana*, we see the intensity of her facial expression and how she uses her hand to enhance it.

Other *copla* singers had smoother singing voices and greater vocal ranges, but Piquer was a consummate actress in song who was utterly compelling when she told a story and incarnated characters. And this combination of role-play and narrative enabled the defeated to fully immerse themselves in her songs' fictional worlds, which were some of the only places where it was safe for them to work through their intense feelings.

But it was equally crucial to her audience that, however emotional her *copla* performances were, she never allowed her feelings to overpower the shape of the song. Ángel Zúñiga praised

> la viva emoción de la artista que la domina hábilmente y, si se humedecen sus ojos, como cuando canta *Ojos verdes* ... jamás pierde el pulso de la canción. Ni se excede ni se queda corta: medida, medida, medida.

> the deep emotion of the actress, who controls it with her talent. If her eyes tear up, as they do when she sings "Green Eyes" ... she never misses the beat of the song. Never too much or too little: right down the middle, every time. (qtd in Plaza 118)

2.3 Piquer's hand on her cheek, and her facial expression, indicate her immersion in the roles she played, and give an idea of how those feelings were conveyed to her audiences. Photograph from the private collection of Manuel López-Quiroga y Clavero.

2.4 Conchita Piquer performing on stage in the opening sequence of Luis Marquina's *Filigrana* (1949). Videocassette. King Home Video: Polygram Home Video (distributor). Vídeo Mercury, S.A. © 1991.

Piquer's masterful control of her own feelings made it safe for the defeated themselves to play the roles of protagonists in heart-rending situations that were comparable to their own. By imitating Piquer, who had supreme control over her emotional expression, they could access their own pain and control their own feelings without becoming overwhelmed.

Piquer's performances invited her radio listeners to play roles. León and Quiroga's *coplas* would have made listeners want to sing along in any case, but the way Piquer acted them was absolutely infectious. In 1978, twenty years after Piquer retired from the stage, in her memoir-novel *El cuarto de atrás* (*The Back Room*), Martín Gaite wrote about her temptation to imitate Piquer. The narrator-protagonist quotes a line from a Piquer *copla*. Her male interlocutor doesn't recognize the reference. The protagonist comments:

> Podría aclararle que se trata de un texto de la Piquer, o incluso ponerme simplemente de pie, echarme por los hombros un chal negro y, sin mediar otra introducción, apoyarme en la pared y cantarle la copla, que ahora se me viene a la memoria palabra por palabra, y a la garganta, y a los lagrimales.
>
> I could clarify that I was quoting Piquer, or even simply stand up, throw a black shawl over my shoulders and, with no other introduction, lean against the wall and sing him the *copla*, which I can now remember word for word, and which is welling up in my throat and in my tear ducts. (*Cuarto* 104)

Piquer's characters took on a life that seemed autonomous. They were not unlike the characters in Balzac's vast *Comédie humaine* or Galdós's *Novelas contemporáneas.* These characters of realist fiction seemed truly alive because they did not disappear when the novel of which they were the protagonist came to an end. Rather, they continued to exist, popping in and out of subsequent novels in minor roles for another twenty years. In this way, they seemed to exist outside the texts. This is what happened with Piquer's memorable characters, as we see in figure 2.5, where she holds the glass of brandy in which the nameless heroine of "Tatuaje" drowned her sorrows.

In 1947, when Piquer returned from two years in Argentina, a "metasong" called "Concha Piquer" was written for her by Ochaíta, Valerio, and Solano. In it, she describes being in Latin America and missing Spain so much that she knew it was time to come home. So she got out her red, high-heeled performing shoes,

> Y con un sollozo dije
> a mis canciones:
> Allí nos espera
> la luna de España.
>
> And with a sob I said
> to my songs:
> The Spanish moon
> is there waiting for us.

She addresses her songs and her characters, telling them it's time to go visit a Spain populated by her characters, inviting them to Madrid, where her character Almudena is selling violets, to the town of Moguer, where

2.5 Piquer with her emblematic liquor glass. Photograph from the private collection of Manuel López-Quiroga y Clavero.

they will find the lovers of La Parrala, and to that dark alley where the prostitute of "Ojos verdes" is crying over her perdition. And she tells her characters how crucial it is that they return to Spain:

Vamos, Lirio y Petenera,
vamos, Doña Sol y Lola
que si no estáis a su vera
con la Concha por bandera,
España, España se queda sola.

Let's go, Lily and Petenera.
Let's go, Doña Sol and Lola
For if you're not by her side,
With Concha as your emissary,
Spain will remain all alone.

Remarkably enough, there was a lot of truth to this. For Piquer and her characters did more to break the isolation of people cut off from friends and loved ones than almost anyone or anything else. These characters became their companions, alive in their own right, and they started to take over reality. Bars called "La Parrala" proliferated all over Spain; some can be seen to this day. People who were indecisive or who contradicted themselves would be told, "Eres como La Parrala" ("You're just like the Wine Lady") (Manuel Román 131).

There were many other stars who sold out their shows and were widely listened to, but Piquer was the era's quintessential performer. Richard Dyer brings together some definitions of charisma that are helpful in understanding the "Piquer effect." First, he quotes Max Weber's definition of charisma:

> Charisma is defined as: "a certain quality of an individual personality by virtue of which he [*sic*] is set apart from ordinary men and treated as endowed with supernatural, superhuman, or at least superficially exceptional qualities."[36]

Dyer goes on to explore the conditions under which a person will be seen as charismatic:

> E.A. Shils in "Charisma, Order and Status" suggests that: "The charismatic quality of an individual ... lies in what is thought to be his connection with ... some very central features of man's existence and the cosmos in which he lives. The centrality, coupled with intensity, makes it extraordinary."[37]

Finally, S. Eisenstadt suggests that "charismatic appeal is effective especially when the social order is uncertain, unstable and ambiguous and when the charismatic figure or group offers a value, order or stability to counterpoise this" (Dyer 58).

Eisenstadt's definition is highly relevant here. In a Spain that was deeply divided and starving, and where official political discourse about Spain's imperial destiny bore no relationship to people's hunger, fear, or suffering, Piquer did actually speak to all Spaniards, not just to the winners. For the losers of the war, she expressed what was most central to their lives and what was being denied in every other discourse: deep emotional pain and the constant experience of injustice and exclusion. Vázquez Montalbán argues that no other songs would reflect people's true experience in this way until the protest songs of the late 1960s and early 1970s (*Cancionero* xxi).

Piquer's songs were also a vital means for Spaniards to answer a pressing question that all of them faced: How were they going to get along together after they had spent three years killing each other? Because *coplas* offered double readings, both sides were able to engage passionately with them. The meta-song "Concha Piquer" alludes to this in veiled form:

Si canté para dos razas
Y las dos me han entendido,
Ya puedo morir tranquila.[38]

If I sang for two races
And both have understood me,
I can die content.

On the surface, these lines could refer to the two races that populated the *coplas*, the whites and the gypsies. Or they could refer to the indigenous races of Latin America, from which Piquer was returning when she sang this song, and the Spaniards. No Spaniard at the time would have been permitted to suggest that Piquer was appealing simultaneously to the winners *and* the losers of the war. Yet her Spanish listeners were able to hear in this line a recognition that her songs had something important to say to Francoists and Republicans alike.

Attending one of Piquer's stage performances became a sacred ritual in which both sides could participate. As Juan Eslava Galán puts it:

> Conchita Piquer, Estrellita Castro, Lola Flores y las otras folklóricas ... oficiaron de carismáticas sacerdotisas con cuyas voces unánimemente comulgaban la España triunfante y la España doliente.
>
> Conchita Piquer, Estrellita Castro, Lola Flores and the other folkloric singers ... officiated as charismatic priestesses, and both the triumphant Spain and the suffering Spain were unanimous in taking the communion they offered. (Eslava Galán 107)

Martín Gaite, too, uses the term "ritual" when she evokes the rapt attention and emotion of the public at Piquer's live performances. Having underscored that Piquer knew how to keep the tragic thread of the story going even during the silences, she points out that the audience already knew how the story ended:

> Los espectadores solían conocer [el final de la historia] por habérselo oído otras veces referir a ella misma, lo cual no era obstáculo, sino aliciente para que lo esperaran en su exacta literalidad y volviera siempre a emocionarles. La fidelidad a aquellas palabras del texto se propagaba, pues, a los espectadores de forma ritual; nadie hubiera podido consentir que se alterara una sola letra de él, porque en la literalidad consistía su esencia.

> The audience generally knew [the ending of the story] because they had heard her tell it to them before. But this wasn't an obstacle, but rather an incentive. They waited for it in its exact literalness and it always moved them all over again. Her faithfulness to those words of the text spread to the spectators as a ritual; no-one could have allowed a single letter of the text to be altered, because its essence lay in its literal repetition. ("Cuarto a espadas" 170)

Thus, whereas real priests were part of the apparatus of persecution, Piquer was a figure endowed with charisma, who had both the majesty and the empathy necessary to "officiate" in the crucial emotional work of mourning. What is crucial is that, along with Hollywood movies, Piquer's *coplas* were something about whose value both sides could agree. This made them important in solving the problem of how to live with the enemy, in the same apartment buildings and workplaces, on the same streets.

In postwar Spain, Franco ruled by terror, not because most people saw him as their legitimate ruler. There was no agreement as to who should rule and no consensus about what was meant by "Spain." In the Francoists' view, the left was the "anti-Spain," having been brainwashed by Russia; the losers, for their part, remembered that the Spanish Republic had been democratically elected and that Franco had come to power with the aid of Hitler's and Mussolini's weapons, not through support by a majority of Spaniards. At a time when values were in crisis, Piquer was one of the few Spanish figures who was endowed with legitimacy by both sides. Her effect was so intense partly because it was compensating for the lack of consensus about Spain's political leaders.

Dyer argues that social groups that are partly excluded from the dominant culture (he is speaking of male, heterosexual culture) are more likely to develop particularly intense relationships with the stars of the culture industry. He points to studies of women, adolescents, and gay men in this regard (59). In Spain, half a country was excluded from the benefits of social membership, and the women among the defeated were especially vulnerable to exploitation. Piquer incarnated both the plight and the dignity of the excluded as she brought to life her marginalized female characters. And she did so with all her being, as no one else could. This is another major reason why her impact on her audience was so intense.

But we can go further than this, and follow Dyer in asking which particular cultural instabilities and contradictions were incarnated by Piquer ("Charisma" 58). Her songs deal with various forms of social injustice, but first and foremost with women who have sex out of wedlock and live out the consequences. In this regard, Piquer both acted out and lived out a key contradiction in Francoist culture. The regime's rhetoric of Catholic chastity and its relentless persecution of any sexual contact among unmarried people made sex taboo. Yet brothels flourished quite legally as places to exploit defeated Republican women who had no other way to support themselves. Piquer's songs, and her own love life, pointed to these contradictions.

Piquer's *coplas* thus served anyone who was socially excluded by posing the problem of injustice in the form of the denial of personhood to people who did not deserve such treatment. And they did so specifically through the figure of the woman who was supposedly sexually "sinful." In a society declared by Franco and the Church to be God-given and perfect, Conchita Piquer had the impact she did because here was someone declaring, in a majestic voice that could not be ignored, that this world was actually profoundly unjust and that the suffering caused by the injustice was immense.

Another reason for Piquer's charisma is, I believe, aesthetic. Human beings need beauty. And in a world where everything was sordid, grey, and mediocre, and where most performances were hastily put together with second-hand materials and poorly trained actors, Piquer's performances offered the very rare experience of first-class talent and good taste.[39] And the songs she sang had a musical quality that made them lasting treasures many later artists would want to record. The combination of music, lyrics, and performance created an experience that in postwar Spain would have been unique indeed.

Other reasons for the immense impact of Piquer's *coplas* had as much to do with the *copla* form itself as with Piquer's remarkable performances. Crucially, *coplas* were sung by one singer accompanied by instruments. According to music therapists, listening to a single singer can break through a patient's isolation. Some of what makes this sort of listening therapeutic has to do with the music itself, even before the words are considered. Says Lucanne Bailey:

> Generally, music that initially matches the mood and the need of the patient is most beneficial. For example, a lonely patient would identify with a musical selection containing a solo instrument supported by other instruments, or vocal soloist pieces that verbally express desire for contact and comfort ... A depressed and withdrawn patient can initially identify with music that is characterized by minor modes, solo instruments, and music that conveys the sorrow a patient may be feeling. Often vocal music is most helpful with fragile, anxious and distressed patients. (26–7)

But the content of the words is also crucial. For people who are under attack, without resources, and cut off from one another, the effect of hearing someone else sing of the same trouble they have been carrying around and trying to hide is of the utmost importance. Clinical psychologist Terry Vance points out that one of the most important ways that therapy provides relief for patients lies simply in the power of the feeling that someone else knows who you are under the mask you ordinarily wear, that they know what your trouble is, and that they care.[40] Under systems of state terror, the singer may be substituting for a human being who can listen to the trouble and understand it; we know that the defeated often hid their traumatic experiences even from their own families in order to protect them.

A lone singer who convinces the listener that she understands the trouble, shares it, and cares, has created the indispensable conditions for the listener to do emotional work. And that is something Piquer was able to do. A listener who feels utterly alone in the world will avoid his own emotional pain because he cannot bear it alone and because he doesn't feel he has anyone to help him if he becomes overwhelmed. The healing effect of catharsis, the release of emotional tension, can only be obtained if a person has sufficient protection to be able to express the feelings (Andersen-Warren and Grainger 87). Thomas Scheff argues that catharsis, the purging of our own emotions, has everything to do with putting ourselves in the role of another person. He traces its origins to early childhood experiences: "The child draws into himself [*sic*] to feel the pain, puts his head down and cries, but frequently looks at his mother to see if the situation is still safe. While feeling the pain, the child also sees himself through the mother's eyes."[41] Andersen-Warren and Grainger explain that this allows the child to establish a degree of distance from his own suffering: "The distance between child and mother – the fact that they are two separate people – allows the child to draw on someone else's love in order to gain courage to endure what is happening ... In fact, the mother's reaction to her child's pain helps to establish the reality and acceptability of the pain for the child" (89).

And so it happens with the theatre. Plays give us permission to weep. When we identify with the feelings of the actor on the stage – or in the case of the *copla*, the singer – this reinforces our ability to bear our own feelings. It is precisely the distance between us and the singer on the stage, the fact that he or she is other than us, that enables us to safely feel our own feelings (Andersen-Warren and Grainger, 89).

The analogy between the singer and the mother of the small child helps us get to the heart of one of the most important effects of Conchita Piquer on her audience. Piquer was capable of caressing the listener with her voice, of making the listener feel that she cared. When the narrator of "La Ruiseñora" asks, "¿Qué te pasa, Ruiseñora?", her tenderness enables the protagonist to come out with her inner pain: "Que tengo un nido de pena y celos en la garganta" ("It's that I have a knot of sadness and jealousy in my throat"). Piquer's tender question, "¿Qué te pasa?" ("What's the matter?"), would have been moving to the listeners, who were living under conditions in which Piquer might have been the only one to ask them such a question.

In sum, Conchita Piquer's unequalled skill at playing roles in song made it safe for her audience to do their painful emotional work. Piquer played such a crucial role in the emotional lives of the losers of the war because she was the guarantor of a fictional, alternative world that the defeated could enter and, by using their voices, learn new ways to respond to chronic terror and grapple with the feelings associated with traumatic grief. They could do all this in the safety of the alibi that the fictional role provided. Piquer made the characters come alive so that they were available to be used in this way. She acted at times as a mother, her tender voice breaking through the isolation of people who had lost so many loved ones, making it safe for them to grapple with their sadness. At other times, she acted as a high priestess, creating an atmosphere of solemnity and reverence that removed her listeners from ordinary time and space into a symbolic world in which they could carry out rituals of mourning. Piquer was thus the *copla* performer who best brought to life an alternative world in which the defeated could use the four mechanisms of role play, ritual, narrative, and music to do the emotional and existential work of survival. And it was undoubtedly because of these qualities that León, Quiroga, and their collaborators wrote many of the most tragic and most immortal of their *coplas* for her.

Chapter Three

Coping with Terror through Popular Music: "La Parrala" ("The Wine Lady")

LA PARRALA
Valerio/León/Quiroga

La Parrala disen que era de 'Mogué',
otros aseguran que fue de 'La Parma';
pero nadie pudo[1] de fijo sabé
de dónde sería Trini La Parrala.
Las malas lenguas desían
que las claritas del día
siempre le daban bebiendo,
pero ninguno sabía[2]
el porqué de la agonía
que la estaba consumiendo.
Unos desían que sí,
otros desían que no,
y pa' dar más que desí
la Parrala así cantó:

ESTRIBILLO 1º

Que sí, que sí, que sí, que sí,
que a la Parrala le gusta el vino;
que no, que no, que no, que no,
ni el aguardiente ni el marrasquino;
que sí, que sí, que sí, que sí
que si no bebe no pué cantar;
que no, que no, que no, que no,

THE WINE LADY
Valerio/León/Quiroga

They say the Wine Lady was from Moguer,
others claim she was from Palma;
but no one knew how to find out for sure
just where Trini the Wine Lady might have been from.
Malicious tongues said
that the break of dawn
always found her drinking,
but nobody understood
the reason for the agony
that was eating her up.
Some said yes,
others said no,
and to add fuel to the gossip
the Wine Lady sang as follows:

FIRST REFRAIN

You're right, you're right, you're right, you're right,
the Wine Lady likes her wine;
you're wrong, you're wrong, you're wrong, you're wrong,
neither brandy nor kirsch;
you're right, you're right, you're right, you're right,
if she doesn't drink she can't sing;
you're wrong, you're wrong, you're wrong, you're wrong,

que sólo bebe para olvidar.
¿Quién me compra este misterio?
Adivina, adivinanza:
¿por quién llora,
por quién bebe,
por quién sufre la Parrala?

II

Dos hombres riñeron una madrugá
dentro del colmao donde ella cantaba
y el que cayó herío dijo al expirá:
por tu culpa ha sío, Trini la Parrala.
Los jueces al otro día
a la Trini preguntaban
si a aquel hombre conosía
y la Trini contestaba:
yo no lo he visto en mi vía
ni sé por qué lo mataban.
Unos dijeron que sí,
otros dijeron que no,
y pa' dar más que desí
la Parrala así cantó:

ESTRIBILLO 2º

Que sí, que sí, que sí, que sí,
que la Parrala tiene un amante;
que no, que no, que no, que no,
que ella no quiere más que a su cante;
que sí, que sí, que sí, que sí,
que si no bebe no pué cantar;
que no, que no, que no, que no,
que sólo bebe para olvidar.
¿Quién me compra este misterio?
Adivina adivinanza:
¿por quién llora,
por quién bebe,
por quién sufre la Parrala?

she's only drinking to forget.
Who'll buy the answer to this mystery?
Guess a riddle:
Who is the Wine Lady crying over?
Who is she drinking over?
Who is she suffering over?

II

Two men fought at dawn one morning
in the bar where she sang
and the one who fell, wounded, said with his last breath:
'this happened because of you, Trini the Wine Lady.'
The next day the judges
asked Trini
if she knew that man
and she answered:
I've never seen him before in my life,
and I don't know why they killed him.
Some said yes,
others said no,
and to give them more to talk about
the Wine Lady sang as follows:

SECOND REFRAIN

You're right, you're right, you're right, you're right,
the Wine Lady has a lover;
you're wrong, you're wrong, you're wrong, you're wrong,
she only loves her singing.
You're right, you're right, you're right, you're right,
if she doesn't drink she can't sing;
you're wrong, you're wrong, you're wrong, you're wrong,
she only drinks to forget.
Who'll buy the answer to this mystery?
Guess a riddle:
Who is the Wine Lady crying over?
Who is she drinking over?
Who is she suffering over?

"La Parrala" ("The Wine Lady") was first performed by Conchita Piquer in January 1940, less than nine months after the end of the war, when the bereavements of the war were freshest, imprisonments and executions were ongoing, and the shock of living under the new system of terror would have been most acute. It would remain on the radio for many years, becoming a favourite with the public and one of Piquer's biggest hits. It was an upbeat, zippy *pasodoble* with many jocular, teasing moments on the part of both performer and orchestra. I read "La Parrala" here in terms of the ways it would have been useful to those Spaniards living in chronic terror.

This *copla* has a number of distinctive features. One of these is the made-up name of the protagonist. "Parrala" is a neologism created for the song. It comes from the word "parral," or vineyard, and is a nickname referring to the protagonist's passion for wine. La Parrala is shrouded in mystery; no one knows where she is from, and she tells us nothing about herself during the song. Her indulgence in alcohol and her flamboyant behaviour make her unique. Also, in this song, as in "La Ruiseñora," a singer (Piquer) plays a singer: La Parrala sings all night at a bar. Finally, the upbeat music and the playfulness of parts of the performance coexist with themes of suffering and danger.

The fact that the song appeared in 1940 made it a tool that the defeated could begin to use just a few months after the war's end, when the terror and the investigations were at their height. As noted in chapter 1, instilling terror through mass executions was crucial to the strategy of the generals who had organized the coup against the Spanish Republic. By 1940, many Spaniards in areas conquered by the Nationalists early in the Civil War had been terrorized by large-scale killings for more than three years. After the war, the terror spread throughout the entire country.

"La Parrala" presents an isolated protagonist. Isolation is extreme for those oppressed under a dictatorship, since it is the regime's intention to break up social networks and groups in order to destroy the enemy as a political entity.[3] For this to happen, people must fear not only the authorities but also one another. Analyses of more recent dictatorships

---

in the Southern Cone (Argentina, Chile, Uruguay) will help illuminate the psychological threat posed by fear under the Franco regime. Ángel Rodríguez Kauth explains the process whereby, under the military junta in Argentina (1976–83), everyone came to be afraid of everyone else:

> Por aquellos tiempos los argentinos tuvimos muchos miedos que nos atenazaban, que nos paralizaban en nuestros quehaceres habituales. Tuvimos temor a que los "otros," los que estaban cerca nuestro pudieran ser "soplones" de los Servicios y que por una venganza de tipo personal nos denunciaran como supuestos subversivos, o efectivos subversivos. Cualquiera, sin distinción de género, clase social, militancia política o lo que fuese, podía ser miembro de los Servicios [...]
>
> El miedo a los "otros" – una estrategia usada por el Terrorismo de Estado para romper los lazos del entretejido solidario social – lo comenzamos a sentir cuando el régimen nos enseñó, a través de los medios de comunicación masiva, que el vecino – con el que compartíamos el mate de las mañanas y las noticias del día – bien podía ser un terrorista, un subversivo o un comunista, y paradojalmente, eso nos llevó a sospechar [...] que ese mismo vecino también podía ser un agente encubierto de los Servicios. Ese fue el momento en que comenzamos a levantar barreras de recelo y suspicacias hasta frente a los propios amigos de toda una vida. Y no vaya a creer el lector que estos temores eran el producto de un delirio paranoide individual [...] dado que la realidad exterior era verdaderamente persecutoria [...] [El miedo] era avalad[o] por hechos objetivos y concretos de los que todos en alguna oportunidad fuimos o actores u observadores.

> During that time we Argentines were gripped by multiple fears that paralyzed us in our everyday activities. We were afraid that the "others," those around us, could be informants of the intelligence services, and that to take vengeance for any personal matter they could denounce us as supposed or actual "subversives." Anyone, of whatever sex, social class, or political party could be a member of the Services [...]
>
> We began to feel the fear of "others" – a strategy used by State Terrorism to break the bonds of solidarity in the social network – when the regime taught us, through the mass media, that our neighbour – with whom we shared tea every morning and the news of the day – could well be a terrorist, a subversive, or a communist, and paradoxically, this led us to suspect [...] that this same neighbour could be an undercover agent for the Services. That was the moment when we began to put up barriers of fear and suspicion even with our own lifelong friends. And let my reader not believe

> that those fears were due to simple individual paranoid delirium [...] because external reality was really persecutory [...] [The fear] was validated by objective, concrete events in which all of us on some occasion had either participated or which we had observed. (2–3)

People were also afraid of fear itself. For, as Salimovich and colleagues and Rodríguez Kauth make clear, people were afraid that their fear would be noticed and that the regime would begin to suspect them of having done something ("ya que el sujeto tenía miedo y éste 'por algo' podría ser" ["since if the person was afraid, 'there must be a reason'"]) (Rodríguez Kauth 2). Numbness was the result of trying to hide the fear, not only from others, but also from oneself, in order to remain safe (Salimovich 89; Rodríguez Kauth 2).

The final fear, says Rodríguez Kauth, was of oneself. People were afraid to express any dissident thoughts or feelings aloud to anybody else; but they were also afraid of betraying their deepest political convictions:

> Llegamos al punto de tener miedo de mirarnos al espejo cada mañana y descubrir que la luna del mismo nos dijera que ése que estaba en el vidrio era un traidor, un cobarde que prefería disimular, ocultar y hasta traicionar su ideología para evitar ser sancionado con las conocidas represalias del régimen gobernante.

> We got to the point of being afraid of looking at ourselves in the mirror every morning and discovering that the face reflected in it was that of a traitor, a coward who preferred to cover up, hide, and even betray his ideology to avoid suffering the well-known reprisals of the regime. (3)

Fear, as it became generalized, reduced people's active participation in public activities and prevented them from imagining a future. The psychological effects of this generalized fear could be devastating:

> Fear of physical harm and of economic insecurity is only the tip of an iceberg whose bulk is obscured. The hidden mass is anxiety: diffuse, apparently objectless fear that eats away at everything, crumbles hope, flattens emotions, and saps vitality – a cold that invades and paralyzes [...] Fear can kill us before we actually die. (Lechner 26)

Terror is the most basic human feeling, because it is designed to help us survive in the face of immediate danger. All other emotions, including grief, must be put on hold as an individual copes with terror. Yet, as discussed in chapter 1, if the fear response becomes chronic, it can turn against us, creating disorganization, paralysis, generalized anxiety, and withdrawal from places and activities. The terror generated by the mass executions and tortures in Franco's Spain was so deep that even today, more than thirty-five years after the dictator's death, some survivors fear to talk about what happened. How could the defeated cope with this intense terror when it was immediate, in the 1940s? How could they retain enough courage and wherewithal to venture out in search of food, which had to be obtained illegally? How could they avoid revealing their fear when confronted by Falangist militia on the streets? The testimony of Spanish intellectuals in the 1970s suggests that one of the principal therapeutic functions of postwar *coplas* was to help keep that ongoing terror at bay:

> Eran ... canciones para sobreponerse a la oscuridad, el vacío, el miedo.
>
> They were ... songs to overcome the darkness, the void, the fear. (voiceover, *Canciones para después de una guerra* [*Songs for After a War*])
>
> Las coplas de posguerra tenían una función narcótica: acunaban el miedo, convocaban el olvido, conjuraban el horror al vacío.
>
> Postwar *coplas* had a kind of narcotic function. They soothed our fear, helped us to forget, kept at bay our terror of the void. (Carmen Martín Gaite, "Cuarto a espadas" 171)

I believe that "La Parrala" offered the defeated an especially important resource as they grappled with their fear. The foundation of the song's therapeutic effect lies in the analogies between the situation of the protagonist and that of the losers of the civil war. La Parrala is promiscuous. She's an alcoholic. She's out all night singing at a violent bar. And when she's not singing, she's crying. She couldn't be more different from the respectable woman of Francoist propaganda, who is chaste and pure, who is home before dark (and curfew), and who, eternally optimistic, gets up early to do the exercises recommended by the Women's Section of the Falange (Martín Gaite *El cuarto* 83). La Parrala will never be assimilated into respectable society. Yet her very marginalization and perhaps even degradation may have been enormously functional for many of the losers as they listened to the song and played her role. By 1940, it had been made emphatically clear to them that the political stain on their past meant that they would never again be included in Spanish mainstream society; like the alcoholic Parrala, they would forever be social pariahs. And the working class was further degraded by the subhuman conditions in which they lived. The fact that La Parrala, like other female characters created by Conchita Piquer, was beyond the pale in so many ways created a bridge between her story and the lives of the defeated, who were also irredeemably marginal and who existed in public discourse solely as objects of vilification.

La Parrala is a woman full of secrets, and many on the losing side would have identified with her situation. The first thing we learn about her is that no one knows where she is from. In the 1940s, many Spaniards were recent arrivals in towns where they knew no one, and many of them could not reveal where they were from and why they had moved. Some had fled their villages during the war for fear of being killed by the Francoists. Others couldn't stand living next door to the people who had killed their loved ones, and left for another town. Still others had been exiled by the new regime to another province of Spain as punishment for the party affiliations they had held during the war.

But the song's main secret, which forms the refrain, is this: For whom is La Parrala crying, drinking, and suffering?

Adivina, adivinanza:
¿por quién llora,
por quién bebe,
por quién sufre la Parrala?

Guess a riddle:
Who is La Parrala crying over?
Drinking over?
Suffering over?

We don't know the answers to these questions. All we do know is that her suffering is so intense that it is described as an *agony* that is *eating her up*. The song was the first of several important postwar *coplas* that named and enacted intense emotional pain – pain that was usually denied by the regime's rhetoric of forced cheerfulness. Thus it may have been a means for the defeated to validate their own feelings, which were so invisible on the social surface.

Crucially, La Parrala never reveals the identity of the person she is crying over. Nor could many of the defeated reveal whom they were suffering over, or why, given the danger attached to mourning their dead. Because the pain could not be expressed, it could not be alleviated. Many, like La Parrala, would have sought to dull the pain through drink. But the song offered those who were in emotional pain another way of coping – by playing the role of La Parrala and singing along with her. This would allow them to express in full voice both the fact that they were suffering and the fact that they couldn't say why.

Another of the secrets La Parrala keeps is whether she has lovers, and if so, how many. Many of the losers of the war shared with her the need to keep secrets about forbidden love. The sexual relations they had established, legally or otherwise, under the Spanish Republic were now illegal. Homosexuals, who had been more tolerated under the Republic, were now ruthlessly persecuted.[4] Even married people committing garden-variety adultery could become the subjects of an investigation under the Causa General.

But the most chilling parallel between La Parrala and the defeated who sang her song relates to the fact that the protagonist is subject to investigation by the authorities. How many of the losers of the war, denounced by neighbours, must have had to say to the authorities about a loved one exactly the words that La Parrala uses, the *only* words she speaks in the first person: "Yo no lo he visto en mi vía / ni sé por qué lo mataban" ("I've never seen him before in my life and I have no idea why they killed him")?

La Parrala is portrayed as isolated; her only social relations are possible lovers, one of whom may have just been murdered. She is a solitary character whose mission is to try to keep at bay all the other characters in the song, who are trying to learn what she is hiding. This sort of dilemma must have resonated with many defeated Republicans, who were cut off from friends and family and trying to hide their left-wing past.

The song's first stanza constructs La Parrala as an object of ongoing investigation by presenting her circumstances exclusively through the conjectures of the townspeople:

> ...*disen que* era de 'Mogué',
> *otros aseguran que* fue
> de 'La Parma' ...
> *Las malas lenguas desían* ...
> pero *nadie comprendía* la razón
> de la agonía ...

Unos desían que sí,
otros desían que no ...

They say she was from Moguer,
others claim she was
from La Palma ...
Malicious tongues said ...
no one understood the reason for her
suffering ...
Some said yes,
others said no ...

In the first stanza, investigation is represented as habitual and ongoing (the present tense and the imperfect tense, indicating repeated action in the past, are used). Also in the first stanza, the topics of investigation are where she is from, how much she drinks, and why she is suffering. While the theme of a character being subject to town gossip is hardly new in Spanish literature, it is striking that Rafael de León wrote these lyrics at the time of Franco's call in the Causa General for people to monitor their neighbours' political and moral behaviour.[5] The second stanza intensifies the theme of being under suspicion and tightens the surveillance of La Parrala. Now she is being investigated for her role in a murder. She is being investigated by judges, and the nosy neighbours have become witnesses; their habitual gossip about her in the imperfect tense ("Unos desían que sí") becomes their testimony about one particular event, in the preterit tense, at the trial ("Unos dijeron que sí"), as they answer the question about whether she knew the dead man. A telltale plural form suggests a broader political subtext to the barroom fight between the two men. La Parrala says, "[No] sé por qué lo *mataban*"("I don't know why *they* killed him"), implying that there is a larger organization behind one of the men.[6] Thus the predicament of La Parrala in this fictional story may have resonated with the defeated, who were also isolated individuals facing a state apparatus of terror.

Jurij Lotman has shown that each work of art creates a model of the world, a vision of how the world *is*, through what it includes within its frame (265). The bar where La Parrala sings is a microcosm of Spain in 1940 and later.[7] Within its walls, some people are killing others and everyone else is either an informant or a target of investigation. The song mirrors the worst aspects of social relations under Franco: people related to one another by investigating and informing on each other. The time of day portrayed in the song is also significant. Both stanzas refer to the early morning hours, first as the time La Parrala is drinking away her sorrows, and then as the time of the murder. Under Franco's dictatorship, "respectable" citizens were home in bed. But what was going on while they slept belied the false cheer and triumphal rhetoric of daylight. For dawn was the time of the *paseos* – that is, when people were taken from home or jail to the outskirts and shot.[8] So while dawn in the regime's Fascist rhetoric was associated with optimism, fresh air, and exercise, for the defeated it was associated with the time when their relatives had been killed and their secret mourning had begun.

Coping with Terror through Role Play: Lessons from La Parrala

"La Parrala" offered the defeated a powerful tool for managing their fear. Its story reflected a multitude of circumstances with which many people had to deal on a daily basis: witnessing the violent death of loved ones, hiding their past from neighbours, convincing the authorities that they knew nothing. In real life, these things were often a matter of life and death, or at the very least of avoiding jail or torture.

The song's therapeutic value lay in the ways it evoked people's real fears even while making those fears seem more manageable. Through its form, the song takes what in real life is an ongoing, chaotic, dangerous situation without hope of an end, and *contains* it in a narrative structure with a beginning, middle, and end, making the violence and the fear seem finite. And its protagonist, "La Parrala" offered those who sang along with her a series of coping mechanisms that perhaps lessened their fear slightly. In the song, what La Parrala does with the malicious neighbours trying to uncover her secrets is to *play with them.* She belittles them by role-playing them, parroting them even as she mocks their descriptions of her conduct: "Que sí, que sí ... que la Parrala tiene un amante" ("That's right, that's right ... the Wine Lady has a lover"). She generates contradictory versions about her secrets by then singing the opposite, to keep them guessing: "que no, que no, que no, que ella no quiere más que a su cante" ("No, no, no, no, she only loves her singing").

Many among the defeated were in danger of being overwhelmed by their fear and their pain and throwing in the towel.[9] In contrast, La Parrala has retained a highly developed sense of play despite the depth of her suffering. She takes her own tragic story ("Who is La Parrala crying over, drinking over, suffering over?") and turns it into a guessing game, drawing on the formula used in children's guessing games in Spain: "Adivina adivinanza" ("Guess a riddle"). The losers of the war could join in by playing the role of La Parrala as she in turn played the role of her nosy neighbours. In fact, they could hardly *not* play the role; the refrain is so catchy that it is almost impossible not to sing along. The song's *pasodoble* rhythm meant that many who sang along may also have danced to it, lightening the fears raised in the song by loosening up bodies used to walking in fear and controlling every gesture. This had consequences for real life, for playing the role of a playful person who is not afraid can help a person develop that courage "for real."[10]

La Parrala uses a playful discursive strategy to stay safe. The refrain begins with the neighbours debating her circumstances, then says, "Y pa' dar más que desí, La Parrala así canto" ("And to give them more to talk about, the Wine Lady sang as follows"). Her strategy is to play the role of the outrageous one. She appears to say to her listeners: "If they're going to talk about you anyway, add to the rumours. Maybe they'll focus on your drinking and your love life rather than your political leanings." But La Parrala is also clever, speaking of herself only in the third person and echoing the discourse generated by her neighbours. In the first person, she only says what she *doesn't* know. Significantly, the result is phrased by Piquer as: "Nadie *supo* de fijo *saber* / de dónde sería Trini la Parrala" ("Nobody could figure out how to find out just where Trini the Wine Lady was from"). The neighbours' goal is to *saber* (to know), and they fail. The song ends with La Parrala repeating the same questions the neighbours had in the beginning.

My readers may object that in real life, such tactics would not really succeed in keeping the enemy at bay. And that singing the song wouldn't magically make things any safer. This is true, up to a point. But the song could have had very real effects nonetheless, by making people feel less helpless and more in control as they responded to real interrogations. In working-class neighbourhoods in Pinochet's Chile, opposition groups taught people how to play roles to cope with their terror when the police burst into their homes with machine guns drawn, searching for dissidents or simply trying to spread panic. Verónica Feliú was a leader of theatre workshops for women under the protection of *vicarías* (parish churches) in Santiago. The technique that she and other leaders were taught was developed by the Brazilian playwright Augusto Boal, and was called "Teatro del oprimido" ("Theatre of the oppressed"). As described by Carlos Ochsenius and José Luis Olivari,

> El sentido del método es percibir, mediante la construcción dramática de una acción real, cómo se estructuran situaciones y roles de opresión y cómo es posible mediante la acción de los afectados romper o modificar dichas situaciones y roles. El espectáculo teatral se vuelve, de esta manera, un pre-

> texto o estímulo para que el público ensaye nuevas actitudes e iniciativas prácticas que conduzcan a su liberación.
>
> The idea of the method is to become aware through the dramatic construction of a real event, how roles and situations of oppression are structured, and how the oppressed can, through their own action, break down or modify these roles and situations. The theatrical performance becomes, in this way, a pretext or catalyst for the public to try out new attitudes and practical initiatives that can lead to their liberation. (Ochsenius and Olivari 31)

In Feliú's workshop, working-class women began by acting out the situation that terrified them: a woman was surrounded by soldiers with rifles pointed at her. Next she encouraged them to rewrite the scene. They had the soldiers now turn to embrace one another, with flowers coming out of the rifles, which now pointed at the ceiling. The women's feedback indicated that being able to control the outcome of the theatrical scene made them feel less helpless in their real situation in the shantytowns of Santiago.[11] Singing "La Parrala," playfully laughing and dancing to a story about investigation and interrogation, surely had similar effects.

Thus, I believe that "La Parrala" served as a mechanism of desensitization to fear. Behaviour therapists use *systematic desensitization* to help free clients from debilitating, unrealistic fears. This technique, when used in a therapist's office, involves relaxation training to produce deep-muscle relaxation in the client, who then imagines a series of increasingly aversive situations related to his anxiety (Goldfried and Davison 112, 124). For example, a client who is terrified of flying might begin by imagining his boss telling him he will have to make a plane trip in six months. At a later session, he might imagine himself in line checking baggage, and still later, on the plane in turbulence (121–2).

Systematic desensitization is used to treat fears that are considered unrealistic and neurotic. At first glance, it would seem counterproductive and harmful to desensitize people to fears that are real, for our instinctual fear response helps protect us against danger and is our most basic survival mechanism. But our fear response is most adaptive in situations of *transitory* fear, to evoke a fight-or-flight response. When fear becomes chronic, it can be debilitating enough to impair basic activities. Under conditions of totalitarian terror, survival requires ways to cope well enough with the fear to keep functioning and to obtain basic necessities. It also requires ways to control the fear well enough not to give oneself away to neighbours and police. Thus, some desensitization is necessary *even though the basis for the fear is real.*

The imagination has a critical role to play in reducing the fear. In the therapist's office, the client is asked to imagine himself in increasingly anxiety-provoking situations, evoking all the sensations, the setting, and so on. As Goldfried and Davison assert, the crucial assumption behind desensitization is that "an imaginary aversive scene is a functional equivalent of the real situation; enabling a person to confront a fantasized representation of what he is afraid of is assumed to be analogous to his learning to face the situation in real life." (113)

In my use of the concept of desensitization, I draw on drama therapy to take Goldfried and Davison's principle one step further: it is just as effective to imagine oneself *as a fictional character* in an anxiety-provoking situation, and to identify with that character as she copes with increasingly aversive circumstances. In fact, doing the work of desensitization by identifying with a fictional character rather than working directly on one's own life actually has advantages: it can happen unconsciously, without a specific decision to try to conquer the fear. It is therefore much less threatening.

The music of "La Parrala" helped reinforce this desensitization process.[12] The tune is happy, zippy; the song begins with the clash of cymbals and quickly introduces a *pasodoble* dance rhythm. Wind instruments are prominent, and the strings are often pizzicato, maintaining a lightness throughout. In the refrain, when "La Parrala" repeats her neighbours' words ("Que sí, que sí ..."), the orchestra answers each line by running playfully up and down the scale. Many other lines of the song are answered by brief orchestral flourishes. When people moved their bodies to this music (and they would have found it hard not to), the process had the added benefit of being active. Instead of simply imagining the fictional situation, people were singing, acting, and possibly dancing to the *pasodoble* rhythm, wholly absorbed in the activity, in a state of "flow."[13] This would have created a state of relaxation that might allow them to desensitize the fear that had been evoked.

In sum, singing "La Parrala" could help the defeated desensitize themselves to their ongoing fears of being investigated. The song presents the anxiety-provoking situation of the prying neighbours in the first stanza, then intensifies it with the murder and the investigation in the second stanza. The song evokes the fear, then turns it into a playful guessing game, and shows the game to be successful. It desensitizes, then, by combining anxiety-provoking material with play, song, and dance.[14] Wherever fear is evoked in the content of the song, the music envelops that fear in a light spirit.

Terror versus Mourning: More Lessons from La Parrala

As we now know, the Francoist terror blocked normal expressions of mourning. A crucial dilemma faced by the defeated in postwar Spain was how to express their intense grief without putting themselves in danger. "La Parrala" enacts the conflict between self-expression and terror by showing its listeners a character who suffers openly and who is investigated as a result. The song thus provided the defeated with a fictional representation of one of their most acute problems. And it did more: it offered them an example of how to grieve safely. For within the song is a character who is a singer. For La Parrala, and for other Piquer characters like La Ruiseñora, singing is a way of coping with pain and responding to pressure. The song, with its catchy refrain, trains its listeners to use singing to cope with pain and fear. And specifically, it invites them to use the alibi of playing the roles of the colourful characters in the *copla* to let out their own pain and to regain a sense of play. La Parrala taught her listeners early in the dictatorship, then, that singing was a safe way to break the thick silence that weighed on them.

Specific features of the music did much to facilitate the expression of suffering by those who sang along. The song never acknowledges fear; however, the emotional suffering at the core of the song's mystery is given great significance by a marked change in the music: the playfulness stops completely. After "La Parrala" has repeated all of the neighbours' contradictory versions of her in mocking tones, with the orchestra answering playfully, the accompaniment suddenly stops, and the narrator's voice rings out, louder than at any other point in the song, piercing, majestic: "¿Quién me compra este misterio?" ("Who'll buy the answer to this mystery?"). A soft arpeggio pizzicato introduces the challenge, which is sung softly and urgently: "Adivina, adivinanza" ("Guess a riddle"), followed by a single chord. A significant ritard follows as Piquer draws out the words of each question, lyrically and with intense emotion, but also softly amidst the silence, as if to accentuate those words' importance. Each of the questions is followed by a single, simple chord from the orchestra, creating a pause during which to consider the question's meaning. This is in marked contrast to the flourishes that answer other lines of the song. Piquer asks:

¿Por quién llora,
por quién bebe,
por quién sufre la Parrala?

Who is La Parrala crying over?
Drinking over?
Suffering over?

Piquer introduces a soft sob between some of these questions. The listener cannot help but focus on the suffering as the song pauses over it. But then it is contained again, because after she slowly sings the words "la Parrala," the orchestra resumes the original faster tempo. After the first refrain, a light pizzicato up the scale returns us to the zippy introduction; after the second refrain, the song ends with a loud, brassy, playful orchestral flourish.

Role Play for Survival: Lessons from Conchita Piquer

Those who sang along to "La Parrala" could learn how to play roles not only from the character, La Parrala, but also from the performer, Conchita Piquer. For in this *copla,* Piquer uses multiple different tones and nuances to convey the words of different speakers. Each stanza begins with a third-person narrator, who, in a serious storytelling tone and with strong momentum, gives us the background in four lines of verse. Then the tone becomes more intimate and gossipy, as the narrator reports what "las malas lenguas," the neighbourhood gossips, are saying. We return to the more serious voice of the narrator, who reports how no one understands La Parrala's suffering. The gossipy tone resumes as Piquer reports, "Unos desían que sí, otros desían que no" ("Some said yes, others said no"). Then we go into La Parrala's refrain: "La Parrala así cantó" ("La Parrala sang as follows"). Here, Piquer must convey the tone of La Parrala, who is herself playing the role of the nosy neighbours and mocking their words. Piquer conveys a false earnestness as La Parrala sings, "Que sí, que sí, que sí, que sí, que a la Parrala le gusta el vino" ("Yes, yes, yes, yes, La Parrala likes her wine"). But the apparent earnestness quickly gives way to mockery and impishness as she then negates these words: "Que no, que no, que no, que no, ni el aguardiente ni el marrasquino" ("No, no, no, no, neither brandy nor kirsch"). Then the narrator pulls back entirely, taking us out of the character's voice, and looking at the events of a song from a distance as she suddenly addresses the listeners directly: "¿Quién me compra este misterio?" ("Who will buy the answer to this mystery?"). Then, a lyrical, more emotional tone, punctuated by soft sobs, characterizes the refrain's final questions about La Parrala's suffering. Within the space of about three minutes, then, Piquer has played the narrator, repeated the words and tone of the neighbours, and created the tone of La Parrala herself, as well as that of La Parrala playing the neighbours. She has gone from her suspenseful, storytelling tone, to gossipy, mocking, majestic, and grief-stricken. As the listeners sang along and imitated her performance, they may have been schooling themselves in the consummate acting skills they needed to survive without realizing they were doing so. And in their conscious attempts to capture the nuances of the role, they would have recovered some of the sense of control that was being taken away from them in everyday life now that even the smallest personal decisions were mandated from above.

Finally, "La Parrala" functioned as a wonderful alibi to give people a little relief from the restraint that was mandated in everyday life. By playing her role, they could safely break the rules. La Parrala was an outrageous, over-the-top kind of character, whose life was the opposite of that of the obedient woman under National Catholicism. But she was also a recognizable character from popular culture, one whom everyone knew. By playing her role, the defeated could get some relief from the stifling restrictions of curfews, muted conversations, pretended piety and chastity, and above all the lack of spontaneity that was the result of terror and the micromanagement of every small behaviour. They could let it all hang out as they sang, thus refusing to "participate in their own execution." Yet their outrageous behaviour would not be punished, for they were simply singing a radio song that everybody knew.

Thus, in 1940, León, Valerio, Quiroga, and Piquer created a song and a character that the defeated could use to meet the first challenges of survival in Franco's Spain. To stay alive, they had to be able to play to perfection the National-Catholic roles imposed on them. They had to be able to fake courage in the face of the authorities, rather than letting their fear show through. They had to remain active and manage their fear. And they had to be able to invent alibis that would conceal their left-wing past and help them stay alive. "La Parrala" offered them a vehicle with which to master all of these most basic tasks of survival.

In "La Parrala," the role play is primarily about *concealing, hiding,* which may have served the defeated in their immediate goal of remaining physically alive despite terror and investigation. Though it names and briefly pauses on the existence of the suffering underneath, the song does not dwell there. In the next three chapters, we will see how role play could be used to *express* that suffering safely. Under the alibi of playing a fictional role, the defeated could simultaneously reveal and conceal the grief underlying the terror, as three of Piquer's most famous *coplas* offered them the chance to carry out substitute rituals of mourning.

Chapter Four

Paradise Lost: "Ojos verdes" ("Green Eyes") as Ritual of Separation

Introduction: Mourning Denied

Fear trumps all other human emotions; terrified people devote all of their energy to getting out of danger. In Franco's Spain, the terror and executions lasted for decades, and this created intense and chronic psychological difficulties that involved not only fear but also grief. The defeated faced cumulative traumatic losses that generated intense anguish, yet they were forbidden to mourn. For them to survive psychologically, they needed to gain control of their terror and then find safe ways to express at least some of their grief. This chapter, and the two that follow, discuss three of Piquer's most famous *coplas* – "Ojos verdes" ("Green Eyes"), "Tatuaje" ("Tattoo"), and "Romance de la otra" ("Ballad of the Other Woman") – all of which deal with loss and grieving. Here, role play remained important but had a different function. If "La Parrala" showed the defeated how to conceal information about themselves through role play, the three mourning *coplas* offered them ways to express and to work through some of their grief in the code of a fictional role.[1]

These mourning *coplas* foreground another key survival mechanism: ritual. Popular songs in many cultures involve repetition and familiarity and thus can be considered a kind of ritual behaviour. I contend that in Franco's Spain, the three *coplas* just mentioned took the place of rituals that are so basic to human beings as to actually define our species: burial and mourning rites.[2] Each of these songs offered the defeated a substitute for one of the three phases of rituals identified by anthropologist Arnold van Gennep. In the phase of separation, the body is prepared and buried in specified ways. A long phase of transition follows during which the mourner withdraws from certain social activities and may wear special clothing. Finally, a ritual of incorporation ends the period of isolation and welcomes the mourner back into society. Such rituals exist in every culture, and when they are denied, the psychological suffering of the relatives is so intense as to last a lifetime.

For the defeated under Franco, all three phases of mourning were blocked. The separation phase typically involves identifying the body, recovering the deceased's personal belongings, acquiring a death certificate, preparing the body for burial, and gathering the community to bury and say goodbye to the deceased. But the defeated Republicans often did not know where their loved ones were or whether they were alive or dead. Those who did know that their relatives had been shot often did not know where their bodies had been buried. And those who knew where a loved one had been killed often did not dare go there to identify the body, fearing that if they acknowledged their connection to the deceased, they would become the next victims (Reig Tapia 100–1). The regime acknowledged few of these deaths and prohibited the defeated from wearing the black clothes of mourning. Widows who defied the prohibition had their heads shaved by Fascist militiamen and were forced to drink castor oil (101; Casanova, "Dictadura" 47). The defeated could not perform funeral rites for their loved ones and were often forbidden even to mention their names.[3]

The phase of transition was equally problematic. In normal circumstances, mourners separate themselves from society, entering a limbo state between their past life with the deceased and a future life with new roles and relationships, toward which they gradually move emotionally. For the defeated, this sort of transition was almost impossible. If they relinquished their attachment to those who had died, they would have felt extremely disloyal, as if they were betraying their own values. Nor could they prepare to take on new roles, given the extremely limited opportunities open to the defeated in 1940s Spain. They were caught in a limbo state that threatened never to end.

As for rites of incorporation, while movies, songs, soccer, and bullfights provided opportunities for all Spaniards to enjoy the same activities, the division of society into winners and losers, fuelled and perpetuated by the "Causa General," made true incorporation impossible.

Thus, the regime acknowledged neither the death itself, nor the idea that a deceased Republican deserved to be mourned, nor the right of a Republican survivor to mourn his or her dead. The bereaved were what Ken Doka has called "disenfranchised grievers."[4] They experienced not only deep, chronic grief and anguish but also a traumatic denial of personhood.

OJOS VERDES
Valverde/León/Quiroga

I

Apoyá en er quisio de la mansebía,
miraba encenderse la noche de mayo;
pasaban los hombres y yo sonreía,
hasta que en mi puerta paraste er cabayo.
Serrana, ¿me das candela?
y yo te dije: gaché,
ven y tómala en mis labios,
que yo fuego te daré.[5]
Dejaste er cabayo
y lumbre te di
y fueron dos verdes luseros de mayo
tus ojos pa' mí.

ESTRIBILLO

Ojos verdes, verdes
como la arbahaca,
verdes como el trigo verde
y el verde, verde limón.
Ojos verdes, verdes
con briyo de faca,
que s'han clavaito en mi corasón.
Pa' mí ya no hay soles, luseros ni luna,
no hay más que unos ojos que mi vía son.
Ojos verdes, verdes
como la arbahaca,
verdes como el trigo verde
y el verde, verde limón.

II

Vimos desde el cuarto despuntar el día
y anunciar el alba la Torre la Vela.[6]
Dejaste mis brazos cuando amanesía
y en mi boca un gusto de menta y canela.

GREEN EYES
Valverde/León/Quiroga

I

Propped against the doorway of the brothel,
I watched the May night light up.
Men passed by and I smiled at them,
until you stopped your horse at my door.
Babe, got a light?
and I said to you, 'Dude,
Come get it from my lips,
I'll light your fire.'
You left your horse
and I gave you a light
and your eyes were two green May stars
to me.

REFRAIN

Green eyes, green
as basil,
green like green wheat,
and green, green lemons.
Green, green eyes
shining like daggers,
which have stabbed me in the heart.
For me there are no longer suns, stars or moon,
there are only those eyes which are my life.
Green eyes, green
as basil,
green like green wheat,
and green, green lemons.

II

We saw the day break from our room
And we heard morning ring out from the Torre la Vela.
You left my arms when dawn was breaking
and in my mouth you left the taste of mint and cinnamon.

Serrana, para un vestío yo te quiero regalá;
yo te dije: estás cumplío,
no me tienes que dar ná..
Subiste ar cabayo y un beso te di[7]
y nunca otra noche más bella de mayo
he vuelto a viví.

AL ESTRIBILLO

Babe, I want to give you enough for a dress;
and I told you, you're paid up,
you don't have to give me anything.
You got on your horse, you left me,
and never have I lived another May night
as beautiful.

TO THE REFRAIN

The bewitching music and words of "Ojos verdes" ("Green Eyes") captivated audiences. First performed before the war, in 1935, it would become one of the most famous *coplas* of all time. It was also groundbreaking; it was one of the songs that launched the *copla* as a genre, gradually pushing aside the erotic cabaret songs called *cuplés* (Manuel Román 25).[8] This chapter explores this song, not as it would have been received by its first listeners in 1935, before the civil war, but as it may have functioned for the defeated after the war, in the dark years of the 1940s. Its postwar reception was strongly associated with Piquer, who did not perform it before the war but would record its most famous version in 1940. I read "Ojos verdes" as offering the defeated a ritual of separation that compensated for the lack of opportunity to say goodbye to loved ones, and as a vehicle for an elegy to all that the Spanish Republic had represented for those who had gotten their first taste of democracy between 1931 and 1936.

The song would have had extra pathos for anyone familiar with the poetry of Federico García Lorca, who had been executed by the Nationalists at the beginning of the civil war. For Rafael de León's refrain was a direct allusion to the beginning of Lorca's famous Surrealist poem "Romance sonámbulo" ("Sleepwalking Ballad"). León had befriended Lorca before the war. Singer Miguel de Molina, who would later perform "Ojos verdes" as well, recalls having a drink with the two poets in 1935, and hearing León recite his new lyric for Lorca:

> Rafael llamaba "poeta" a Lorca y Federico le decía "marqués" porque descendía de una familia de la nobleza. Y en la conversación, Rafael comentó que estaba escribiendo, con su colaborador Salvador Valverde, una nueva canción que ya habían titulado *Ojos verdes.* Cuando comenzó a recitar algo del estribillo, "Ojos verdes, verdes como la albahaca ...," Federico, evidentemente en broma, le dijo que eso estaba inspirado en su *Romance sonámbulo,* "Verde, que te quiero verde. Verde viento. Verdes ramas" ...
>
> Rafael, entre ofendido y siguiendo la broma, le preguntó si se creía "el dueño del color verde en la poesía española."
>
> Los dejé así conversando en la mesa ... y cuando estreché la mano de Federico al despedirme, no sabía que no lo vería nunca más y que sus días ya estaban contados.

Rafael would call Lorca "poet," and Federico called him "Marquis," because he was from a noble family. In the conversation, Rafael mentioned that he and his collaborator Salvador Valverde were writing a new song, which

> he had called "Green Eyes." When he began to recite part of the refrain, "Green eyes, green as basil," Federico, jokingly, told him that the words came from his "Sleepwalking Ballad": "Green, I want you green. Green wind. Green branches ..."
>
> Rafael, half offended and half joking, asked him if he thought he was "the owner of the color green in Spanish poetry."
>
> I left them there, talking at the table ..., and when I shook Federico's hand as I said goodbye, I didn't know that I would never see him again and that his days were already numbered. (Miguel de Molina 109)

The very way Molina tells of his encounter with León and Lorca shows it as a fleeting moment of creativity and humour that was soon to disappear forever.[9]

Reminiscences of Lorca can be found throughout "Ojos verdes," not just in the refrain. We find them in the piano that plays the introduction, recalling Lorca's piano accompaniment to the popular ballads he recorded with La Argentinita in 1931.[10] We find echoes of Lorca in the taste of mint and cinnamon that the lover leaves in the protagonist's mouth. We find them in the song's setting and atmosphere. Though it was written before Lorca's death, the song could have functioned after the war as a eulogy to him. For in this song, the idyllic world that has been lost is not just a fleeting night of love for the protagonist; it is also Lorca's poetry, which has been snuffed out by the Nationalist terror. And it is, by extension, the whole world of hope and promise that many Spaniards passionately embraced in the years of the Spanish Republic.

Paradise Lost

Basilio Martín Patino's fictional Marqués de Almodóvar, in the 1995 "mockumentary" titled *Ojos verdes*, compares this *copla* to the Bible's Song of Songs. Some of its distinctive features help account for its powerful effect on listeners. This *copla* draws us immediately out of our ordinary world into an alternative space and time, replete with intense sensations. It places us in that alternative world even before Piquer begins to sing. Unlike later *coplas*, which would be accompanied by an orchestra, "Ojos verdes" features a guitar, a piano, and an orchestra, as if the song were a compendium of the *copla*'s history, for the genre's popular origins were in flamenco, which is accompanied by the guitar. When Lorca collected and recorded popular Andalusian songs, he accompanied them on the instrument of the bourgeoisie, the piano. The music had made its transition to the stage that way, in the show created by Lorca and La Argentinita. And its future lay in accompaniment by an orchestra before large urban audiences. "Ojos verdes" combines all these stages in its especially rich instrumentation.

As the song begins, the piano commands our attention immediately with a single deep bass note, then a chord, then an imitation of the guitar flourishes of flamenco, with sixteenth-note triplets high in the treble. These dramatic flourishes are then answered by the guitar. By the time the orchestra comes in, at a slow, lyrical tempo, the listener is already hypnotized. This introduction takes longer than that of most *coplas*, giving listeners time to immerse themselves in the alternative space before the singing begins. When Piquer does begin to sing, the guitar and the piano continue to play along with the orchestra, sweeping us away in the lush instrumentation. The *copla*'s flamenco roots are emphasized throughout, with either the piano or the guitar answering Piquer with triplets after many of her lines.

A close reading of the lyrics reveals the meanings they could have taken on for the defeated. The first line is crucial:

Apoyá en el quisio de la mansebía

Leaning against the doorway of the brothel

This is probably the most famous single line of any *copla*. It immediately marks the difference between the Republic and the Franco dictatorship, for this overt reference to prostitution was permitted under the Republic, when the song was written, but censored under Franco.[11] León would later write new, blander lines to substitute for the censored first four lines of the song. Many performers sang the blander version, obeying the rules, but not Conchita Piquer, who always put art before politics and insisted on singing the censored version, both in live shows and on recordings – indeed, she paid stiff fines for doing so.[12] For listeners who sang along with her, then, the song, from its first line, must have felt like an act of resistance, in that it created a complicity among members of the audience or groups of radio listeners, who knew the line was forbidden. It also forged an alliance between Piquer and the defeated in her audience, because, however right-wing her ideology may have been, whenever she sang those lines, she was placing herself on their side. In this way, from the very first line, the theatre or the radio opened up an alternative space with laws that differed from those of the regime.

The prostitute stands on the brothel's threshold. That liminal space parallels the space the listeners occupied during the singing of the song as they, too, looked back on another, happier world. The time, too, is liminal: the protagonist watches the lights turn on in the town at dusk on a May evening. She portrays herself as plying her trade, smiling at passing men. She flirts shamelessly as she tells the man on the horse she'll be happy to light his fire. Such overt references to female desire were anathema in Franco's Spain. The song thus drew female listeners into an alternative space where, by singing along with Piquer, they could affirm their own sexual desire and imagine themselves acting as seducers – a role the regime forbade them.[13]

The entire first stanza is built around images of light, beginning with the oxymoron of the May night lighting up, and continuing through the puns on lighting a cigarette as lighting a sexual fire. Finally, the stranger's eyes become two green stars, with the chosen word for stars being *luceros* rather than *estrellas*, thus containing the word *light (luz)*. So, the green-eyed horseman is the bringer of light. The scene takes place in the idyllic atmosphere of a May evening, May being associated with spring, greenness, sprouting, renewal. The vocabulary (*gaché, candela*) and pronunciation locate us in Andalucía, as do the flamenco-style flourishes.

Then comes the refrain, with its slow, step-by-step musical descent reminiscent of a nursery rhyme or lullaby, transporting listeners even deeper into the song's alternative world. The refrain has a hypnotic effect, just like the eyes of the horseman, as we hear it repeated and sing along with it throughout the song. The comparison of the stranger's green eyes to basil initially appears to be simply a borrowing from Lorca's "Romance sonámbulo" ("Sleepwalking Ballad"). But the next two images complicate the message:

verdes como el trigo verde,
y el verde, verde limón.

Green like green wheat,
and green, green lemons.

Since neither wheat nor lemons are automatically thought of as green, León must repeat the word green in these images. Why, if the stranger's eyes are so green, does the poet not choose images of plants or foods that, like basil, are *always* green? "Verdes como el trigo verde" might initially strike one as bad poetry. But far from it. For both wheat and lemons are green only *fleetingly*, their greenness quickly giving way to yellow. The two images, repeated throughout in the incantatory refrain, contain the song's most important message: happiness is fleeting, ephemeral. The encounter with the green-eyed stranger only lasts a night; spring doesn't last; green wheat and lemons turn yellow before you know it. So the green wheat and the green, green lemons are already impregnated with the experience of loss. The amorous encounter will not last until they ripen; it will be snuffed out before it comes into its own. The three similes in these lines all refer to food. León wrote them before the war, when only the working class was hungry. In the 1940s, these images of food would have been poignant, for most of Spain was chronically malnourished due to government policy; wheat was especially scarce.[14] Those who had had enough to eat before the war and who no longer did would have had additional reasons, then, to think of satisfaction, plenitude, or fullness, as fleeting.

The green eyes begin as light, then turn into nourishment. But suddenly they turn into weapons as their light shines like a long-handled knife plunged into the protagonist's heart. Light, and greenness, associated with life, quickly yield to images of death. Then the lights go out; neither sun, nor moon, nor stars shine for the protagonist any longer, because the only thing that could light up her life and make it meaningful would be those green eyes, which are now gone.

The first stanza is set in the transitional time of dusk; the second, in the equally ephemeral dawn, as the day "awakens" and the bells announce the morning. The stranger leaves the prostitute's arms as the sun comes up, leaving the delightful aftertaste of Lorca's mint and cinnamon in her mouth. And now the song redeems the prostitute. The horseman offers her money for a dress, which she refuses, saying he has already given her enough. The protagonist's encounter with the stranger is thus taken out of the realm of commercial exchange. She refuses pay because, as all the food images indicate, she has had the experience of plenitude; nothing further is required. The stranger then gets on his horse and leaves, and for the protagonist who remains behind, no other May night will ever equal that one. At the end of the song, as she repeats the refrain, she cries inconsolably, for when she loses her lover, food comes to an end and all the lights go out. It is no wonder that Spaniards in Franco's Spain, living amid hunger, curfews, and frequent cuts in electricity, could identify with the song.[15]

The idea that no other May evening will ever bring the protagonist an equally marvellous encounter may have had a special meaning for those living in Franco's Spain. Many writers have indicated that in the postwar period, it was as if time had stopped. Carmen Martín Gaite describes the entire forty years of the dictatorship as a single, indivisible block of time that she cannot differentiate (*El cuarto* 133). In a short story by Juan Marsé set in postwar Barcelona, time is out of whack; April seems like November, and everything seems paralyzed ("Historia de detectives" 8). And in Fernando Fernán-Gómez's play, *Las bicicletas son para el verano* (*Bicycles are for Summer*), the characters recall as the war is ending how the father of the family had promised just before the war began to buy his son a bicycle the following summer. Now, trapped in the Spain of Franco's victory, the father says in the play's final line: "Sabe Dios cuándo habrá otro verano" ("God knows when there'll be another summer") (208). For the protagonist of "Ojos verdes," after the stranger leaves, the sun, moon, and stars no longer exist. Time has effectively stopped for her as well.

The song thus draws the listener-performer into a bewitching, idyllic space full of Lorca, food, and light, an uncensored space where a woman can claim sexual desire, a space of happiness and plenitude, which is then lost. This *copla*'s narrative structure fleshes out the scene, appealing to the senses; we can see the characters and the place. And the feelings that go along with all of this are put into words and expressed through Piquer's voice. The listener-performer, playing both the role of the protagonist and the role of Piquer, projects herself into the idyllic space. She experiences the magical encounter along with the protagonist and feels along with her what it is like to lose the person who meant everything to her, and with him, the whole surrounding world.

"Ojos verdes" and the Loss of the Spanish Republic (1931–6)

"Ojos verdes" was written just a year before the Spanish Civil War, when the Republic, although no one knew it, was in its last months. What did this vanished state mean to those who remember it?[16] It was their first taste of real democracy, where both sexes could vote, and where votes actually counted. It meant dignity, in that Spanish working-class people were recognized as citizens in the very first lines of the Constitution: "España es una República democrática de trabajadores de toda clase" ("Spain is a democratic Republic of workers of all classes.")[17] It meant participating in the creation of a new kind of country, as "un proyecto colectivo que tenía como principal objetivo la justicia social, en un país asolado por la pobreza y la falta de oportunidades" ("a collective project whose principal objective was social justice, in a country devastated by poverty and lack of opportunity").[18] It meant a collective hunger for education and culture and a state whose priority was to satisfy that hunger. Ten thousand schools were created in the first two years of the Republic, and teachers were trained according to the best humanistic values of liberal Spain; many who were children then remember even now how much they learned from their inspiring teachers in those years (*Víctimas todavía*). Working-class organizations had long provided popular libraries in their local headquarters, but now this was joined by a massive effort by the state to bring books and culture to the most isolated corners of Spain. This effort did not stop even during the civil war. More libraries were founded during the years of the Spanish Republic than at any time before or since.[19] The Republic meant new opportunities for women, who could now enter the professions and began to go to university in numbers. The Republic also witnessed a flowering of Spanish cultural life that perhaps has never been equalled, with intellectuals and artists of the stature of Unamuno, Ortega, Lorca, Dalí, Buñuel, and countless others, and with many writers brought into the Republican government. Exclaims writer José Luis Sampedro, remembering his youth in the years of the Republic: "¡Cómo se dilataba el horizonte español! ¡Cómo se respiraba en libertad!" ("How the Spanish horizon opened up! How we could breathe in freedom!")[20] It was for reasons like these that, when the generals carried out their coup d'état, many were proud to take up arms and fight.

With the end of the Republic, the whole cultural elite was exiled or killed, leaving Spain frozen in a mediocrity that many describe as a *darkness* akin to that experienced by the prostitute of "Ojos verdes" when the green-eyed stranger leaves and the lights go out.[21] It meant "cuarenta años de oscurantismo y represión ..." ("forty years in the darkness of reactionary ignorance and repression") (Sampedro). It meant that the children of postwar Spain would grow up in silence, "un silencio que llenó la vida pública de mi país, y que fue la respuesta a todas mis preguntas e inquietudes" ("a silence that filled the public life of my country, and that was the response to all my questions and worries") (Regás). It meant growing up "en un país oscuro e inmóvil, [donde] llegamos a creer que España había sido condenada desde siempre a la oscuridad de la caverna, a la inmovilidad de los años iguales, feos, grises" ("in an obscure and immobile country, [where] we came to believe that Spain had always been condemned to the darkness of the cavemen, and to the paralysis of years that were all the same, ugly and grey") (Grandes).[22]

Many spent the forty years of the dictatorship hoping for the return of that May evening upon Franco's death. But such was not to be. For the Spanish democracy that came after 1975 grew out of the dictatorship and refused to acknowledge any link to Spain's first democracy, that of the Republic. What this meant was that, although those Republicans who lived to see that day had their votes and their freedom restored, the cause for which they had sacrificed so much continued to be either forgotten or distorted. As Rosa Regás put it at the Concierto-Homenaje a los Republicanos, the defenders of the Spanish Republic "no sólo no fueron reconocidos, sino ni siquiera recordados" ("not only were not recognized, they were not even remembered"). This contrasts with the treatment given to those who fought Fascism in other countries, and who were honoured in state ceremonies and commemorated in films (Elordi). Instead, the Republic is remembered the way the Francoists wanted it to be: only for its social unrest and burning churches. And the civil war is remembered as equal in savagery on both sides, the implication being that there is no reason to remember the Spanish Republic. Its great achievements and the people who contributed to them have been consigned to oblivion.

For my purpose here, what this means is that the personhood, the visibility, the citizenship, and the dignity conferred on people for the brief five years of the Spanish Republic have not returned to this day. Only in 2004 was the first ceremony held in homage to the surviving Republicans. And even then, it was organized by left-wing associations rather than by the government. Only since 2004 has the government made even timid efforts to rehabilitate the names and the memory of those who remained loyal to the democratically elected Republic when the civil war broke out.[23] This continued invisibility and stigmatization, in turn, means that those survivors of the Spanish Civil War have remained in the marginal, unrecognized situation of the nameless protagonist of "Ojos verdes." That May night has indeed never returned, and the defeated still mourn it even as they continue to mourn their lost loved ones. In a photograph by Eloy Alonso projected on screens during the 2004 concert in homage to the Spanish Republicans, we see a memorial with a plaque listing the names of some of Franco's victims. In front of the plaque stand four elderly men and women holding a Republican flag in front of them. On the flag is the slogan, "¡Viva la República!"[24]

"Ojos verdes" as Leave-Taking Ritual

At a deeper level, I contend that "Ojos verdes" may have functioned in postwar Spain as a covert mourning ritual, corresponding to the separation phase, in which the surviving relative reacts to the death and says goodbye to the loved one. Onno van der Hart, who pioneered the use of ritual in grief therapy, proposes that such invented rituals enact a farewell, but that they also acknowledge the difficulty of letting go: "This can be done by producing a symbol and allowing it first to intensify the relationship. For example, a mourner might give a photograph a special place in the house before destroying it or putting it away" (Rando 327–8).[25] Thus, the ultimate goal of leave-taking rituals is gradually to diminish preoccupation with the deceased and bring about a farewell, but for this to happen, the feelings of grief must first be intensified in the ritual, as they are in "Ojos verdes."

To be effective, a mourning ritual must take participants out of ordinary space and time and immerse them in an alternative space in which they perform symbolic acts that allow them to reflect on the loss and discover its meaning (Lubin and Johnson 77–8). Rituals are most effective when they function on several levels and involve the senses; this helps engage the unconscious. In "Ojos verdes," the alternative space is especially compelling not only because of the beauty of the musical accompaniment, but also because of the rich, sensual imagery: greenness, mint, cinnamon, basil, wheat, lemons, the sound of bells on a May evening. "Ojos verdes" evokes our senses of taste, smell, and sight even as we use our hearing to listen and to sing along.[26] And performing it requires both singing and acting, involving the whole body, which makes it especially effective as a ritual.

Rituals of separation involve revisiting the experience of the loss along with its attendant tangle of sadness, anger, guilt, and fear. When they sang "Ojos verdes," the defeated had an opportunity to re-experience, at the safe distance provided by the role of the fictional protagonist, all the past happiness of being with their loved ones, and then relive the despair of their loss, the feeling that all the beauty had gone and that time itself had stopped moving. "Ojos verdes" represents the relationship with the deceased or absent person as its only horizon; it contains no verbs in the future tense, for in the terms of the song there can be no future without those green eyes that supplanted the sun, moon, and stars.

The fact that "Ojos verdes" is addressed directly to the absent lover is crucial to its potential use as a ritual of separation. This *copla* could function like the daily letters that psychotherapists prescribe today for mourners who have difficulty acknowledging the death of their loved one. Clients are instructed to address those letters to the deceased as if he were alive (Witztum and Roman 150). This enables mourners to express all their mixed feelings about the death itself and about the person who has died. And this in turn helps them gradually assimilate the loss. In "Ojos verdes," the protagonist is able to tell her lost lover how much their encounter meant to her, how it changed her life forever, how he satisfied and nourished her, and how he was the light of her life, but also how all this nourishment has turned into mortal wounding, since his departure has left her unable to go on living without him. The song thus expresses complaint and anger as well as the pain of loss.

In other songs, Piquer sometimes sobs as she takes a breath between lines. At the end of "Ojos verdes," she sobs her way all the way through the last words she sings: "y el verde, verde limón." "Ojos verdes" represents the desolation of the worst moments of grief, but it does so through the safe distance of a fictional story. People suffering from post-traumatic stress and complicated grief tend to oscillate between the overwhelming emotions of painful flashbacks and the numbness of avoidance. "Ojos verdes" provided a middle ground. When the defeated performed the role of the song's protagonist, they poured themselves into her painful feelings, which may also have been their own as mourners. But they simultaneously remained aware of the inflections, the intonation they were giving to each phrase as performers of the song.[27] According to drama therapist Robert Landy, healing occurs in the back-and-forth movement in and out of the fictional role.[28] When Conchita Piquer cries as much as sings the last lines of the song, she enables the tears associated with the listener's grief to come out, under the safe cover of imitating her magisterial performance. It is hard to remain numb while hearing this song, let alone while singing it. The song, then, provided a channel for the pain to rise to the surface and be released, even as its plot progression and brevity provided a container which guaranteed that the mourner would not have to stay in touch with the pain indefinitely and become overwhelmed. Critics praised Piquer for the fact that, even though she became very emotional while singing, her emotions never ran away with her; they were always controlled. Thus the listener who sang along with her could safely end "Ojos verdes" by sobbing along with her in a contained way, and then come out of the song and end that episode of mourning. The repeated singing of "Ojos verdes" allowed for the repeated re-experiencing of the loss with safety built in, until it had been processed to a large degree and had lost some of its initial force, that is, until the mourner had adjusted somewhat to the loss.

When we consider who was being mourned by the defeated in those years, we are brought back to those green lemons and that green wheat, never allowed to ripen. For many of those who were executed were men in the flower of youth. The 2003 documentary *Les fosses del silenci* (The Silent Graves) tells of Asunción Álvarez's brothers, who in 1937 were young men. They initially fought for the Republic, but when the Nationalists took over their province of León, they reported for duty, thinking they would simply be sent to the front as Nationalist soldiers. Asunción remembers how they got dressed in their best clothes, "muy guapos los dos, como unos soles." And of course they were executed. In 2002, Asunción, then eighty-seven, was still searching for their remains, still seeking closure, the ability to say goodbye, even if she would only be addressing their bones ("quiero abrazar los huesos"). As the first bones appeared at the excavation site where they were believed to have been buried, she burst into tears (figure 4.1).

Many among the defeated would have found that the protagonist's predicament in "Ojos verdes" resonated with their own. For both, mourning was not legitimized by the surrounding society. In the song, the prostitute's love relationship is illicit by definition. Because of the illegal and transitory nature of her relationships, she cannot declare her mourning for the horseman, nor can she have it recognized. That is why the song is addressed directly to him rather than to a third-person public. The song is a private communication between the prostitute and her absent lover, or between mourner and deceased, on which the public eavesdrops. Thus the song provided the defeated with an opportunity to make their mourning public and audible in coded form, by performing the role of that other disenfranchised griever, the prostitute.

As she expresses to her absent lover and to her listeners the full depth and range of her experience, the prostitute shows herself to be a person of deep feeling and dignity. The regime may have marginalized her as a sinner, but her first-person account of her experience and feelings belies that official version. By performing her role in the first person, the defeated were able to declare before the world that their own experiences of love and loss were as worthy of attention as anyone else's. In

4.1 Asunción Álvarez cries as the first bones are discovered in an exhumation at Piedrafita de Babia (León) in 2002. Photograph by Eloy Alonso González. ©

this way, the song vindicated those whom the regime had declared to be outcasts, whose experiences were ordinarily denied, distorted, or simply made invisible.

Even in the most favourable political and socio-economic circumstances, a bereaved person in the separation phase of mourning may dream repeatedly about the deceased and the past (Rando 328). The bereaved in Franco's Spain were especially vulnerable, because the desolation of their psychic life was reflected in the objective desolation of the physical landscape of postwar Spain. The feeling, common in bereavement, that one will never be able to move on to another loving relationship actually had empirical validity for women in postwar Spain, for the census of 1940 showed 1 million more women than men, in a total population of 26 million.[29] Demographics thus increased the risk that the bereaved would fall into total despair, or into numbness, a form of giving up on life. To be able to say out loud what they had lost and how they felt about it, even through a song, would have been their best chance at remaining alive to their own grief, desires, and discontent, and thus coming to terms with their loss. "Ojos verdes" could be especially effective in this regard because it was already famous before the war. It could therefore activate people's memories of a time before all the death and destruction. The song thus had a real link, through memory, to the world they had lost and needed to mourn.

Given the brutal, vindictive atmosphere, a mourning ritual had to be available, and it had to be repeated in small doses over a long time in order to be effective. This would enable the mourners to enter the alternative space of the ritual repeatedly, and access their real feelings briefly, while hiding them the rest of the time. "Ojos verdes," as the second most famous *copla* after "Tatuaje" ("Tattoo"), was available on the radio for decades to be used as a ritual marking traumatic separations from those one loved. And its ability to create an idyllic and spellbinding atmosphere was therapeutic in and of itself, for it introduced beauty into an otherwise grey and sordid world, a world of dirt, mediocrity, silence, hunger, and fear. The experiences of beauty and sexual desire expressed so vividly in the song would have helped the defeated recall how it felt to be profoundly alive and to remember that such feelings were possible.

Finally, "Ojos verdes" had a therapeutic function as an expression of resistance and discontent. Given that it was written in 1935, the song clearly had not been conceived as a gesture of protest. However, the censoring of the opening stanza under Franco opened up a whole new set of functions for the song: it could protest both censorship and sexual repression, and it could create a community of people united in the complicity of singing the forbidden lines. We know that the regime strove to depoliticize social life through the mass media's products (Vázquez Montalbán, *Crónica* 35). It also worked very deliberately to fragment the old communities on the left. Nevertheless, the regime's own censorship combined with the people's resistance to it created a new kind of interpretive community. By telling a fictional story about losing the good life, and by claiming that nothing since had been anywhere near as good, the defeated could express, in full voice and in the first person, their deep discontent with their present life. The mere singing of lines that were once permitted but now censored involved an assertion of their memory of, and preference for, the past of the Republic. The defeated could use such lines to convey to one another their ongoing dissent against the Franco regime, without having to express it directly. This made the song what Harriet Senie calls an instance of "mourning in protest" (Senie 41).

Chapter Five

"Tatuaje" ("Tattoo"), the Unburied Dead, and Complicated Grief

TATUAJE
León/Valerio/Quiroga

Él vino en un barco de nombre extranjero.
Lo encontré en el puerto un anochecer,
cuando el blanco faro sobre los veleros
su beso de plata dejaba caer.
Era hermoso y rubio como la cerveza;
el pecho tatuado con un corazón.
En su voz amarga había la tristeza,
doliente y cansada, del acordeón.
Y ante dos copas de aguardiente
sobre el manchado mostrador,
él fue contándome entre dientes
la vieja historia de su amor.
Mira mi brazo tatuado
con este nombre de mujer.
Es el recuerdo de un pasado
que nunca más ha de volver.
Ella me quiso y me ha olvidado,
en cambio yo no la olvidé;
y para siempre voy marcado
con este nombre de mujer.

Él se fue una tarde con rumbo ignorado
en el mismo barco que lo trajo a mí;
pero entre mis labios se dejó olvidado

TATTOO
León/Valerio/Quiroga

He came on a boat with a foreign name.
I met him at the port one nightfall,
when the white beacon let fall
its silver kiss on the sailboats.
He was beautiful and blond as beer;
his chest tattooed with a heart.
In his bitter voice was the pained and tired
sadness of the accordion.
And with two glasses of brandy before us
on the stained countertop,
he gradually told me, in whispers,
the old story of his love.
Look at my arm, tattooed
with this woman's name.
It's the memory of a past
which will never again return.
She loved me and she's forgotten me,
but I haven't forgotten her;
and I am marked forever
with this woman's name.

He left one afternoon for an unknown destination
on the same boat that brought him to me;
but between my lips he left, forgotten

un beso de amante que yo le pedí.
Errante lo busco por todos los puertos;
a los marineros pregunto por él,
y nadie me dice si está vivo o muerto
y sigo en mi duda buscándolo fiel.
Y voy sangrando lentamente
de mostrador en mostrador,
ante una copa de aguardiente
donde se ahoga mi dolor.
Mira tu nombre tatuado
en la caricia de mi piel;
a fuego lento lo he marcado
y para siempre iré con él.
Quizás ya tú me has olvidado,
en cambio yo no te olvidé
y hasta que no te haya encontrado
sin descansar te buscaré.

Escúchame, marinero,
y dime qué sabes de él;
era gallardo y altanero
y era más rubio que la miel.
Mira su nombre de extranjero
escrito aquí, sobre mi piel.
Si te lo encuentras, marinero,
dile que yo muero por él.

 Facing English translation mine.

a lover's kiss I'd asked him for.
I wander, looking for him at every port;
I ask the sailors about him,
and no one tells me if he's alive or dead
and I continue, in my doubt, looking for him faithfully.
And I go bleeding slowly,
from bar to bar,
with a glass of brandy before me
to drown my pain.
Look at your name, tattooed
on the caress of my skin;
I marked it on with a slow fire,
and I'll wear it forever.
Maybe you've forgotten me already,
but I haven't forgotten you
and until I've found you
I'll look for you without resting.

Listen to me, sailor,
and tell me what you know about him;
he was gallant and confident
and he was blonder than honey.
Look at his foreign name
written here on my skin.
If you see him, sailor,
tell him I'm dying for him.

The song that towers over the entire postwar period is "Tatuaje" ("Tattoo"). It was omnipresent on the airwaves for at least twenty years and has never ceased to be performed since. After Franco's death, when people could write freely about the 1940s, "Tattoo" was unanimously singled out in essays, novels, and films by intellectuals who had grown up in those years. The right-wing but anti-Francoist writer Francisco Umbral wrote that for "la generación del piojo verde" ("the generation who grew up with green lice in their hair"), "Tatuaje" was a kind of street version of Beethoven's Fifth Symphony (Umbral 140). On the left, Carmen Martín Gaite could still recall, thirty years later, the radio announcer intoning: "E.A.J. 56, Radio Salamanca; van a escuchar ustedes 'Tatuaje,' en la voz de Conchita Piquer" ("E.A.J. 56, Salamanca Radio; you're going to hear 'Tattoo,' sung by Conchita Piquer"). Her comment: "Aquello era otra cosa, aquello era contar una historia de verdad" ("That was something different. That was telling a *real* story ...") (*El cuarto* 154). Manuel Vázquez Montalbán refers to "Tatuaje" as a "canción de protesta no comercializada" ("non-commercialized protest song"), one that the women of the 1940s sang "con toda el alma ... a través de sus ventanas de par en par" ("with all their hearts ... through their windows opened wide") (*Crónica* 43).[1] And Basilio Martín Patino, in his documentary film *Canciones para después de una guerra* (*Songs for After a War*), juxtaposes "Tatuaje" with images of the hard work of women's survival in Franco's Spain. He shows us women sewing in factories, washing clothes, and standing in line at the market with their ration cards, all to its rhythm. And he fades out the song momentarily to have an elderly female voiceover reflect: "Eran canciones para sobrevivir" ("They were songs for survival").

Even today, once you hear "Tatuaje," you never forget it.[2] The lyrics tell an intense story in few words (Mira Nouselles 348). The rhythm of the song, and the bitter urgency of Piquer's performance, leave you hanging on every word, knowing that something of great importance is happening as the song is being sung. "Tatuaje" has also absorbed what little attention has been focused on the *copla* genre by critics.[3] I cannot think of any single song in English that has stood out as much from the pack and maintained its status over so many decades. In this chapter, I read "Tatuaje" as the period's supreme ritual of mourning. It had such a profound impact on the defeated, I believe, because it offered them a way to respond to the cumulative, traumatic losses arising from mass executions, jailings, disappearances, and exile.

Making It Safe to Mourn: The Mask of Fiction in "Tatuaje"

The lyrics, music, and performance of "Tatuaje" worked together to make the expression of pain bearable for the listeners who sang along to it with all their hearts. This *copla* created a compelling fictional world and a protagonist with whom listeners could easily identify. People who entered the protagonist's story, by listening or singing along, were able to bypass their defences against their own pain and thereby address their own real situation and feelings even as they acted out those of the protagonist.

Several aspects of "Tatuaje" establish this emotional protection. The first eight lines create a vivid alternative world. As Silvia Bermúdez has pointed out, the exotic setting of the port is associated with both danger and desire; it is a place inhabited by outlaws, a place where rules can be broken with impunity (47). It is a liminal place, linking land with sea. The time, too, is liminal; dusk is the hour at which "repressed desires are unleashed under the protective cover of the night" (39). In Franco's Spain, where people had to be home by curfew, this place and time represented an escape from stifling norms. The foreign sailor is especially exotic: he is tall and blonde in a Spain of short, dark men (Vázquez Montalbán *Crónica* 43), and he has arrived on a foreign ship from places that Spaniards in those years could not imagine going, due to their penury and to the regime's many restrictions on travel. This foreign lover sets "Tatuaje" apart from many other *coplas,* which are uncritical representations of everything Spanish.

In the first stanza, Rafael de León builds on this exotic setting by accumulating elements that were either unavailable or forbidden in Franco's Spain. Food, the most necessary yet the most absent element for most Spaniards, is introduced through *metaphor*: the sailor's blonde hair is as nourishing as beer or honey. Sex, too, is introduced initially as metaphor; nightfall is heralded by the lighthouse pouring a *kiss* of light on the sailboats in the harbour.[4] The sailor is handsome, introducing beauty into an otherwise seedy world.

The music, too, draws the listener into the song. The brief orchestral introduction is light and lilting, in a major key, imitating the rocking of the waves; the pizzicato of the cellos reinforces this effect. The song's first two lines are in a major key, affirming this carefree air. Then the key changes to the tonic minor, returns briefly to major, and the stanza ends in a minor key. The listeners are thus taken gradually from major to minor, going through the steps of accessing their own sad feelings.

The second four lines are entirely in a minor key, with heavy orchestral bowing replacing the light pizzicato of the first stanza. Here, the world of the song differs from people's daily lives in that negative feelings may be named and expressed. In two short lines, the words "*amarga,*" "*tristeza,*" "*doliente,*" and "*cansada*" ("bitter," "sadness," "painful," and "tired") are used to describe the handsome sailor. These words are emphasized by a ritard that begins at the word "*amarga,*" pauses on the words "*tristeza*" and "*cansada,*" and culminates in the drawn-out word "*acordeón.*" All of these emotions ran counter to what people in Franco's "New Spain" were supposed to be feeling. In this way, listeners on the losing side found almost all of their hidden feelings named within the space of a few short lines. These words would not have been available in any other song genre. In the song, the sailor's sadness is compared to the music of the accordion; thus, the role of this music in expressing sadness is reflected within the song itself. The accordion, evocative of the bandoneón used in the Argentine tango, again sets this *copla* apart from those influenced by flamenco or other Spanish regional music.

Then begins an urgent, suspenseful, forward-moving rhythm, reminiscent of a tango, as the sailor tells his painful story in the second half of the first stanza. The accumulation of forbidden elements continues – there is the brandy, which burns and kills the pain; and there are the stains on the bar's countertop, the antithesis of the spotless Francoist kitchen, in whose maintenance women were exhaustively instructed. The stains, like the tattoo later in the song, cannot be erased; they are indelible marks of experience, the "objective correlative" of the sailor's painful feelings, which also cannot be erased.[5]

Finally, the tale of an old love story emerges. The story has to be told "entre dientes," in a hushed voice. This must have resonated for many among the defeated, since it was extremely dangerous for them to refer to painful stories from their past, and they could only do so in whispers.

By the end of the first stanza the images and feelings that created the alternative space become intensified. The stains on the countertop yield to the song's main symbol – the tattoo. A countertop is stained involuntarily; but a tattoo, even more indelible, is deliberately inscribed on the skin. The tattoo is associated with rebellion against social norms, with sailors, outlaws, and other marginal people. The tattoo, as the sailor tells us, is a memory: "the memory of the past which will never return." The sailor's love story is all the more poignant because the woman whose name was tattooed on his arm once loved him but has now forgotten him, yet he has not forgotten her. The first section of the song ends in a minor key.

The first part of "Tatuaje," then, creates an alternative space, a provisional space between two worlds, in which everything that is absent or repressed in the listener's world is made present and named.[6] Above all, feelings are named, feelings that have left a mark – on the sailor's voice, on the music, on the countertop. The part fulfils several key functions for the listener. The plot, setting, and characters create a story that is exotic, mysterious, outside the norm. The feelings expressed are painful, perhaps dangerous. The listener, as she put herself in the place of the protagonist and sang of the encounter with all her heart, could think of herself, too, as someone who had an important, colourful story to tell, as someone who was interesting because she had been marked by her painful past. Even her own fatigue, as she worked, cleaned house, and stood in eternal lines at the market, acquired an exotic frame. By identifying with, and helping re-create, the protagonist of the song, the listener could recapture some belief that she was special.[7]

The orchestral bridge offers the listener some relief from the grieving process, returning as it does to the happy lilting of the waves. The first lines in the second part, like those in the first part, begin in a major key, then alternate major and minor, and end in minor as they tell of the sudden departure of the sailor on the same ship, for parts unknown, after he has given the protagonist the single night of love that she initiated. The second part thus draws the listener gradually into the intense state of grief that will be described and enacted as the song continues. For the protagonist has been forever changed by her encounter with the sailor. She remains in the liminal space of the port, neither on land nor on sea, wandering. She insists on asking the sailors about him, refusing to acknowledge that he is gone forever. As in the first part, a long ritard with significant pauses gives added weight to the lines, "y nadie me dice si está vivo o muerto / y sigo en mi duda buscándolo fiel" ("and no one tells me if he's alive or dead / and I continue, in my doubt, looking faithfully for him"). Unable to get any definitive answers, she nevertheless develops a philosophy of loyalty, the adjective "loyal" ("fiel") being one of the two words that mark climactic pauses in the second stanza. Piquer then sobs prior to the line "Y voy sangrando lentamente ..." ("And I go bleeding slowly ..."), and builds up to the word "*dolor*" ("pain"), which is the climax of the song, drawn out over several beats and a long ritard. The protagonist will remain in this state between life and death – that is, wounded – as she goes along, "bleeding slowly" from bar to bar, drowning her sorrows in what is now a lone glass of brandy, unaccompanied.

Then the protagonist speaks directly to the absent sailor, telling him she has tattooed his name on the *caress* of her skin. Again, León's lyrics introduce through metaphor precisely the things that were most sorely lacking in postwar Spain, in this case, caresses, love.[8] And again, the protagonist manages her emotional pain through a physical burning ("I marked it on my skin with a slow flame"), intensifying the initial burning effect of the brandy.

The protagonist now creates her own mission in life. Here, the song makes the transition from the past and present tenses that have been dominant, to the future tense: "Para siempre iré con él [el tatuaje]" ("I will walk with it [the tattoo] forever"). The grief continues throughout this mission; Piquer sobs again between the words "yo" ("I') and 'no te olvidé" ("haven't forgotten you"), allowing the listeners singing along to do the same. Unresolved grief defines the protagonist's future role; she refuses to accept the absence of her lover and has made it her mission to find him:

y hasta que no te haya encontrado
sin descansar te buscaré.

and until I've found you
I'll look for you without resting.

In the final stanza, the drunken, hoarse voice of the protagonist demands that the sailors listen to her as she requests information about her lover's whereabouts. And she sends him a message about her liminal status between life and death: "If you see him, sailor, tell him I'm dying for him." In the song's final line, Piquer sobs again after the word "yo" ("I"): "dile que yo muero por él" ("tell him I'm dying for him").

The song's end exemplifies something found in other *coplas:* the contrast between the lack of resolution in the narrative and the definitive resolution of the music. The protagonist ends the song not knowing whether her sailor is alive or dead, still searching, unable to get information; nothing has been resolved. The music, however, ends in a ritard followed by a conventional resolution that moves from a seventh chord to the tonic minor chord. There is no doubt that the song has come to an end. The ritard prepares the listener to wrap up his or her grieving session and enter ordinary life again. The control needed to imitate

Piquer in her sob, the ritard, and the final chord resolution all invited the listeners to move away from their own pain so as to focus on the performance of the last line. In this way, they could make the transition out of the song's story (and their emotional lives) and back into the practical struggle for survival that was their ordinary life in the 1940s.

Two other factors made this painful story a safe means for the defeated to cope with their losses. One was that songs about a woman pining for her absent lover had been a staple of Spanish oral literature since the Middle Ages.[9] This masked the relationship between the theme and the present moment in which they were singing. The second was the plot's enigmatic twist: the fact that the sailor was in love with a woman who no longer cared for him, rather than with the protagonist, made the story unique; it would have prevented the song from becoming too transparent to serve the defeated as a safe expression of loyalty to the victims of Francoist repression. The chain of unrequited loves gave the story meat, something people could ponder. The story leaves us full of questions: Why did the absent woman forget the sailor? Why does the woman at the port fall so hard for someone who is in love with someone else? In addition, the rhythm of the song, and Piquer's performance, drew the listener into the role of the fallen woman. Engrossed in the plot of the story, and in the nuances of the performance, the listeners who sang along could express their own feelings without necessarily having to recognize them as their own. This would have kept them from being overwhelmed by their grief as they expressed it in song.

Extra Camouflage: The Double Reading

For the defeated to use it as a mourning tool, "Tatuaje" had to be safe politically as well as emotionally. This safety came from a reading that suited the values of the winners, and was readily accessible. "Tatuaje" appeared in 1941, at the height of Spain's Germanophilia. The blond foreigner seems most obviously to be a Nazi, given that German soldiers had been a familiar presence in the Francoist zone during the civil war. So the exotic, gallant foreigner could fuel a fascination with Fascism on the part of right-wingers. Their reading may have served as a mask for a different, left-wing reading of the blond sailor. The sailor arrives at the port as a broken man: bitter, sad, tired, preoccupied with his own troubles – hardly a poster boy for the Nazi ethos. For left wingers, the sailor might well have evoked memories of the International Brigades, whose members had arrived by ship from a number of countries, including

Germany, to fight for the Spanish Republic. The International Brigades had been sent home by President Juan Negrín in 1938 as a gesture of conciliation (a futile one) with the Francoists, in the hope of promoting negotiations. In other words, the International Brigades actually did leave one day on a ship.

But the blond sailor could also function in a more general, symbolic way. Franco's propaganda proclaimed that he had saved Spain from foreign influences and that it was now self-sufficient. In this context, the sailor would have represented what did not fit the stifling mould of Francoism. Finally, we may read his foreignness metaphorically, as his inaccessibility, on that other shore owing to death or exile. The defeated were thus protected politically by the multiplicity of possible readings, which made the song usable by right and left alike.[10]

Confronting Complicated Grief: Protagonist and Listener

With the mask of fiction firmly in place to protect listeners, "Tatuaje" presented a protagonist whose circumstances were analogous to those of the losers of the war. In the song, the woman's lover leaves suddenly, for parts unknown, just like so many of the listeners' family members. The defeated were lonely and marginalized; the song's protagonist is so socially isolated as to be nameless. She drinks a lone glass of brandy, disconnected from the rest of society. Like the defeated, she is a disenfranchised griever, a person whose mourning is not socially sanctioned, since no one recognizes the importance of her one-night stand with the sailor. And her degraded social position as a fallen woman who wanders the ports asking for information means that she is ignored, if not scorned. In Franco's Spain, the defeated, too, often wandered "de mostrador en mostrador" ("from counter to counter") in office after office, searching in vain for information about their loved ones.

After the protagonist loses her sailor, her behaviour is striking. She is obsessed with her lost lover. Her pain continues as intensely as when the loss first occurred, forcing her to self-medicate with strong drink. She exhibits chronic yearning and searching behaviour, indicative of separation distress and trauma. Her life is in upheaval; she wanders, aimless, restless, drunk, out at night. She refuses to construct a life without the sailor, as indicated by the indelible tattoo. She refuses to acknowledge that he is gone forever, and tells him she'll keep looking until she has found him. Since she can't get him back, she adopts his behaviour herself, wandering from port to port, drinking brandy, duplicating his story of loving someone who has forgotten him, and tattooing his name on her body just as he tattooed the other woman's name on his. And she characterizes herself as wounded and dying, feeling partly dead herself in identification with her missing lover.

The protagonist's behaviour shows all the symptoms of a condition that psychotherapists call "complicated grief." It is diagnosed when the bereaved person, more than a year after the loss, suffers "recurring, unintended, and uncontrollable recollections (e.g. memories, images, dreams and nightmares), often related to the feeling that the deceased is still alive" (Maercker et al. 1119). The survivor exhibits symptoms of separation distress, such as yearning, longing, and searching for the deceased. As with PTSD, these intrusive feelings and thoughts alternate with persistent efforts to avoid reminders of the deceased; this involves avoiding activities, people, and places as well as thoughts and feelings (Jacobs and Prigerson 491–2).

The surviving relative feels a sense of purposelessness and futility. He or she feels numb and detached, as if just going through the motions of life. The state of shock or of being dazed, which most people experience immediately after bereavement, continues. The survivor has difficulty assimilating the fact that the death has occurred, but also feels that part of himself has died and has difficulty imagining a fulfilling life without the deceased. He displays ongoing anger and bitterness related to the death. The mourner's world view has been shattered, and his ability to function in daily life is significantly impaired (492). Many of the symptoms that are present for a limited time in "normal" grieving have become chronic.

Complicated grief carries significant risks to physical and mental health. Psychiatrists have linked it to heart disease, cancer, high blood pressure, lasting changes in eating habits, and increased suicidality. It is often accompanied by depression or PTSD (Prigerson et al.). In one study, about 50 per cent of patients who were being treated for complicated grief had no previous history of mental illness. Almost all of them subsequently developed psychiatric disorders, such as major depressive disorder, panic disorder, or generalized anxiety (Melhem et al. 885).

Whether a person's grief will become complicated and chronic depends on a number of factors. Sudden death and violent death are most likely to result in complicated grief. The closeness of the relationship of the bereaved person to the deceased is directly related to the likelihood of complications in grieving, with spouses being the most at risk, followed by parents. Complicated grief is also much more likely when an adequate social support system is lacking, so that the survivor is isolated, less able to come to terms with the loss or to share the experience of it with others and thus connect to the world again. The question of social support also involves whether the individual is encouraged or discouraged from expressing the emotions associated with the grieving process.

In Franco's Spain, the defeated faced a particularly severe situation of complicated grief. They had been prevented from mourning for those who had been killed during the civil war itself. Now they faced the further loss of friends and family throughout the 1940s, as the vast apparatus of Francoist repression was consolidated and as people continued to be taken from their homes or from jail, never to return. This meant that the bereaved were suffering cumulative traumatic losses through numerous violent and unjust deaths. And they were facing this with almost no social support to mitigate the effects of complicated grief, for the deaths were compounded by other losses of friends and family due to exile and jailing. And the few friends who were left did not dare to get together for fear of arrest.

The winners of the war had enormous advantages over the losers as far as mourning was concerned, since their dead (the "fallen for God and for Spain") were glorified and were being acknowledged through official burials, and ceremonies, and monuments, and anniversary processions. They could grieve with their community without fear. But this does not mean that they did not also suffer from complicated grief. Many of them, too, had lost loved ones in horrific circumstances that were difficult to assimilate.[11] The official ceremonies were probably unsatisfactory for many, since not everyone who had fought on the Nationalist side was a devout Catholic.[12] And even the devout might have felt the need for a less political, more individualized form of mourning. While I focus here mainly on the defeated, it is important to remember that "Tatuaje" met the grieving needs of many winners as well as losers. This fact was important for the losers themselves, since only songs that served the needs of both sides were safe vehicles for the emotional expression of the defeated.

For those who sang it along with Conchita Piquer, "Tatuaje" was an unsurpassed vehicle for expressing complicated grief. The disappeared sailor represented all of those who were absent from their lives, whether they were dead, missing, or jailed. The sailor is the vehicle to bring to the surface the listener-performer's own mourning. I contend that many of the defeated who sang "Tatuaje" were working to resolve their own complicated grief vicariously, through the grief of the protagonist.[13]

The Dead, the Missing, and the Absent: Who Addresses Whom in "Tatuaje"

> y nadie me dice
> si está vivo o muerto
> y sigo en mi duda
> buscándolo fiel.
> Quizás ya tú me has olvidado,
> en cambio yo no te olvidé
> y hasta que no te haya encontrado
> sin descansar te buscaré.
>
> and no-one tells me
> if he's alive or dead
> and I continue, in my doubt,
> looking for him faithfully.
> Maybe you've forgotten me already,
> but I haven't forgotten you
> and until I've found you
> I'll look for you without resting.

By asking ourselves who in 1940s Spain might be singing these lines, and to whom, we can begin to understand the depth of the pain that people across the country were expressing by singing "Tatuaje." Let's begin with the winners of the war. "Tatuaje" appeared in 1941, two years after the end of the civil war. That was a significant year for the winners, for it was the year that Franco sent soldiers to fight for Hitler in Russia in the "Blue Division." Many right-wing Spaniards, then, had sons or boyfriends fighting in foreign lands and did not know whether they were alive or dead. This provided cover for the defeated, who could use the song to mark losses that could not be so publicly acknowledged.

For the defeated, these lines gave voice to many kinds of suffering. As they sang along, they could address them, first and foremost, to those who had disappeared in the Francoist terror. At the time, people were trying to get information about those who had been executed, only to run up against denials that they had been killed. The line "y nadie me dice si está vivo o muerto" ("and nobody tells me if he's alive or dead") retains all its potency today; many relatives still have no official information about the deaths of their loved ones or about where they are buried.

They are still searching loyally today, as we see in documentaries, in the press, and on the Internet.[14]

But they were also expressing their loyalty to those in jail.[15] Antonio Ferres's novel *Los vencidos* (*The Defeated*) tells the story of Asunción, a woman from southern Spain who has not heard from her husband for five years, since he left to fight in the war.[16] She obtains safe-conduct papers and saves her pennies to go to Madrid, where she inquires among his old friends. They direct her to the jail at Guadalarreal, where she finds out he has been killed. In other cases, women saved their money to go to the prison where they had heard their husbands were being held, only to hear that they had been transferred. They had to go home and save money again for many months before being able to go to the second prison. And they might or might not find their husbands alive.

Then there were those last seen in a concentration camp, or those who had fled to the mountains and were conducting guerrilla warfare against Franco's Civil Guard. There were the half million Spaniards who had fled into exile and who could not write home without endangering their loved ones in Spain.[17]

But the litany of the missing does not end here. Nor does that of the possible speakers of these lines. For there were also many on the Republican side whose *children* were missing. The documentary *Els nens perduts del franquisme* (*The Stolen Children of the Franco Dictatorship*) tells the heart-rending story of several categories of missing children.[18] One such category was the children of female prisoners. At the end of the war, these children were initially taken to jail with their mothers. But the regime wanted to eliminate all "Reds" from Spain, and Franco's chief military psychiatrist, Antonio Vallejo Nágera, theorized that children should be separated from the pernicious influence of their Republican parents, lest they turn out the same way. Accordingly, many children were taken away on buses to the orphanages of Auxilio Social. Most often, their mothers never saw them again.

The documentary includes testimony about the lasting emotional impact on these parents of the loss of their children. Emilia Girón had never participated in politics in her life, but she was the sister of one of the most famous of the Spanish maquis – that is, guerrillas who fought against Franco after the war from the mountains. She paid dearly for that blood tie. When she gave birth to a child in a hospital in Salamanca, her baby was taken from her to be baptized and she never saw him again. As an old woman, she describes the effect on her of this loss:

> Y con esta angustia estoy toda mi vida, porque sé que lo parí y que lo traje nueve meses encima de mí y no lo conocí siquiera. La angustia me durará hasta que esté en el otro mundo.
>
> I've spent my whole life with this anguish. Because I know I gave birth to him, and that I had him inside me for nine months, and that then I never even got to see him. This suffering will last until I'm in the other world. (Vinyes et al. *Los niños perdidos* 149)

During the war, many Republican parents had sent their children to France, England, or Russia to save them from the the Francoists' massive bombing raids. The Franco regime launched a vast propaganda campaign about bringing back to Spain the "children the Reds stole from us" (*Canciones*). But the regime did not return these children to their families, even when the families came to claim them. Rather, they were placed in the orphanages of Auxilio Social (Social Services), and then, in some cases, adopted by right-wing families.[19] And here the year 1941, the year "Tatuaje" appeared, becomes important again. For in that year, Franco signed a law permitting the regime to change the names of the children whom Francoist agents had repatriated, sometimes by kidnapping them from their adoptive families in Europe (Vinyes et al. 63). The children often went through several name changes, having been given one name at birth, a second name by the regime, and further new names by adoptive parents. Siblings were separated, given different names, and sent to different families. Florencia and María García were sent to different families in France during the war. After the war, they were brought back to Spain separately. Florencia was sent to an orphanage, where she spent her childhood in utter loneliness. María was adopted by a family whom, she was told, were her parents. She learned from the children of her new neighbours that she was not really their child. The sisters remembered each other from when they were very small, and kept looking for each other. They were lucky enough to find each other sixty years later through a television program (*Els nens perduts*, 2ª part; Vinyes et al. 170).

And then there were those whose whereabouts *were* known but who were irremediably absent. This was the case of loved ones in exile. It was also the case of those serving long jail sentences, whose loved ones could see them only very briefly and at very long intervals. In Dulce Chacón's novel *La voz dormida* (*The Sleeping Voice*), the protagonist, Pepa, saves money all year in Madrid to go visit her boyfriend in jail in Burgos. After the brief conversation they have across the bars of the *locutorio*, Jaime has to return to his cell. Pepa shouts across the distance that separates them, "Volveré el año que viene, amor mío" ("I'll be back next year, my love"). And the waiting begins again (326).[20]

Finally, "Tatuaje" provided a vehicle for expressing the painful quest of those who were searching for *themselves*. As *Els nens perduts del franquisme* reveals, many of those children who had their names changed became engaged in a search that would last a lifetime. María Lucas García, who was told initially that she was the real child of her adoptive family, explains: "Te ha criado una familia. Pero tú no eres tú. Y entonces, eso es lo que te hace buscar" ("A family has brought you up. But you are not you. And that is what makes you search"). Having gone through four names, the only way she could find out her age was to go to a forensic doctor. He looked at her teeth "igual que le miran a los caballos" ("as if I were a horse"). She demands: "¿Yo no soy una persona igual que otra, que yo pueda tener mis papeles y mis cosas y sepa de quién he nacido, quién soy, y de dónde he venido, y cómo, y de qué manera?" ("Am I not a person like everybody else, who has my own papers and my own things, and who knows whom I was born to, and who I am, and where I came from and how?") (*Els nens perduts*, 2ª part).

Thus some of the people who sang "Tatuaje" were searching not only for their missing loved ones, but also for their own missing selves, their own stories. The line "y sigo en mi duda buscándolo fiel" ("I continue in my doubt, looking faithfully") could then also function as an expression of loyalty to self, loyalty to one's own past memories of who one had once been, memories that the regime attempted to eradicate.

The immense impact of "Tatuaje" can thus be explained if we hear the song as the expression of the immense pain and anguish of vast numbers of people who, in the 1940s, were criss-crossing Spain in search of lost loved ones, or who were stuck at home suffering, without information. It was the expression of people who had lost spouses, parents, and children. Crucially, the protagonist of "Tatuaje" addresses the lines "Y hasta que no te haya encontrado / sin descansar te buscaré" ("And until I've found you / I will search for you without resting") directly to the absent person. This was key to the song's function as a mourning ritual that stood in for ordinary funerals (i.e., those that are held after a natural death). Singing "Tatuaje" was a way for survivors to speak to the dead, in much the same way as the poetry that was found everywhere in New York

City after the 9/11 attacks of 2001. In New York, people wrote poems to the dead in the ash that settled over the city; on index cards in store windows; and on butcher's paper provided for them in Union Square. Steve Zeitlin has posited that these poems worked to create a sacred space. They functioned, he writes, as "portals" that could "pierce the very barrier that separates the living from the dead" (110). Through these portals, the living could "mend ruptures" with the dead, who had been torn from them without the chance to say goodbye (114). In "Tatuaje," as in these poems, the living and the dead could meet again, and the defeated could tell the dead, out loud and in the first person: "I haven't forgotten you, I'll always keep searching for you." Today, sixty to seventy years later, surviving relatives and their descendants are keeping that promise to the dead, as volunteers dig up the bones in Franco's mass graves.[21]

Loyalty is represented in the song not only by the words the protagonist addresses directly to her absent lover, but also by the words she addresses to another character, the anonymous sailor she accosts as she wanders the ports looking for her lover. León, Valerio, and Quiroga brilliantly introduced a recited section into this song, unusual in the *copla*, which made possible the most direct expression of the pain of those searching for their loved ones, and may have cemented even further the connection between the protagonist, Piquer, and the listeners who sang along. Piquer, in a drunken voice, addresses a sailor at each port, telling him to listen to her, and asks what he knows of her missing lover, whom she describes as gallant, confident, and blonder than honey. Not every listener would have had a good singing voice, but every listener could have recited that question along with Piquer. Piquer's voice quavers as she imitates drunkenness; the listener's voice might have quavered with emotion as she asked very similar questions of prison guards and bureaucrats at counters. Piquer's voice could stand in for their hoarse, tired, grief-ridden, downtrodden voices as they repeated time after time their questions about the fate of their loved ones. When Piquer sings again, it is with urgency: "Mira su nombre de extranjero" ("Look at his foreign name") as she gives her interlocutor a message for her missing sailor. By stepping out of her singing role, Piquer lessens the distance between herself and her listeners, as if she understands and shares in their ongoing search. This would have helped break through the listeners' feeling of isolation, allowing them to feel support as they recited along with her their demand to be listened to and given information about their missing loved ones.

Condemned to Wander: "Tatuaje" as Ritual of Perpetual Transition

Complicated grief involves the problem of how to go on living when the person one held most dear has been lost forever, along with the way of life associated with that person. The mourner yearns to return to that way of life but cannot do so. She also cannot abandon it and find new people, places, and experiences to which to reorient herself. So she is in an in-between, limbo state. "Tatuaje" enacts this problem and grapples with it in its plot and imagery, as the protagonist wanders on the shore, between land and sea, searching for her missing sailor.

Anthropologist Arnold van Gennep identifies three phases of ritual mourning: separation, transition, and incorporation. The longest is the transition phase, which may last a year. During it, the deceased makes the journey to the world of the dead, and the survivor is in a kind of limbo, no longer living the life he or she did with the deceased person, but not yet having returned to social life to make new relationships. Another way of talking about complicated grief, then, is to say that the transition phase of mourning has been made perpetual. This was almost inevitable in Franco's Spain, because the dead were denied ritual burial. There is an ancient belief in Western culture that a dead person who remains unburied, or who died in unjust circumstances, cannot rest and is condemned to wander until the living have corrected the situation.[22] In Virgil's *Aeneid*, where we see the ferryman Charon take the souls of the dead across the river to the underworld, we learn that the souls of those who have not been buried are condemned to wander on the river bank for 100 years before they can find rest.[23]

When the dead wander, so do the living. If their dead lie in ditches, the living cannot rest until they are properly buried. And if it is not clear whether their lost loved ones are dead or alive, those who remain alive can find no peace until they have found them. But knowing where their bones lie is not enough. The suffering of the relatives continues until the bones have been exhumed from the mass graves, definitively identified, and properly buried.[24]

The need to bury transcends religious belief. In the 2003 documentary *Les fosses del silenci* (*The Silent Graves*), we are introduced to two elderly women, Isabel González and Asunción Álvarez, both of whom have brothers buried in a ditch in Piedrafita de Babia, in the province of León. Asunción is an ardent Catholic who doesn't believe in politics. Isabel does not consider herself religious and was active in left-wing unions. But both need to see their brothers buried:

ASUNCIÓN: Soy cristiana, católica, apostólica y romana. Quiero llevarlos al cementerio donde están mis padres porque creo que Dios quiere que yo viniera aquí a verlos, porque quiero abrazar los huesos, por deber, por obligación, y por mis padres. Porque mi padre y mi madre descansarán tranquilos sabiendo que sus hijos están allá con ellos.
ISABEL: Más de una vez he soñado que estaba yo misma levantando con mis manos las piedras y la tierra para encontrarlos. Yo no soy tan creyente como Asunción ... pero, a pesar de eso, yo creo que los cementerios se han hecho para llevar allí los seres queridos cuando mueren. Yo tengo la ilusión de hacer un panteón y poner los huesos de mi hermano con los de mis padres.

ASUNCIÓN: I am a Christian, a Roman Catholic. I want to take them [her brothers' remains] to the cemetery. [I'm here] because I think God wanted me to come here to see them. Because I want to embrace their bones. Out of duty. Out of obligation. And for my parents. Because my mother and my father will rest in peace knowing that their children are there with them.
ISABEL: I've dreamed more than once that I myself was lifting up the stones and earth with my own hands to find them. I'm not a believer like Asunción ... but still, I believe that cemeteries were made to take loved ones there when they die. My dream is to make a mausoleum and put the bones of my brother with those of my parents. (*Las fosas del silencio* 189)

I believe that this irrepressible need to bury is part of the reason for the enormous impact of "Tatuaje" and one of the principal reasons people sang it with so much intensity in the postwar period. The female protagonist of "Tatuaje" is the inheritor of the classical tradition as she wanders from port to port, the tormented living counterpart of the unburied dead. Left on the shore in that liminal space between land and sea, she can find no rest:

Errante lo busco	I wander, looking for him
por todos los puertos	at every port

But she cannot get to that unreachable world where the lost person is, where he went on a foreign ship. I contend that in the 1940s, when the defeated acted the part of the nameless protagonist in her quest for her missing sailor, they were carrying out symbolically the quest that we now see Isabel, Asunción, and thousands of elderly Spaniards like them carrying out literally, by seeking the bones of their relatives in Franco's mass graves, burying them, and erecting memorials with the names of those whose remains cannot be found. In figures 5.1, 5.2, and 5.3, we see elderly relatives of the executed holding up photographs of their missing loved ones. To do so is to bear witness and to affirm their mission to remember, to be faithful, and to search, just as the protagonist of "Tatuaje" does by wearing the tattoo.

"Tatuaje" and the Problem of Meaning

In her memoir *The Year of Magical Thinking*, Joan Didion captures the greatest threat attached to complicated grief:

> Grief turns out to be a place none of us know until we reach it ... In the version of grief we imagine, the model will be "healing." A certain forward movement will prevail. The worst days will be the earliest days ... We imagine that the moment to most severely test us will be the funeral ... We have no way of knowing that this will not be the issue ... Nor can we know ahead of the fact (and here lies the heart of the difference between grief as we imagine it and grief as it is) the unending absence that follows, the void, the very opposite of meaning, the relentless succession of moments during which we will confront the experience of meaninglessness itself. (188–9)

Survivors on the Republican side in postwar Spain faced an existential dilemma. So many of the people dearest to them were absent, whether exiled, imprisoned, disappeared, or dead. The entire world they knew had been destroyed. Many of the defeated felt that their lives had really ended with the losses of their loved ones and their country. Yet they had to deal with the uncomfortable fact that they remained alive. What were they to do, and how were they to conceive their lives, if they felt themselves to be dead inside, and if the state encouraged them to regard themselves as unwelcome holdovers from an era that had ended? The remarkable thing about "Tatuaje" is that it manages both to represent this terrible dilemma and to help solve it. "Tatuaje" provides an answer to this question: What kind of narrative could the defeated compose that would lend some coherence and meaning to their present existence, which was neither life or death?

"Tatuaje" does this in two stages. First, through the tormented searching of its protagonist, it represents the state of complicated grief. It allowed the defeated to express in words their own existential dilemma of feeling between life and death ("bleeding" and "dying," in the words of the song). It enabled them, through the voice of the protagonist, to express their inability to find a place in the new society, to say that they felt like wanderers on the margins, unable either to leave on the ship or to stay on land and integrate.

But then "Tatuaje" offers a new role to the survivors, a role created precisely out of their ongoing suffering and limbo state. It does this through the image of the tattoo, an indelible mark that can never be erased. The tattoo constitutes memory, and what is remembered, branded on the body, is a name. As in many of León's other *coplas*, "Tatuaje" protects the secrets of its characters even as it reveals that they exist; we never learn the name tattooed on the protagonist's body. But the song does reveal that there is a missing person with a name, that there is grief, that there is suffering. The image of the tattoo enabled the defeated to develop a new role for themselves as witnesses to the "past that would never return": by singing the song, they could declare that they would always carry the memory of those who had been taken from them, that it was an indelible mark that could never be erased. The song thus enabled them to say safely that no amount of violence and terror was going to make them forget those who had been so unjustly taken from them. Their social function from this time forward would be to remember the missing, to search for them, and to bear witness to their murder at the hands of Franco's supporters.

Furthermore, the plot progression of "Tatuaje" turns the chronic pain of the defeated and the impossibility of moving on from their losses into an affirmation of identity, values, and agency. The protagonist makes a deliberate choice to brand the sailor's name on her skin and to turn her loss into an opportunity to proclaim loyalty and memory, which is her future mission. Agency was of course discouraged under Spain's authoritarian regime, which advocated a "silencio entusiasta" ("enthusiastic silence") on the part of the populace (Martín Gaite, *Usos* 18), and which proclaimed: "Franco manda: España obedece" ("Franco commands: Spain obeys") (Abella 22). Agency was dangerous. For the defeated, insisting on remembering what really happened to their dear ones was extremely dangerous; the state's official history blamed all the death and destruction of the war on the losers themselves and forbade competing accounts. Without the cover of a fictional story, the defeated would have been unable to declare that the past had left an indelible mark and that they were proud to carry it with them.

So the fact that the protagonist has chosen to burn the tattoo onto her skin is crucial. It is a chosen role. And it contrasts with another, horrific, kind of branding that corresponded to the roles imposed by the Francoists. In the documentary *Els nens perduts del franquisme*, Teresa Martín

5.1, 5.2, and 5.3 (opposite and above) Beside the excavation sites where bones are being dug up, three survivors hold up photos of their executed relatives, whose remains they are still seeking. These three photographs by Eloy Alonso González were originally in colour; the contrast with the black-and-white photographs of the executed relatives points up the many decades that have passed between the executions of the 1930s and the exhumations of the twenty-first century.

recalls how, as a child, she saw a neighbour woman who had been in jail bare her breast:

> Y una vez en su casa ... le enseñó a mi madre el pecho – y no era la única – con el pecho izquierdo marcado a fuego [con] el yugo y las flechas. Perfectamente marcado. Y morado. Y eso sí que no se me olvida. Es una imagen que tengo grabada.

> And once, at her house, she showed my mother her breast – and she wasn't the only one to whom this happened – with the yoke and arrows of the Falange branded by fire on her left breast. Perfectly branded. And blue. And I certainly will never forget it. It's an image that is etched on my brain. (*Els nens perduts*, 1ª part)

This horrific story shows how trauma spreads from the direct victim of torture to those close to her as they learn what happened. The woman prisoner had been branded on her body; the younger Teresa Martín has the image of this branded on her soul. Similarly, a man in the town of Almansa, who was a child when his father was executed after the war, says today, "Eso lo llevo grabado" ("It's etched, or branded, on my memory") (*Víctimas todavía*). Here we can see an important difference between the chosen, active branding of "Tattoo" and the way that trauma brands its victims. Trauma results from terror and helplessness; the branding of the traumatic memory happens outside the victim's control. "Tatuaje" takes that branding and turns it into an active, chosen process – that of deciding to remember forever the names that others have attempted, through terror, to erase.[25] The song thus meets one important psychological criterion for the healing of trauma – that is, that the trauma not be simply *re-experienced* in the singing, but *reformulated*, given new meaning.[26] The song succeeds in creating a space where agency can be affirmed. Thus, "Tatuaje" does not adopt the self-deprecating tone of the victim. Instead, it allows the defeated to turn the desperate fact that their lives were effectively over into an affirmation, even if that affirmation is one of constant suffering by holding fast to the memory of their dead loved ones. "Tatuaje" thus helped the defeated meet the conditions that Viktor Frankl argued were necessary for survival in the Nazi camps: that the person have a mission for the future, and that he find meaning in his suffering in the present (Frankl *Man's Search* 115–27).[27]

In freer, more affluent societies, such a use of "Tatuaje" might appear to be an unhealthy response to loss, one in which the griever refuses to accept the loss, adapt, and build other connections. I contend that in the context of the Francoist terror, the song actually had many adaptive functions. The traumatic circumstances of the bereavements, and the ongoing terror, meant that the survivors were likely to experience a sense of extreme fragmentation and disorganization as a trauma reaction (Herman 34–5). The fact that the song was able to create links between the past of the protagonist's encounter with the sailor, the present suffering of her loss of the sailor, and her future mission to find him may have lent a much-needed sense of coherence and purpose to traumatized, disoriented people. The temporal movement of the narrative, the shape of a plot, should not be taken for granted. For these were years of stagnation, where time appeared to have stopped. The ability to link their past to their present and future would have been especially important for the defeated, who were having to adjust to a "new Spain" that was seeking to eliminate all traces of the Spanish Republic it had supplanted. But a tattoo, of course, cannot be erased. The song thus provided a way for the losers to affirm the continuity of their history and identity, and to gain a sense of psychic coherence.

Symbolic Enactments: "Tatuaje" as Speech Act

Jack Santino, writing about the spontaneous shrines that appear after terrorist attacks such as 9/11, points out that these shrines both commemorate the dead – something often done privately – and suggest a position on a public issue – namely, the social and political conditions that caused the deaths. Such shrines, he says, are both commemorative and performative. He refers to J.L. Austin's examples, in *How to Do Things with Words*, of sentences like "I do," or "I christen this ship," in which words create the event that they declare (Santino 9). In this sense, singing "Tatuaje" was an act that *brought into being*, or achieved, what it declared.

To sing about the protagonist's quest for her missing sailor was the best way available for the defeated to break the silence, both about the dead in the mass graves and their other missing and absent loved ones, and about the anguish and suffering of those who were still present. As a repeated text, it was a covert yet audible ritual of mourning. It was a coded way to express what was otherwise kept silent. As such, it helped alleviate the psychic and physical burden of keeping a traumatic secret, a burden that has been shown to undermine the immune system (Pennebaker, *Emotion, Disclosure, and Health; Opening Up*). It told the secret for all to hear (it was a "secreto a voces"). But it did so in the safe code of fiction; like all rituals, it was symbolic. And since everyone sang "Tatuaje," often collectively through open windows, it also fulfilled part of the function of mourning rituals: to affirm the bond among the living and their common mission to remember and bear witness to the mass murders (Kollar).

"Tatuaje" was a majestic, theatrical, repeated ritual that became a substitute for all the usual rites that had been denied. Since it did not speak the name of the absent sailor, each mourner could slot in the name of his or her own dead. The protagonist, too, was nameless, and this enabled her to represent any mourner. I believe that "Tatuaje," sung for decades, became permeated with the bereavement stories of each person who sang it. For the defeated, it stood in for their loved ones' names, the bodies, the graves, and for the burials and memorials they could not carry out.

"Tatuaje" was also a protest, as Vázquez Montalbán has pointed out (*Crónica* 43). It proclaimed an alternative kind of citizenship for people who had lost their civil rights and been defined as "scum." Singing it was thus an act of "mourning in protest" (Senie), much like the collective act of holding up the photo of a victim in figure 5.4.

The Listener-Performer versus the Protagonist

While the listener-performer would have identified with the grieving protagonist of "Tatuaje," the key to the song's therapeutic value lay in the fact that it functioned differently for the listener-performer than for the protagonist. In the song, the protagonist remains stuck in her grief, *drowning* her pain in brandy as she wanders from bar to bar. She is trapped in the plot structure, contained within it. Conchita Piquer brought the protagonist and her grief to life, mediating between character and listener. In this way, the character's grief had a "velcro effect," attaching to the listener's own grief, which came to the surface in the performance of the song.[28] The listener, rather than *drowning* her grief, would have *expressed* it. She would have sung the word *pain* with all her heart. The word "dolor" ("pain") ends a stanza. It is the word on which the stress is placed, the culmination of the second part of the song. It is drawn out over several beats and a ritard. By naming the pain, the listener likely experienced some relief and liberation as well as some psychological movement. The fact that the character remains stuck in her grief, then, was functional for the listener. For given the traumatic nature of the listener's grief, he or she would have needed to repeat the performance countless times to allow more of the pain to come to the surface. "Tatuaje" was omnipresent on the airwaves for two decades and

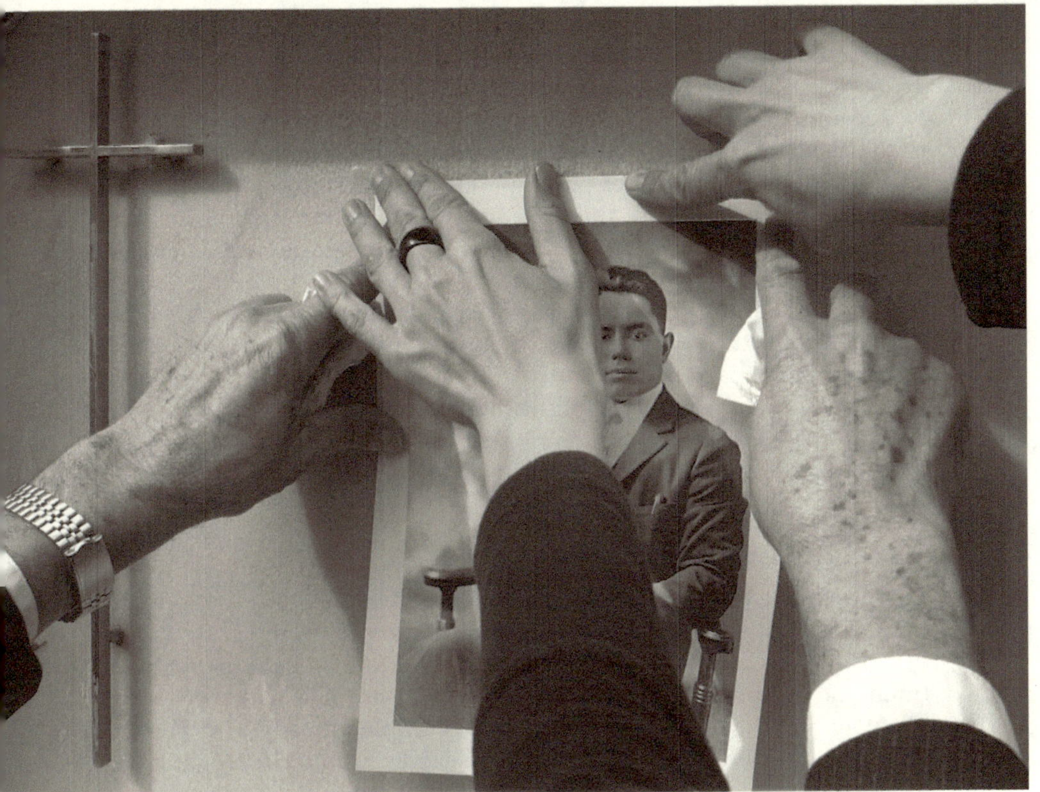

5.4 Hands of survivors hold up on the wall a photo of Emilio Silva's grandfather, Emilio Faba Silva, who was executed in 1936. Photograph by Eloy Alonso González.

could still be heard thereafter. So both the protagonist and Conchita Piquer were always available to make another performance possible.

There may be many reasons why younger generations who never knew the war and who did not even know the dictatorship still know "Tatuaje." Its compelling story and music, and the incomparable performance by Conchita Piquer, are enough to account for that. But given that traumatic mourning is passed down the generations, I wonder if this is not one of the unconscious reasons for the continued return to this song. Those who survived the period still need to remain tattooed with the names of their dead, for they still have not been exhumed and reburied, and the government has made only timid efforts to rehabilitate their names. Until the twenty-first century, many survivors never spoke of their losses. They have thus been the only ones to keep alive the memory of the injustice done to their dead. Today, their grandchildren have joined them in the struggle to get the Republican dead found and properly buried. The grandchildren are thus participating in the same mission of loyalty to those who died, and in the fight for the full recognition and citizenship of both the dead and the living, that their grandparents enacted in code by singing "Tatuaje." In the documentary *Semillas*, the camera shows a close-up of the black-and-white photograph of a young soldier, then pans out to reveal a collage of photos of the victims made by their relatives; the collage occupies an entire wall. This reminds us that singing "Tatuaje" was not only an individual ritual, but also a collective one, just as today's effort to find missing relatives is not simply a private, family matter, but one that affects and involves Spanish society as a whole.

Conclusion

The preceding discussion has suggested that "Tatuaje" was the song that was heard the most and that was sung most intensely in the postwar years because it was the song that most directly addressed the irresolvable, traumatic mourning that the defeated otherwise had to keep hidden. "Tatuaje" was the best vehicle they had to grapple with and work through this major burden. Thus it became the period's supreme surrogate ritual of mourning.

As we have seen, "Tatuaje" was a ritual for coping with a transition that had been made perpetual by the regime's refusal to allow the defeated to bury their dead. As in "Ojos verdes," the protagonist of "Tatuaje" directly addresses her missing loved one at key points in the song. But unlike "Ojos verdes," which represents the protagonist's life as effectively ending at the moment her lover departs, "Tatuaje" articulates a mission for the protagonist to carry out, using future tenses. In this way, "Tatuaje" provided the readiest answer available to the existential question of what meaning life might have when everything one most loved and valued had disappeared.

"Tatuaje" was so effective as a way to work through complicated grief because of the way the lyrics, the music, and Piquer's unforgettable performance all worked together. Each of these aspects offered means for the defeated to access, express, and reformulate their intense grief. But each also built in protective devices to ensure that the defeated would not become overwhelmed by their own feelings.

The lyrics presented the defeated with a protagonist who was also suffering from complicated grief, as well as a story with important analogies to their own. By playing the protagonist, the defeated could name all their emotional states (pain, bleeding, dying ...) and affirm their commitment directly to their dead. Yet the song avoided despair, and it gave the defeated the symbol of the tattoo as something to hold on to. And it provided emotional protection in the form of a compelling tale about a foreign protagonist in an exotic setting. Thus, the defeated were able to engage with the song as fiction, instead of becoming overwhelmed by their own pain.

The music's passage from light and lilting to heavier, and from major to minor, expertly drew the defeated into the grieving process in stages. Ritards and pauses allowed emphasis on all the significant feelings in that process, such as bitterness, fatigue, sadness, pain, but also loyalty to the dead. And the song's clear musical resolution contrasted with the unresolved plot, marking off this grieving episode from the rest of the day.

Piquer's performance is by turns intimate, bitter, urgent, majestic, dignified, and grief-stricken. Her drunken *recitative* allowed the audience to *speak* their quest and to tell the truth in speech rather than only in song; it also brought the protagonist, Piquer, and the defeated who sang along even closer together.

"Tatuaje" is an excellent example of the psychotherapeutic benefits a song can bring to people whose bodies and souls have been targeted for annihilation. "Tatuaje" involves the deepest and most sustained working-through of the main dilemma of the defeated: they were branded by traumatic loss and condemned to perpetual grief. This song, like no other, allowed them to grapple with that grief and to emerge from it with a mission that turned their branding into a tattoo they chose to wear, a tattoo that signified a mission that gave them a reason to go on living. It is no wonder that people sang it with all their hearts.

"Tatuaje" is the central song in a triptych of three *coplas* that served respectively as rituals of separation, transition, and incorporation. In ordinary circumstances, about a year after a death, mourning rites are lifted, and rituals mark the re-entry of the mourner into the surrounding society. The losers in postwar Spain were unable to cease mourning the dead, the missing, or the improperly buried. But the vengeful nature of the Franco regime, the way it kept society starkly divided between winners and losers, also made true incorporation into the surrounding society impossible. The next chapter shows how "Romance de la Otra" ("Ballad of the Other Woman") responded to this perpetual marginalization.

Chapter Six

The "Other Woman": "Romance de la otra" as Ritual of Marginalization and Disenfranchised Grief

ROMANCE DE LA OTRA
Quintero/León/Quiroga

I

¿Por qué se viste de negro – ¡ay, de negro! –
si no se le ha muerto nadie?
¿Por qué está siempre encerrada – ¡ay, por qué! –
como la que está en la cárcel?
¿Por qué no tiene familia,
ni perrito que la ladre,
ni flores que la diviertan,
ni risa que la acompañe?
Del porqué de este por qué,
la gente quiere enterarse...
Cuatro suspiros responden
y no los entiende nadie,
y no los entiende nadie.

ESTRIBILLO

Yo soy la otra, la otra,
y a nada tengo derecho
porque no llevo un anillo
con una fecha por dentro.
No tengo ley que me abone,
ni puerta donde llamar

BALLAD OF THE OTHER WOMAN

Quintero/León/Quiroga

I

Why is she dressed in black – why! –
if no one dear to her has died?
Why is she always shut in – why! –
like someone in jail?
Why has she no family,
nor a little dog to bark at her,
nor flowers to distract her,
nor laughter to accompany her?
People want to know
the reasons for this enigma...
A few sighs are her response,
and no one understands them,
and no one understands them.

REFRAIN

I'm the other woman, the other one,
and I have no right to anything
because I don't wear a ring
with a date engraved inside it.
I have no law to protect me,
and no door to knock on

y me alimento a escondías
con tus besos y tu pan.
Con tal que vivas tranquilo,
¡qué importa que yo me muera!...
Te quiero, siendo ¡la otra!,
como la que más te quiera.

II

¿Por qué no fueron tus labios – ¡ay, tus labios! –,
que fueron las malas lenguas
las que una noche vinieron – ¡ay, por qué! –
a leerme la sentensia?
El nombre que te ofresían
ya no es tuyo, compañera;
de azahares y velo blanco
se viste la que lo lleva.
Como fue tu voluntá,
mi boca no te dio queja;
cumple con lo que has firmao,
que yo no valgo la pena,
que yo no valgo la pena.

AL ESTRIBILLO

 Facing English translation mine.

and I nourish myself, in hiding,
on your kisses and your bread.
As long as you're without worries,
who cares if I die!...
I love you, as the other woman,
and the one who loves you the most.

II

Why was it not your lips – oh, your lips! – ,
but evil tongues,
who came one night – why! –
to read me my sentence?
The name they offered you
is no longer yours, comrade;
the woman who bears it wears
orange blossoms and a white veil.
Since it was your will,
my mouth made no complaint;
carry out what you've signed,
for I'm not worth the trouble,
for I'm not worth the trouble.

TO THE REFRAIN

Introduction

Like "La Parrala," "Romance de la otra" ("Ballad of the Other Woman") begins with a female protagonist presented in the third person through the eyes of the neighbours, who want to know the circumstances of her life. They ask a series of questions: Why is she always dressed in black if no one has died? Why does no one visit her? Why is she always shut up in the house? Why is there no laughter in her life? She responds only with sighs, sighs the neighbours cannot understand.

However, whereas in "La Parrala" (and in "La Lirio," another Piquer favourite), we never learn the protagonist's secret, in "Romance de la otra," the protagonist tells the audience her secret directly, in the first person. A man had promised to marry her and then married someone else, leaving her as his lover, legally unprotected and leading a clandestine life off the crumbs of food and love he now doles out to her. Not surprisingly, she feels that her life is of little value.

In "La Parrala," the jocose music belies and helps make manageable the violent and threatening subject matter; in contrast, the accompaniment to "Romance de la otra" is heavy and sombre, especially in the stanzas. The piano accompanies the orchestra, outlining chords so that every eighth note of the 2/4 time has a heavy beat on it, rather than only the first and third eighth notes of each measure. The pattern of this heavy piano accompaniment is as follows: measure 1 – root, chord, chord, chord; measure 2 – root, chord, root, chord; and so on. The minor key and the heavy beat on every note combine to create a funereal atmosphere. Piquer sings the neighbours' questions in a serious, mournful way, with an increasing intensity that conveys both the tragic situation and the vehemence of the neighbours' desire to know. Her tone and the musical accompaniment lighten up as she sings "Del por qué de este por qué" ("People want to know the reason for this enigma") in a more intimate tone.

Then in the refrain, the song switches to a major key and the tempo accelerates. Piquer changes her tone to reflect that the protagonist is now speaking in the first person. In the few lines of the refrain, she conveys a range of feelings. She sobs as she sings "Yo soy la otra, la otra" ("I'm the other woman, the other one"). She is indignant about being ostracized because she doesn't wear a ring with a date engraved inside it. She is angry and defiant as she sings "No tengo ley que me abone, / ni puerta donde llamar" ("I have no law to protect me, no door to knock on"). And the song emphasizes the hypocrisy of the married man with a big ritard on "y me alimento a escondías / con tus besos y tu pan" ("and I feed myself in hiding / on your kisses and your bread"). The protagonist's anger reaches its height as she sings "Con tal que vivas tranquilo, ¡qué importa que yo me muera!" ("As long as you're carefree, who cares if I die!"). The music reinforces this with a brief return to the minor key. But the anger immediately gives way to love, and minor to major, as she sings "Te quiero siendo [sob] ¡la otra!, como la que más te quiera." ("I love you as [sob] the other woman, the one who loves you most."

In the second stanza, the protagonist is the one asking questions of her lover: Why did you let me learn of your marriage from the neighbours rather than from your lips? Piquer conveys the cruelty of the neighbours as they answer in the lover's place, reporting that his name will never be hers. And she expresses the grief-stricken resignation of the Other Woman as she sings the last five lines of the second stanza: "Como fue tu voluntá ... que yo no valgo la pena" ("Since it was what you wanted ... I'm not worth the trouble").

In 1944, five years after the war's end, the defeated continued to be excluded from the dominant, Francoist society. Seen in this light, "Romance de la Otra" can be read as the anthem of the disenfranchised in Spain. This interpretation lets us hear the voices of sectors of the population that were otherwise condemned to silence. In this sense, the song was a tool the defeated could use to grapple with the fact that they could not complete the third phase of ritual mourning – reincorporation into society.

Republican Women as "Other"

As Manuel Vázquez Montalbán reminds us, "Romance de la otra" served as an eloquent protest against the circumstances that many women on the Republican side faced under Franco (*Crónica* 36). The regime had created a legal situation that retroactively defined many women as sinners for behaviour that had been perfectly legal before the dictatorship began. It also punished women for any sexual behaviour unsanctioned by the state, while allowing men – particularly wealthy men – to satisfy their sexual needs outside of marriage. This placed many women in an untenable position. Some had divorced legally under the Republic and begun new relationships, only to find their divorces annulled by the new regime, which considered them guilty of adultery. Others had gotten married in civil ceremonies that were now treated as invalid; even worse, some had adopted the anarchist doctrine of "free love" during the war. All were now excluded from the category of "respectable" women.

In the postwar period, poverty left many Republican women vulnerable to sexual exploitation. The double standard of sexual morality meant that upper-class society turned a blind eye to the many wealthy married men who kept mistresses in furnished apartments. These women were expected to stay off the streets, like "the Other Woman," so as not to compromise the men who were keeping them. As well, many widows and orphans of Republican soldiers, having been barred from receiving state pensions, turned to prostitution (Abella 32–3). They were then declared to be degenerates. Social norms dictated that, having fallen, these women could not be incorporated into respectable society, even if a man fell in love with one of them and would have liked to marry her. In doing so, he would have been going against his mother. Carmen Martín Gaite tells us that it was relatively common to hear of a young man who had fallen in love with a prostitute, taken her off the streets, and put her in an apartment:

> "Lo que no me explico es por qué no se casa de una vez con ella," se comentaba a veces en círculos de amigos enterados del caso. Y la respuesta era casi siempre la misma: "Hombre, yo lo comprendo, por no darle un disgusto a su madre." De hecho alguna de estas relaciones, que incluso fueron monógamas y duraron años, solamente acabaron santificadas ante el altar con la muerte de una señora de misa diaria, ropas oscuras y gesto de reina destronada, sobre todo si era madre de hijo único.
>
> "What I don't understand is why he doesn't just go ahead and marry her," they would say in the circle of friends who knew what was going on. And the response was almost always the same. "Well, I can understand that, he doesn't want to upset his mother." In fact some of these relationships, which were even monogamous and lasted many years, only were sanctified before the altar after the death of one of those women who went to daily mass, wore black, and cultivated the gestures of a queen who had lost her throne – especially if she was the mother of an only son. (*Usos amorosos* 107)

Such permanent marginalization from mainstream society made the bodies of Republican women permanently accessible to the winners.

Finally, many working-class girls who, under the Republic, would have had opportunities to earn a living wage independently, now were obliged to work as live-in servants in the houses of the winners. And it was not uncommon for the young man ("señorito") of the house to seduce one of them with false promises of marriage (Mir 167–8).

All of these predicaments were part of a general trend pointed out by Conxita Mir: the regime first achieved social control by persecuting political crimes and then intensified that control by exerting power over the most intimate relationships. The Franco regime repressed women's sexuality in order to maximize conformity and control (Mir 160). Thus women whose circumstances had put them beyond the pale of narrow National Catholic sexual respectability were subject to ostracism, gossip, and even denunciation (165).[1] Many of León and Quiroga's *coplas* expressed the consequences of these social and legal controls for women on both sides of the line separating the respectable from the fallen. In "Romance de la otra," the Other Woman has been denied all social legitimacy because her lover has married another; she lives shut up in her house "como la que está en la cárcel" ("like one in jail"). But as the next chapter will indicate, *la otra*'s more fortunate rival, who wears white to the altar, is also shut up behind bars.

In "Romance de la otra," we again hear the voices of Republican women expressing their anger at the loss of employment opportunity that left them vulnerable to exploitation. Under the Republic, many women had held jobs and gained some measure of economic independence; under Franco, work was seen as something a woman did out of strict necessity, and only until she married and had a family (Martín Gaite *Usos* 47–9). Many women must have felt "encerrada[s] ... como la que está en la cárcel" ("shut up ... like someone in jail"), just like the protagonist, especially when they saw the schedule prescribed for them by the Women's Section of the Falange, which told them what to do from seven a.m. to ten p.m., seven days a week and twelve months a year.

The refrain of "Romance de la otra" allowed women to protest the condition to which they had been relegated. They could do so in full voice, in the first person, under cover of playing the role of the fictional protagonist. The song also allowed them to assert their moral integrity: the state might not recognize the legitimacy of their love relationships, but that didn't keep each of them from being the one who loved the most fully and who had been the most forthright.

Gay Men as "The Other Woman"

By all accounts, Rafael de León was gay. Martín de la Plaza, biographer of Conchita Piquer, reports that she recognized it at once (*Conchita*

Piquer 50). Alberto Mira Nouselles notes that Josefa Acosta Díaz, Manuel Gómez Lara, and Jorge Jiménez Barrientos, in their book about León's work, chose to say nothing about his personal life, supposedly out of respect for the poet's wishes. Mira makes the obvious point that no gay person under Franco dared to come out of the closet, but that this is no reason to continue the stigma on gay people today by holding back such information. León was a poet as well as a songwriter, and Mira points out that in his poems there is a great deal of gender ambiguity on the part of the speaker, and that the relationship between the speaker and his/her male lover breaks with stereotypes. The speaker, who in a heterosexual relationship would be the female, is neither chaste nor submissive. The relationships are secret, guilty, and subject to persecution. León dedicated many of these genderless poems to a man (García Piedra and Gil Siscar 68–9). And he would return to these themes repeatedly for years in his songs as well, even though they ran counter to Francoist values (Mira 347).

Whatever the truth of León's life, it is clear that gay men could and did identify intensely with many of his *coplas*. Mira's explanation of why this was the case could also apply to many of the defeated who were not gay but who were similarly invisible and degraded:

> Estas canciones reflejaban la experiencia *emocional* de aquellos cuya sexualidad el franquismo había condenado al silencio. Éstos exprimían hasta la última gota de significado de las letras para encontrar en ellas una verdad que la institución acaso no podía ni sospechar ...
>
> En parte la gran necesidad de encontrar un correlato a sus experiencias, silenciadas en cualquier otro ámbito, les convertía en lectores especialmente receptivos, quizá no siempre conscientes de lo que les unía a las canciones, pero con gran simpatía por aquellas situaciones ... El referente directo de las letras de Rafael de León eran amores que el franquismo consideraba marginales, pecaminosos o incluso detestables. La dignificación que se produce a partir de las interpretaciones emocionales de las tonadilleras constituye una respuesta a estos rigores. Pero la fuente de tales sentimientos estaba en una percepción de la propia posición de marginalidad.

These songs reflected the emotional experience of those whose sexuality had been condemned to silence by Francoism. These people would squeeze every last drop of meaning out of the lyrics to find in them a truth that the censors couldn't even suspect ...

In part, it was their great need to find a correlative for their experiences,

> which were silenced in every other arena, that made gay people especially receptive readers. They were perhaps not always conscious of what linked them to these songs, but they identified greatly with the situations [recounted in them] ... Rafael de León's lyrics told of love relationships that were considered marginal, sinful, even despicable under Franco. The songs countered this harsh atmosphere by restoring the dignity of the protagonists through the impassioned performances of the *copla* stars. But the deep feeling people had about these songs came from their awareness of their own marginal position.[2] (Mira 344, 347–8)

Gay men could thus easily identify with the "Other Woman," who loves her man more than his wife does, but who is condemned to unhappy marginality, constant surveillance and gossip, loneliness, and internalized self-hatred.

Conchita Piquer as the "Other Woman"

In chapter 2, I contended that what made Piquer the "queen of the *copla*" was her enormous talent as an actress in song, her ability to project herself onto her fictional protagonists and bring them to life. Naturally, in some cases, there were commonalities between herself and her characters, such as being a singer, like La Parrala and La Ruiseñora. But never was there so much overlap as with "la Otra," and this meant that the audience could identify, not just with the fictional character, but also with Conchita Piquer as a flesh-and-blood woman with an emotional and sexual life of her own. For Piquer had been living with a married man, the bullfighter Antonio Márquez, since 1933 (Plaza *Conchita Piquer* 46). And this gave her a special relationship with this song, one that was apparent the first night she sang it in Madrid, at the Teatro Fontalba, in 1944. Martín de la Plaza quotes the reviewer of opening night, José Montero Alonso, and adds his own comment:

> "Ha puesto la intérprete tal acento de verdad en la canción, que el público se entrega, ganado por el humano temblor de los versos. El triunfo fue fulminante. La melodía era fácil. Los versos sencillos, hondos, certeros. Se adivinaba en la canción una historia real, que cada uno atribuía a una persona determinada." Según la mayoría, la de la propia Conchita con Antonio Márquez.

> "The performer put such true emotion into the song that the public sur-

> rendered, won over by the vulnerable tremor of each line. The response was thunderous. The song was easy. The lines were simple, deep, true. One could glimpse in the song a true story, that each listener attributed to a specific person." According to the majority, it was the story of the relationship of Conchita herself with Antonio Márquez. (84)

The fact that divorce was no longer legal, and that a puritanical morality was being enforced in Spanish society, had a dramatic effect on Piquer's life, one that went far beyond a simple sentimental desire to see her relationship legitimized with a ring and papers. In 1945 she left Spain for two years so that her daughter by Márquez would be born outside of Spain. As a public figure, she could not have a child out of wedlock in Spain without causing a major scandal. In Argentina, Márquez could officially recognize their child. Piquer lived and performed in Argentina and Mexico for two years before returning to Spain in 1947 (Plaza *Conchita Piquer* 87–93). Perhaps this forced exile and the clandestine way in which Piquer became a mother explain why, although she performed "Romance de la otra" on stage for more than a decade, it never lost its emotional impact on her or her audience:

> Conchita Piquer tampoco podía llevar anillo de casada... El público, que sabía esta historia, se conmovía al oírle interpretar ese "Romance de La Otra," con el que conseguía siempre el aplauso enardecido de los espectadores. Y ella mismo se emocionaba. Detrás de una fotografía que se hizo, interpretando ese número, Conchita escribió, de su puño y letra: "Aquí estoy, vestida de 'La otra.' Y qué gracioso. Después de haberla cantado durante diez años seguidos, sigo llorando cada vez que la interpreto."

> Conchita Piquer couldn't wear a wedding ring either ... The public, which knew this story, was moved to hear her perform that "Ballad of the Other Woman," with which she always got the most fervent applause of the audience. And she herself was moved. On the back of a photograph taken of her performing that number, Conchita wrote in her own hand: "Here I am, dressed as 'the Other Woman.' And how funny. After having sung it for ten years in a row, I still cry every time I perform it." (M. Román 133)

Here we see an example of how the figure of Piquer herself could be subject to a double reading. Piquer had performed risqué cabaret songs in her youth, in both New York and Spain. During the Spanish Civil War, according to Mira, she had "reinvented herself" as Doña Concha, the representative of respectable, Francoist values (343). Her political views and links with prominent government figures made her acceptable to right-wingers, who were more than willing to forget her less than Catholic past and embrace her marvellous performances. Yet at the same time, for the left, the fact that she had a sexual past that she had to bury, the fact that her current relationship was unsanctioned by law, and the fact that her pregnancy compelled her to go into temporary exile, all created a bridge between her situation and their own that may have made her performance of "The Other Woman" profoundly consoling. For here was someone on the winning side, who was not a "degenerate Red," yet who was affected by the same social injustice and felt moved to protest it in song.

The "Other Woman" as Half of Spain

I contend that at its deepest level, "Romance de la otra" used gender as a figure for politics, allowing men as well as women to make intense use of the song.[3] The marginalized "Other Woman" could represent *all* of the Spanish Republicans in their weak, symbolically "feminized" position in Franco's Spain. In this reading, the man in the song represents the Spanish state and its power to confer or deny legal rights and protections. The bride and the "other woman" represent the "two Spains" that had fought each other in the war. One is legitimate, recognized, with all its papers in order, wearing white on her wedding day in an ostentatious display of moral purity; the other is marginalized, without legal recourse or social support, wearing the black that represents both mourning and moral "stain." One looks to the future in her white wedding dress; the other looks to the past by wearing mourning.

The protagonist's circumstances can be read as mirroring the situation of the defeated Republicans. We begin with the voice of the neighbours, who evoke the threatening framework of the Causa General, as a network of people who gained power and social status by informing on their neighbours. If we follow Mikhail Bakhtin and listen for echoes of the winners' world view in their lines, the neighbours' question:

> ¿Por qué se viste de negro ...
> Si no se le ha muerto nadie?
>
> Why is she wearing black ...
> If no one has died?

takes on new meaning. For in this Spain of executions that were never officially recorded, and disappearances without the possibility of official information, how could the neighbours know that no one had died? We can hear in these lines not only the neighbours' inability to recognize the Other Woman's illegitimate relationship, but potentially their refusal to recognize the losers' mourning because it would mean admitting that they, as winners, had executed people and left them in ditches. On a more general level, the neighbours' lack of understanding of the Other Woman's mourning could reflect the winners' unawareness of the sadness of the Republicans over all kinds of losses that were not death: the loss of family and friends to jail, concentration camps, exile. The defeated, then, could use the song to assert the existence on the Republican side of many kinds of mourning that remained unofficial and unrecognized. The mournful minor key of the music reflects the subject matter.

Why doesn't the Other Woman go outside her house? Why does no one come in to visit? Why is there no laughter in her life? Many of the defeated who had been politically active could not receive visits from friends without putting both parties in danger. Many had fled to other towns to avoid being denounced and had no family or friends where they now lived. When the neighbours press her, the Other Woman responds with sighs, and the song repeats twice that nobody understands those sighs. Her situation in the first stanza is that of a social outcast. This could well have resonated with the Republicans, who did not have a place in the conventional Francoist world, and who were confronted with the winners' utter incapacity to understand either their circumstances or their feelings. In fact, just as in the case of La Parrala, the sad isolation that results from the neighbours' incomprehension is the best situation the Other Woman can hope for; if the neighbours *did* understand the reasons for her distress, she would likely be punished.

The words of the song repeatedly point to the apparatus of the Francoist repression. The "Other Woman" is "encerrada ... como la que está en la cárcel" ("shut up ... like one who is in jail") – an allusion to real jails and also to the surveillance that made freedom of movement impossible for many of the losers who weren't behind bars.[4] Later in the song, the neighbours come "de noche para leer[le] la sentensia" ("at night to read out her sentence"). In real life, when someone showed up at a home at night with a sentence to read, it was a Falange militiaman, and the person who received such a visit was never heard from again. Near the end of the song, the Other Woman, devastated by her lover's betrayal, tells him to ("cumpl[ir] con lo que has firmado" ("carry out what you have signed") – that is, the sentence. Here we recall images of Franco imperturbably signing large stacks of death sentences.

But the specifics of the Other Woman's sentence, and the results for her, are the most eloquent representation of the situation of the defeated Republicans, one that was both desperate and unjust. The sentence reads:

El nombre que te ofresían
ya no es tuyo, compañera;
de azahares y velo blanco
se viste la que lo lleva.

The name they offered you
is no longer yours, comrade;
the one who bears it wears
orange blossoms and a white veil.

The Other Woman had been promised official recognition of her relationship, just as the left had been promised social legitimacy and legal rights under the Republic. Based on those promises, both had given everything they had. But under Franco, the legal rights and social status had gone to the winners. Those who loved their country, remained loyal, and sacrificed everything for it were now locked in jail, ostracized, defined as "immoral" and "degenerate" like the Other Woman, and punished with constant surveillance and social control. The result was that, like the clandestine lover of the song, they were without any recourse:

No tengo ley que me abone,
ni puerta donde llamar,

I have no law to protect me,
and no door to knock on.

Once citizens with full rights, the defeated had been reduced to living on the so-called "charity" of the winners. The lines

y me alimento a escondías,
con tus besos y tu pan.

And I nourish myself, in hiding,
On your kisses and your bread.

recall the system of rationing that kept the working class close to starvation, since they could not afford the exorbitant food prices on the black market, which the regime tolerated throughout the period. These lyrics also recall the bread lines of Auxilio Social. The regime made propaganda about how generous they were being by offering charity to the losers of the war, although it was they who had impoverished those losers by declaring their currency to be valueless.

The end of the second stanza describes the protagonist's silence and her internalized self-hatred. Again, many on the losing side would have experienced similar feelings. The overwhelming betrayal they had suffered at the hands of the state, and the terror, helplessness, and humiliation that were constant features of their daily lives, could not but take a psychological toll. Traumatic events break trust in such a basic way that the survivor feels utterly alienated and alone, like the Other Woman. Trauma survivors lack a sense of self and suffer from guilt and self-doubt. Psychiatrist Judith Herman explains that trauma victims feel guilty that they were unable to ward off the disaster. They feel this even though traumatic events, by definition, are characterized by helplessness in the face of terror:

> Guilt may be understood as an attempt to draw some useful lesson from disaster and to regain some sense of power and control. To imagine that one could have done better may be more tolerable than to face the reality of utter helplessness ... Feelings of guilt are especially severe when the survivor has been a witness to the suffering or death of other people. (53–4)

As a result, traumatized individuals can be prone to exaggerated self-blame and unable to stand up for what they truly deserve. Some critics have condemned the masochism of the female protagonists in certain *coplas* as the expression of conventional, Andalusian-flavoured *machismo,* but there is another possible reading, in which the songs give voice to the real self-loathing of traumatized and oppressed people:

> cumple con lo que has firmado,
> que yo no valgo la pena.

> Carry out what you've signed,
> for I'm not worth the trouble.[5]

This is why the refrain of "Romance de la Otra" is so important. In real life, the defeated had to remain silent, and thus depersonalized, which rendered them more susceptible to feelings of guilt and inferiority. Keeping quiet out of fear is part of what leads trauma survivors to feel contaminated and unworthy, for they then also must blame themselves for not being more courageous (Rodríguez Kauth 3). "Romance de la otra" would have been profoundly therapeutic, for it reminded the defeated that they *did* matter, that they *were* deserving, and that they *should* have rights. And they could affirm this themselves as they sang along. Thus, the lines

Con tal que vivas tranquilo,
¡qué importa que yo me muera!

As long as you're worry-free,
who cares if I die!

should be interpreted not simply as masochism, but rather as an accusation against the winners, who were living worry-free lives, having ruthlessly taken everything from the losers and cut them off from all legal and social citizenship.

Coplas as Rituals of Marginalization: Disenfranchised Grief and the Impossibility of Reincorporation

"Romance de la otra" completes the trilogy of rituals begun by "Ojos verdes" ("Green Eyes") and "Tatuaje" ("Tattoo"). It expresses how the defeated had been condemned to a life of invisibility, surveillance, and mourning. Ordinarily, rituals of incorporation lift the restrictions on mourners and allow them to rejoin the wider society (van Gennep *Rites* 147–8). In this regard, "Romance de la otra" allowed the defeated to express how, five years after the war's end, Francoist society was still keeping the losers of the war shut in, forever mourning deaths that were not socially recognized, and forever isolated in a pain that the wider society refused to understand, much less share.

La Otra, wearing the black of mourning, but with her grief unsanctioned by the surrounding society, exemplifies what Kenneth Doka has termed the "disenfranchised griever" (4). In societies not under state terror, disenfranchised grief can develop when the mourner's relationship with the deceased is not recognized, as in extramarital relations, homosexual relations, or other relationships that do not involve kinship.

Disenfranchised grief also develops when society does not recognize the loss itself, such as may occur with miscarriage or abortion. Finally, it develops when society does not regard the mourner as a potential griever, as may be the case with children (3–7).

The obstacles that disenfranchised grievers face in expressing their sorrow exacerbate the emotional difficulty of the bereavement process; normal feelings of anger, guilt, and powerlessness are intensified (Doka 7). Concurrent crises such as financial problems often arise, as we see when a lesbian loses the right to the house in which she has lived with her deceased partner. At the same time, the actions that would help in mourning (caring for the dying person, planning the funeral, attending it) are not allowed, which isolates the bereaved from the social support that is crucial to helping them avoid depression and move through the mourning process (Sanders 11–12).[6]

I would add to Doka's description that not all disenfranchised grief involves death. Other kinds of losses require social support, which members of disenfranchised groups do not get. For example, when a marriage breaks up, the separated spouse can talk about his sadness to friends and co-workers. His social network will rally and invite him to dinner and include him in other activities. A gay person living in a homophobic community may well have had to hide the very existence of his relationship. So when it ends, he also has to hide the sorrow occasioned by the breakup.

Psychotherapists often use rituals in therapy with any bereaved person who is having difficulty with mourning. These are all the more crucial for disenfranchised grievers, who cannot participate in official rituals. Therapists may help a client develop an original ceremony involving an object associated with the deceased, or the client may imitate the public ceremony in private. Singing "Romance de la otra" may have functioned in a similar way. It was a vehicle for the defeated to express the double bind of being forbidden to mourn in public and therefore also being unable to *cease* mourning so that they could be welcomed back into society. If ritual is supposed to be about bringing community together, "Romance de la otra," paradoxically, engaged people in a ritual that enacted and named the impossibility of life in community for half of Spain. It named the problem of not being allowed access either to mourning or to reincorporation. It served as an affirmation of marginalization that *substituted* for the denied ritual of reincorporation. It lamented that there was no life in common, no justice, no compassion, and therefore no meaning to life without the lost person. It enacted the reasons why the defeated were stuck in the perpetual limbo state portrayed in "Tatuaje."

Conchita Piquer sang "Romance de la otra" live for more than a decade. Her performances were reverential occasions. In this solemn atmosphere, with her listeners hanging on every familiar word as she sang "No tengo ley que me abone,/ ni puerta donde llamar" ("I have no law to protect me and no door to knock on"), Piquer 's performance may have been creating an unspoken social cohesion among the losers. This *copla* could well have served as a ritualized testimony to their common ostracism, their grief, and their sense of betrayal. Its performance created a space in which they could mourn together as a group. But it was equally important that the winners were also present at Piquer's shows. For the losers, hanging on every word and then enthusiastically applauding "La Otra" allowed them to bear witness in front of the winners, to make themselves visible as mourners and as victims of legal and social persecution. Also, the performance of "La Otra" symbolically affirmed the losers' relationship to their country. Although they had no legal rights, although they were defined as the "anti-Spain," the song allowed them to affirm in code that, however marginalized, they loved their country more than the winners did:

> Te quiero siendo ¡la otra!,
> como la que más te quiera.
>
> I love you, as the other woman,
> and the one who loves you the most.

Conchita Piquer acted as the bridge between the two sides, all the more so because of her unsanctioned love for Antonio Márquez.

"Ojos verdes," "Tatuaje," and "Romance de la otra," all of which were broadcast frequently on the radio, offered the defeated opportunities to move through the three phases of mourning rituals that had been denied them. They could say goodbye to a lost world. They could grapple with the pain of being trapped in a transition made perpetual by the disappearance and murder of their loved ones. And they could protest their permanent condition as pariahs. As they identified with the three protagonists, they could carry out the gradual "working-through" of mourning that allowed them to evolve emotionally despite the silence and prohibitions imposed on them.

Chapter Seven

Reasserting Personhood through Popular Song: "Romance de valentía" ("Ballad of Bravery") and "La Ruiseñora" ("The Nightingale")

Introduction

Key to psychological survival for the defeated was retaining a sense of personhood despite being constantly humiliated and degraded by the Francoists. León and Quiroga's *coplas* provided crucial tools for this, affirming personhood through the kinds of protagonists they created. Their most important *coplas* feature an isolated character who is suffering and who has to struggle against the surrounding society. The protagonist is most often nameless, known only by a nickname: La Parrala (the Wine Lady), La Ruiseñora (the Nightingale), La Lirio (the Lily), La Otra (the Other Woman).[1] Or she may not even have a nickname, like the prostitute in "Ojos verdes," or the woman who wanders the ports in "Tatuaje." In one *copla,* "Yo soy … Esa" ("I'm just 'that woman'") (1952), the problem of not being able to determine even one's own name, symbolic of the denial of personhood, becomes the theme of the song. In it a prostitute complains:

Lo mismo me llaman Carmen,
que Lolilla, que Pilá;
con lo que quieran llamarme
me tengo que conformá.

They might call me Carmen,
or Lolilla, or Pilar;
I have to accept [resign myself to]
whatever they want to call me.[2]

These protagonists usually speak in the first person at some point in the song, explaining their feelings and their way of responding to their situation. The listener-singer identifies with the protagonist, who is shown to have deep feelings and who responds with dignity and integrity despite her social degradation. The process of projecting oneself onto such a character would have worked to counteract the regime's vilifications of the defeated.[3]

In 1940, "La Parrala" dealt with the problem of how to maintain one's physical existence despite constant surveillance and investigation. The three mourning *coplas* of the early 1940s allowed the defeated to mourn the death and absence of others. In the 1950s, terror and mourning came together in two *coplas* that made the problem of personhood, the problem of the existence of the self, their explicit theme. In both "Romance de valentía" ("Ballad of Bravery") (1957) and "La Ruiseñora" ("The Nightingale") (1953), the protagonists assert their personhood in a context of violence, and lose their lives, but gain a moral victory in the end.

ROMANCE DE VALENTÍA
Quintero/León/Quiroga

I

Era mu poco en la vía,
tan poco que nada era;
por no tener, no tenía
ni mare que lo quisiera.
Era un triste afisionao
que buscaba la ocasión
de dejar en un cerrao,
frente a un toro, el corazón.
Romance de valentía
escrito con luna blanca
y gracia de Andalucía
en campos de Salamanca.

1er. ESTRIBILLO

Embiste, toro bonito,
embiste, por cariá ...
Morir se me importa un pito,
pues nadie me iba a llorá.
Aquí no hay plaza, ni nombre,
ni traje tabaco y oro.
Aquí hay un niño muy hombre
que está delante de un toro.
En matarme no repares,
te concedo hasta el perdón ...
Y ya que no tengo mare,
la Macarena me ampare
si me cuelgas de un pitón.

II

Todas las noches saltaba,
sin miedo, la talanquera
y a cara o cruz se jugaba,
al toro, la vía entera.

BALLAD OF BRAVERY
Quintero/León/Quiroga

I

He was very little in life,
so little that he was nothing;
he had so little he didn't even
have a mother to love him.
He was a sad amateur
who was looking for the chance
to leave his heart
in a ring, facing a bull.
A ballad of bravery
written with a white moon
and Andalusian flair
on the fields of Salamanca.

FIRST REFRAIN

Attack, beautiful bull,
attack, for heavens' sake ...
I couldn't care less if I die,
since no-one would cry for me.
Here there is no bullring, nor name,
nor gold and brown suit.
Here is a child very much a man
who is facing a bull.
Don't think anything of killing me,
I even pardon you ...
And since I have no mother,
let the Macarena Virgin succour me
if you hang me over a horn.

II

Every night, fearless,
he jumped the fence
and played his whole life,
at heads or tails, before the bull.

Quizá fuera colorao
er buré que lo embistió
y mordiendo su costao
malherío lo dejó.
Romance de valentía
teñío con luna blanca
y sangre de Andalucía
en campos de Salamanca.

2do. ESTRIBILLO

Adiós, plaza de Sevilla,
ya nunca me habrás de vé
pisar tu arena amarilla
con tanto que lo soñé.
Adiós, capote de sea
que fuiste mi compañero;
morir en esta pelea
es cosa de buen torero.
Ya vestío de alamares
no ha de verme la afisión
y ya que no tengo mare,
la Macarena me ampare
y me dé su bendición.

3do ESTRIBILLO

Y allí quedó ante la fiera,
ninguno lo vio caé,
nadie resó tan siquiera
ni un padrenuestro por é.
Por él ninguna serrana
lloró de luto vestía ...
Por él ninguna campana
dobló amanesiendo el día.
Pero en cambio, entre asusenas
y entre velas enrisá,
en San Gí, la Macarena,
sí que lloraba de pena
por la muerte der chavá.

Perhaps it was reddish,
the bull that attacked him
and, biting him in the side,
left him mortally wounded.
A ballad of bravery
stained with a white moon
and Andalusian blood
on the fields of Salamanca.

SECOND REFRAIN

Goodbye, bullring of Seville,
now you'll never see me
set foot on your yellow sand
despite how much I dreamed of it.
Goodbye, silken cape,
you were my comrade;
to die in this kind of fight
is what a good bullfighter does.
The fans will never see me
dressed in tassels
and since I have no mother,
may the Macarena Virgin protect me
and give me her blessing.

THIRD REFRAIN

And there he remained before the beast,
no-one saw him fall,
nobody even said
the Lord's Prayer for him.
No mountain girl cried for him
dressed in mourning ...
No bell tolled for him
when morning came.
But nevertheless, from among lilies
and braided candles,
the Macarena in the church of
San Gil *did* cry in sadness
for the death of the boy.

A famous Negro spiritual begins with the lament, "Sometimes I feel like a motherless child a long way from home." These words describe the situation of the protagonist of "Romance de valentía" ("Ballad of Bravery"). One of León's rare male protagonists, he is introduced to us precisely as *nothing* (*nada*). The character is in Salamanca, far from his beloved home, Seville. His life's passion is bullfighting, and he has no fear of dying, since, as he tells us, there would be no one to cry for him if he did. Every night he jumps a fence and fights a bull, commending himself to La Macarena, the famous Virgin of Seville, since he has no mother.

One night, the bull mortally wounds him. He says goodbye to Seville, which will never see him realize his dream of fighting in its bullring. He declares that to go down fighting is part of being a good bullfighter. And it turns out to be true that he is completely alone in the world. For when the bull mortally wounds him, no one prays for him, and no bells toll. But the abandoned man who goes down fighting is vindicated in the end by a superior authority, as the famous Macarena Virgin of Seville does indeed cry tears of pain for him.[4]

As in "La Parrala," the music is light and playful, contrasting with the story's tragic content. Fittingly for a bullfighting story, it is a *pasodoble.* The song has five stanzas, three of them set to the music of the refrain, but all advancing the story. Narrator and character alternate as speakers in the five stanzas: the narrator speaks in the first, third, and fifth, the protagonist in the second and fourth. Piquer's storytelling talent is evident as she maintains the momentum and suspense in the narrator's voice, while imbuing it with tragic tones as the bull mortally wounds the young man. When she sings the part of the young man, she conveys his aspirations and his fearlessness in the second stanza, and in the fourth, his grief as he says goodbye to his dreams, recalls that he has no mother, and commends himself to the Macarena. The ritards in the song bring out the pathos of not having a mother, which is emblematic of abandonment. These ritards, which stop the forward movement of the narrative, emphasize the grief at the core of the song and create space in which to feel it. When Piquer returns to the narrative voice in the final stanza, it is a voice that has been profoundly affected by the tragedy and by the protagonist's utter abandonment by society. The first four lines are not sung, but recited dramatically in a voice of deep grief, as the narrator recounts that no one saw him fall, no one said the Lord's Prayer for him. Piquer then returns to singing, ending the song with sobs, to recount how the Macarena cries in grief over the young man's death.

This *copla* presents an abandoned person, utterly insignificant and unnoticed in life, who makes a decision to follow his passion, to act, and to exercise courage, even if it means death, and even if he gets no glory because no one else notices. The protagonist exercises what freedom he has and affirms his personhood in the act that ends his life. The trade-off is more than worth it to him. And for the listener, the song confirms his worth through the response of La Macarena.

I read this song as a political allegory. Because of its shape, Spain is often referred to as the "piel de toro," the bull skin. The bull can be read specifically as Franco's Spain, both because of the symbolism of the bull in Picasso's famous anti-Franco painting, "Guernica" (1937) and because some of Franco's key supporters owned large estates in Andalucía, where they bred and raised bulls for the ring. In this reading, the protagonist has been reduced to nothing and abandoned because he was on the losing side. He has already lost everyone who cared about him, even his mother. Having nothing to lose, he chooses to fight the bull that represents Franco's Spain, exerting his freedom to choose rebellion, even if it means death.

As he faces the bull, the protagonist is utterly alone, though in a proper bullfight he would be assisted and protected by mounted bullfighters known as picadors. As in the other *coplas* we have examined, the protagonist's situation is analogous to that of the defeated in postwar Spain. Before and during the war, they had enjoyed the support of their comrades, organized in powerful unions. But under Franco, each surviving Republican was compelled to face the ferocious beast alone. And the time to face that beast was often at night, which was when people were dragged from their houses and taken out to the countryside to be shot. What distinguishes our protagonist is that he has taken the initiative – to face the bull voluntarily and at a time he chooses. As such, he represents one option for those targeted by the regime: to choose the hour of one's death, and go down fighting.

What makes the song potentially useful as a survival tool for the defeated is that the young man does not reduce his self-perception to "nobodiness." He has become a hero, the hero of a song called "Romance de valentía" ("Ballad of Bravery"). His worth, his personhood, is affirmed by the Virgin, implying a condemnation of the callous mortals who will not cry for him. But there is one human being who does cry for the young man – the performer, Conchita Piquer, who sobs as she recounts how no one marks his death. The protagonist is thus made a person not only by the fictional and supernatural Virgin, but also by the real performer. For the many Republicans who were forbidden to cry over loved ones who had been killed by that totalitarian bull, Piquer's tears may have meant much indeed.

Many of the radio listeners who sang along to "Romance de valentía" were themselves isolated and degraded. Many had lost most of their loved ones. As they sang, they played the role of a marginal figure different from themselves, and the protective distance of fiction allowed them to experience their feelings of abandonment and nothingness without being overwhelmed. And then they could have the vicarious experience of recovering their personhood. By projecting themselves onto the role and playing out the story, they could live out the process whereby the character acts on his talents and passion, asserts his being and his will, even if it means death. In this way, members of Piquer's audience could transcend their abjection and experience vicariously the moving feeling of having their existence validated by the mourning of the Virgin.

But it was not just by identifying with the character that they were able to recover personhood. They were also singing along with the performer, Conchita Piquer. They literally recovered their own personhood by making sound through the mask provided by the fictional character. Indeed, the very concept of personhood is linked to making sound; it comes from the Greek theatre, where the *sound* of the voice is heard *through* the mask (per-sonare).[5] By declaring their personhood in this way, through song, they could say to their oppressors, "We are still here, we are worth something." The most important thing, of course, is that they could do all of this without being killed themselves – after all, they were just playing a role. The song's nameless protagonist had to die in order for the listeners to have the opportunity to remember they were still alive and to assert it in full voice.

In "Romance de valentía," the lone bullfighter asserts his personhood in a song in which there are no other human characters. Another particularly beautiful *copla* called "La Ruiseñora" ("The Nightingale") grapples with the problem of how to achieve voice and personhood when one is oppressed in a specific social context.

The Singer Silenced: Recovering Voice and Personhood in "La Ruiseñora" ("The Nightingale") (1953)

LA RUISEÑORA
Quintero/León/Quiroga

I

En la taberna de 'El Tres de Espadas',
entre guitarras y anís de moras,
¡cómo cantaba de madrugada
por soleares la Ruiseñora!
Se acabó lo que se daba – le dijo Paco Olivares –,
y la llevó hasta el altá;
y ella, que lo camelaba, se puso blanca de
  asahares
y nunca vorvió a cantá.
Pero Paco, antes del año, empesó a vorvé de día
y a bebé sin ton ni son;
y mordiendo el desengaño, la flamenca
  repetía
en los hierros del balcón:

1er ESTRIBILLO

¿Qué te pasa, Ruiseñora?
Que tengo un nío de pena y selos en la garganta,
que hasta er corasón me llora
por seguiriyas, por soleares y por tarantas.
¿Qué sombra lo tiene esclavo?
¿De qué rumbo mardesío
viene este doló de clavo
que m'esbarata er sentío?
¿Dónde está el agonisante
que, entre la noche y la aurora,
se muera cantando un cante
mejó que la Ruiseñora?

THE NIGHTINGALE
Quintero/León/Quiroga

I

At the Three of Spades tavern,
among guitars and anisette,
how beautiful were the flamenco songs
of the Nightingale at dawn!
That's the end of that, Paco Olivares told her,
and he took her to the altar;
and she, who'd been after him, wore white and orange
  blossoms
and never sang again.
But inside of a year, Paco started staying out all night
and drinking like a fish;
and swallowing her disappointment, the flamenco singer
  repeated
behind the bars of her balcony:

FIRST REFRAIN

What's the matter, Nightingale?
I have a knot of pain and jealousy in my throat,
so that my very heart is crying, in
seguiriyas, soleares and tarantas. [flamenco forms]
What ghost has enslaved him?
From what accursed place comes
this terrible pain that is
driving me crazy?
Where is there a dying man who,
between nightfall and dawn,
dies singing a song
better than the Nightingale?

II

A 'El Tres de Espadas' corrió celosa
con la carita despavoría
y vió a su Paco que con la Rosa
en una mesa se divertía.
Subió derecha al tablao: ¡Aquí está la Ruiseñora
pa' lo que gusten mandá!
¡Lo de ése y yo s'ha acabado! ¡Vuervo a sé la
  cantaora!
¡Conque vamos a cantá!
– ¡Pues se va a cumplí tu suerte!–
Y al relámpago de un tiro,
er café se iluminó.
Ella vio llegar la muerte y, en el úrtimo suspiro,
de este modo le cantó:

2do. ESTRIBILLO

¡Dios te ampare, Ruiseñora!
Campanas doblen por er silencio de tu garganta;
resen por su cantaora[6]
las seguiriyas, las soleares y las tarantas.
De un soplo m'has apagao
la lámpara de la vía,
¡Mira qué bien has pagao
lo que yo a ti te quería!
¿Dónde está el agonisante
que, entre la noche y la aurora,
se muera cantando un cante
mejó que la Ruiseñora?

Para FINAL

Tenerle, por Dios, clemencia,
piedá tenerle los jueses,
que yo le he dao lisencia[7]
para matarme sien veces.

 Facing English translation mine.

II

Jealous, she ran to the Three of Spades
with terror on her little face
and saw her Paco enjoying
himself with Rosa at a table.
She went straight up on stage: – Here is the Nightingale
at your service!
What was between me and him is over! I'm a flamenco
  singer once more!
So let's sing!
– Well, you're going to get what you deserve!–
And the café lit up with the
lightning of a gunshot.
She saw death coming, and with her last breath,
she sang to him in this way:

SECOND REFRAIN

– May God protect you, Nightingale!
Let the bells toll for the silencing of your throat;
let them pray in seguiriyas, soleares and tarantas
for their flamenco singer.
With one breath you've blown
out the lamp of my life.
Look how you've repaid me for
all the love I gave you!
Where is there a dying man
who, between nightfall and dawn,
dies singing a song
better than the Nightingale?

ENDING

– Show him mercy, for God's sake,
let the judges have compassion,
for I gave him licence
to kill me a hundred times over.

"La Ruiseñora" ("The Nightingale") was first performed by Piquer in 1953, fourteen years after the end of the Spanish Civil War. By this time, the worst of the hunger was coming to an end. But the silence continued. I read "La Ruiseñora" as providing an opportunity for the defeated to reflect on what they had lost as a result of the denial of their personhood during those fourteen years. This *copla* offered a way for the defeated to express mourning for that loss. And it could function as a fantasy of reasserting one's personhood despite the danger. But the song could also serve as a meditation on the problem of creativity snuffed out, and as a lament for the loss of beauty under Franco's rule. It is to my mind the most beautiful melodically of these *coplas*, with a lyrical orchestral bridge.

In Spanish vernacular, a nightingale is someone with a special talent for singing. (In English, we would say that someone sings like a lark.) Like La Parrala, La Ruiseñora sings in a tavern in the wee hours. She sings flamenco songs (*seguiriyas, soleares,* and *tarantas*) with a beauty that transports her listeners. The place, the time, and the activity in which she is engaged place her, like others of Piquer's characters, on the wrong side of the divide between the "respectable" and the "fallen" woman, although there is no evidence of sexual promiscuity or alcoholism in her case. La Ruiseñora expresses her creativity through her flamenco singing, which is so much a part of her that she is named for it. She's been after Paco Olivares, who, in asking her to marry him, offers her the respectability of wedlock, symbolized in the whiteness of the orange blossoms she wears to the altar. She embraces the dream of romantic marriage, although the price for doing so is high. She never sings again and is confined to the home, waiting for Paco like a caged bird, behind the iron bars of the balcony. Paco's marriage proposal is in fact expressed as a withdrawal of rights: "Se acabó lo que se daba" is an expression that means "enough is enough" but whose literal translation is "What was given has come to an end." What has run out is La Ruiseñora's right to sing, to work in the public sphere, to be out at night, to be independent.

This devil's bargain, in which La Ruiseñora signs away her voice and her freedom in return for the legitimacy of marriage, does not turn out well for her. Paco continues to stay out all night, drinks like a fish, and openly flaunts his adultery with Rosa, sitting at a table with her in the same tavern where La Ruiseñora used to sing. Crazed with pain and jealousy, La Ruiseñora reclaims her right to freedom of movement by following Paco to the tavern. She asserts her right to a voice by stepping onto the stage, telling the public that her relationship with Paco is over, and declaring that she is now a singer again. Paco then asserts his control over her as her husband by shooting her, thus immobilizing and silencing her for good. But before she dies, she wins the moral victory over him with her final song, pointing out the disproportionate nature of her punishment and the fact that her only crime was to love him: "¡Mira qué bien has pagado / lo que yo a ti te quería!" ("Look how you've paid me back / for all the love I gave you!"). The collective voice of the "Greek chorus" in the refrain expresses sympathy for her by pointing out that she continued to sing beautifully even as a dying person.

The metaphor of the bird confined to a cage and unable to do what it naturally does – which is to sing – accentuates the tragedy of a woman who is first silenced and jailed behind the bars of her balcony, then murdered for insisting on doing what came most naturally to her. This story may have been useful to many on the losing side, for La Ruiseñora's predicament bore similarities to their own as they struggled to survive psychologically. Their voices had been silenced like hers, and many of them had been forbidden to exercise their natural talents. Many had been banned from their professions, and their children barred from higher education or decent jobs. Some of the losers found themselves behind bars like La Ruiseñora, while others had only very limited freedom of movement – at certain hours, and with all identity papers ready for inspection. They had given up their voice and their freedom for the very tenuous recognition of their right to remain alive. And many others had died, shot like La Ruiseñora, between nightfall and dawn, for having spoken out.

The double moral standard illustrated in the story of La Ruiseñora and Paco can also be read in multiple ways. One possible reading focuses on gender. La Ruiseñora gives up her right to work, her freedom of movement, her voice, and the thriving that results from making beautiful music (what personality theorist Abraham Maslow would call self-actualization).[8] In return, she gets legal status and the right to wear white at a wedding. She obeys all the conditions imposed on her. Her husband, by contrast, is out all night and is quite open about his adultery.[9] The crimes are his, and the obedience and suffering are hers, yet he retains the right to give her orders, and when she breaks the rules, he exercises his power over her with lethal force. Thus for her, obedience means being jailed and disobedience means death, while he can betray the marriage contract with impunity.

In its presentation of the consequences of marriage for women in Francoist society, "La Ruiseñora" complements and completes "Romance de la otra." The latter song has shown us the fate of the clandestine lover of a married man: she lives shut up "as though in jail." La Ruiseñora gets to wear white to the altar, as La Otra never could, yet she, too, lives shut up and silenced, while her husband Paco spends his time with *his* "other woman," Rosa. So obeying the rules hasn't put La Ruiseñora in a better situation than that of the Other Woman. Piquer's songs, taken together, thus paint a picture of women's oppression under Franco.

The sexual double standard indicated in "La Ruiseñora" was similar to the double standard of conduct between the winners and losers of the war. The losers faced sacrifices, restrictions on movement, silencing, the need to obey every rule to the letter, and disproportionate punishment for any infraction. Many on the winning side, which imposed this "moral purity" on them, were themselves corrupt, packing the brothels, some getting rich with impunity on the black market in food while the losers starved, then using their newfound wealth to set up mistresses in apartments.

La Ruiseñora actively rebels against the man who has power over her, directly proclaiming her right to her voice and her freedom. Although her rebellion ends in death, her defiance and her declarations of her rights would have offered vicarious satisfaction to the losers of the war, who must sometimes have fantasized about telling off their oppressors, whatever the cost. It is perhaps no coincidence that the authority figure against whom La Ruiseñora rebels is called Paco, a nickname for Francisco, which was Franco's given name. The song is also significant in siding with La Ruiseñora against her adulterous husband at a time when it was common for misogynistic courts to blame women for somehow "driving" their husbands to commit adultery (Mir 162).

But the therapeutic effects of "La Ruiseñora" go beyond the level of plot to the act of singing itself. The song can be read as a reflection on the many functions of singing. At the same time, it teaches the listener how to use singing safely as a coping mechanism. La Ruiseñora is characterized as someone who loves to sing. Just as birds naturally sing at dawn ("de madrugada"), so does she, but with a special beauty that comes from the flamenco tradition. La Parrala also sings in a bar at night, but she is characterized by other things as well, such as drinking, crying, suffering, and confounding her neighbours. Her name comes from her alcoholism. By contrast, singing is the essence of La Ruiseñora – it is who she is and what she was born to do. So in a few lines we already know that it is a tragedy for her that she has had to give up singing when she marries Paco: she has entered into a power relationship that keeps her from being who she is, and she will get nothing in return. Thus far in this analysis, then, singing means doing what comes naturally, exercising one's talents, and creating beauty. It also means working in the public sphere.

But now, as La Ruiseñora begins to suffer from Paco's infidelity, singing takes on new functions. This *copla* makes a rare connection between the level of narration/performance and the level of the plot, in that the narrator who has been telling the story in the third person now addresses herself directly to La Ruiseñora:

> ¿Qué te pasa, Ruiseñora?
>
> What's the matter, Nightingale?

The narrator's tender question gives La Ruiseñora an opening to tell us about her pain, and her response has everything to do with the importance of singing as a survival tool:

> Que tengo un nío de pena
> y selos en la garganta,
> que hasta er corasón me llora
> por seguiriyas, por soleares y por tarantas.
>
> What's wrong is that I've got a knot [literally, a "nest"]
> of pain and jealousy in my throat,
> and my very heart is crying,
> in *seguiriyas, soleares* and *tarantas* [flamenco forms].

These lines are significant because they name the emotions of pain and jealousy from which La Ruiseñora is suffering. They also tell us that repressed tears have formed a knot or lump in her throat. But the same singing that *names* the bottled-up grief is also the vehicle for *undoing* that knot and keeping the grief moving: when La Ruiseñora's heart is in pain, the various genres of flamenco, sung deep in the throat, provide the means for the crying to reach the surface. Flamenco not only expresses her natural talent but also gives voice to her deep emotional pain.

As La Ruiseñora follows Paco to the tavern, her singing becomes an expression of rebellion, her protest against injustice, her declaration of agency, dignity, and right to self-expression. But then she becomes the victim of authoritarian violence. And the function of singing changes again, as she sings with her last breath:

> ¡Dios te ampare, Ruiseñora!
> Campanas doblen por er silencio de tu garganta;
> resen por su *cantaora*
> las seguiriyas, las soleares y las tarantas.

May God protect you, Nightingale!
Let the bells toll for the silencing of your throat;
let them pray for their flamenco singer
in *seguiriyas, soleares,* and *tarantas.*

In these lines, La Ruiseñora begins by appealing to God to look after her, since man has done her in. Then she goes on to displace religious ritual, telling her friends in the tavern to toll the bells in mourning for the way her voice has been silenced. In this way she offers the losers of the war an opportunity to affirm, by singing along with her, that the loss of their own voices, their submersion in thick and terrible silence, is also a tragedy worthy of official recognition and mourning. She then asks her friends to pray for her, not through Catholic liturgy, but through the same kinds of flamenco she used to sing. The song thus makes explicit what I have argued in the previous three chapters: that *coplas,* with their roots firmly in Andalusian flamenco, could be used as covert rituals of mourning that substituted for those of the Catholic Church.

The *coplas* explored in previous chapters had first been performed by Piquer in the 1940s. "La Ruiseñora" was first performed in 1953, by which time the mourning the song expressed was of a different nature. In the 1940s, Piquer's most famous *coplas* provided a safe way to mourn family members executed by Franco's apparatus of state terror. By contrast, "La Ruiseñora" presents the violent death of the protagonist herself. And the song is also about the way she is silenced while still alive. Part of the pain in La Ruiseñora's heart is about missing singing itself. When she is shot, she directs the onlookers to mourn, not her death in general, but "the silencing of my throat." The defeated could thus use this song as a vehicle to mourn, not those who died in the war, but their own lost lives and all that they had lost in the preceding fourteen years during which they had remained silent in the hope of staying alive. In 1940, Rafael de León's "La Parrala" had taught people to stay physically alive by playing roles and not expressing themselves directly. By 1953, León's lyrics were beginning to reflect on the terrible trade-off the losers faced: to stay alive, they had to suppress their personhood.

But the most important lesson about singing in this *copla,* and the solution to that terrible dilemma, arises implicitly, from the parallel between Conchita Piquer and La Ruiseñora. Both sing late at night, and both were born to sing. On the level of plot, La Ruiseñora will be killed if she tries to express herself again through song. On this level, singing is *expression* without *protection;* the result is death, physical extinction for the sake of asserting personhood.[10] On the level of performance, however,

Piquer can sing with impunity as she tells La Ruiseñora's fictional story of injustice. The listeners learn that to sing this story is to access beauty, express pain, declare rebellion, and exercise one's talents, all *without* dying, because it is, after all, "just a song" and they are merely playing a role. La Ruiseñora is sacrificed in the plot, but in a way that allows the listener to tell her story in song, yet live on as a person.

First performed in 1953 and recorded in 1955 (Plaza, *Conchita Piquer* 167, 204), "La Ruiseñora" opened up a space for the losers to take stock of the devil's bargain that had allowed them to survive fourteen years of dictatorship. The plot took them vicariously through fantasies of rebellion, allowing them to ask themselves whether it was worth dying to recover their voices. By playing the role of La Ruiseñora, they could express their masochism, derived from traumatization and humiliation – "Que yo le di la lisencia para matarme cien veces" ("I gave him permission to kill me a hundred times over") – while also asserting their moral superiority through their capacity to forgive, something that Paco (Franco) did not possess. And they could point out the extreme disconnect between punishment and crime under Franco, and how their supposed "crimes" were really just crimes of identity, of being who they naturally were.

In the early 1950s, Spain's international isolation ended and American aid began to arrive, putting an end to the worst of the hunger. In 1955, Spain was admitted into the United Nations. The pace of executions had by then slowed. Spain embarked on a neocapitalist path that would lead to rising material prosperity. But these two *coplas* discussed in this chapter, dating from 1953 and 1957, attest to the fact that the problem of being denied personhood, of needing to mourn for the self that had been silenced by terror, persisted. The heyday of the *copla* might have been drawing to a close, but the problems to which these two *coplas* pointed – the silencing, the fear, and the denial of personhood imposed on the defeated Republicans – have not been fully resolved even today.

Chapter Eight

When a Radio Song Is the Meaning of Life: Mending the Torn Fabric of Identity through Narrative, Music, and Interpretation

> All sorrows can be borne
> if we put them in a story
> or tell a story about
> them.
>
> Isak Dinesen[1]

This chapter explores how the narrative form and the music of Piquer's *coplas* worked to address the existential threat to survival that the defeated faced in postwar Spain. Psychiatrist Viktor Frankl developed a theory of survival based on his experiences in the Nazi concentration camp of Auschwitz. He argued that meaning was the most basic human survival need, more urgent even than the need for food. He identified two necessary conditions for a prisoner to survive in the camps. First, he needed a vision of something in the future to live for, a mission that only he could carry out. Second, he had to seek meaning in the present suffering he was enduring in the camp.[2] Both of Frankl's conditions presuppose the ability to tell oneself a story, one that links past, present, and future. Narrative, then, is the essential vehicle for Frankl's requirement to be met.

This is not surprising, for narrative is the principal vehicle that human beings use to understand their own experience and to make sense of the world around them. We construct our selves through narrative. And we come to know the outside world, says Jerome Bruner, even as we represent it in the stories we tell about it.[3] More specifically, we use narrative as we attempt to interpret events that break cultural norms; narratives of adultery, which break the culture's norm of marriage, are a common example. People construct stories every day in an effort to explain the motives behind the actions of others when those actions break norms. Narratives are thus a basic tool for people to solve interpersonal problems (Robinson and Hawpe 112).

It is important to remember that despite the horrific persecution they faced, not all of the losers of the Spanish Civil War lacked a narrative that gave meaning to their existence. Many remained firmly committed to communism, socialism, or anarchism. Strong political beliefs allowed people to hold on to their dignity and self-worth, their sense of belonging to a group, and their sense of what the ongoing struggle for justice meant, even under the most inhuman conditions. One extreme example, recounted in the book *Los niños perdidos del franquismo (The Lost Children of the Franco Regime),* is that of Julia Manzanal, a firebrand of a woman who in 2002 was still a Communist Party militant. In 1939, she was arrested along with her infant daughter and put in prison. She was forced to watch her baby become ill with meningitis and die, while the nuns who ran the prison refused to treat her. Even at this most terrible moment, Julia turned to her ideology for a sense of meaning. She managed to get some red fabric and yellow thread, and used the thread to embroider the hammer, the sickle, and the five-pointed star on the fabric. She then demanded permission to leave her cell and go to the room where her dead daughter's body lay, to say goodbye to her. She threatened to cause a huge scandal if this was not allowed. She kissed her daughter goodbye and slipped the Communist flag into her casket. She gave meaning to her daughter's death this way:

> Una tontería, pero para mí no lo era. Mi hija moría comunista porque iba condenada a muerte desde que estaba en el vientre de su madre. Porque todos esos niños estaban condenados a muerte por ser hijos de rojos.
>
> This might seem silly, but to me it wasn't. My daughter was dying a communist, because she had already been condemned to death from the time she was in her mother's womb. Because all those children were condemned to death for being the children of Reds. (Vinyes et al. *Los niños perdidos* 103)[4]

However, others on the Republican side either had never had such strong political beliefs, or, broken by trauma, had come to question them during or after the war. Some came to doubt their former ideology because of the internecine warfare between Communist and Anarchist forces behind the Republican lines during the war. Others lost hope later, when the Allies failed to come to Spain's aid after defeating Europe's other two Fascist dictators in the Second World War.[5]

Those who lacked a strong framework for meaning in postwar Spain faced both external and internal obstacles to creating such a narrative. Their known world of people and places had been destroyed. They could not live according to their values. The social surface of Francoist discourse made their own experiences invisible; as Helen Graham has put it, "the defeated cast no reflection" (*Spanish Civil War* 137). Francoist rhetoric was triumphant, about the war as a Glorious Crusade, and about Spain's grand imperial destiny. This meant that it was very difficult for the defeated to obtain confirmation of their own feelings.[6] And Spain was economically paralysed, so much so that the bombed-out landscapes that people saw in Barcelona in 1941 were still there in 1948. The passage of time brought no change to their living conditions, their hunger, or their treatment by the winners, as indicated by the expressions "los años de piedra" and "los años de plomo" (the years of stone, the leaden years).[7] Hope for a future was thus hard to come by.

For many of the defeated, this predicament was undoubtedly compounded by the internal disruption to their sense of time caused by trauma. Many survivors compartmentalize traumatic events, separating them from ordinary experience. Because those events were so horrific, they cannot later be integrated into a verbal narrative as one more event in an ongoing life story. This cuts people off from a part of their past, which they may remember only in fragments, or only as a series of images or sensations, or only as words with no feelings. In the process, this past that cannot be fully remembered hijacks the present, for as Judith Herman explains,

> Long after the danger is past, traumatized people relive the event as though it were continually recurring in the present. They cannot resume the normal course of their lives, for the trauma repeatedly interrupts. It is as if time stops at the moment of trauma. (37)

All of these dislocations of time, reinforced by censorship, prevented people from articulating in language the connections between their past, present, and future; this in turn made it difficult for them to conceive of a purpose or meaning in life.[8]

The content and form of León and Quiroga's tragic *coplas* had distinctive characteristics that made them ideally suited to help the defeated restore a sense of meaning in life. Carmen Martín Gaite has referred to these *coplas* as "narrativa pura" ("Cuarto a espadas" 169–70). As narratives, they created a convincing and consistent alternative world by presenting unique characters with specific traits and eccentricities, as well as plot events occurring in particular geographical settings that the listener could visualize (Neimeyer "Narrative Disruptions" 218).[9] Narrative became the means of creating a stable alternative world in which to take refuge from the surrounding, false world of the dictatorship.

Furthermore, as the previous chapters have indicated, the protagonist's situation in many of León and Quiroga's *coplas* was analogous to the marginal, grief-stricken, and terrorized condition of the defeated. As Martín Gaite has described, when Piquer's voice was heard on the radio incarnating these characters, it pierced through the covering of denial and the forced cheerfulness to reveal the void underneath (*El cuarto* 153). Her voice plumbed the depths, hooked on to the silenced material of suffering, terror, grief, and loneliness, and brought it to the surface, giving voice to it. I believe that, as listeners who sang along to these *coplas* felt their own feelings mirrored and validated by Piquer and by the protagonist of the song, they began to recapture a sense of meaning in life. Paradoxically, then, to help her listeners survive, Piquer through her *coplas* first had to bring them face to face with the void that inhabited them. Only then could her songs help listeners investigate the void and find meaning in their present suffering.[10]

The content of Piquer's tragic *coplas* helped create meaning, too, by providing a powerful antidote to Francoist values. In these songs, the idyllic family, the "eternal values," and the forced cheerfulness of the regime's propaganda are nowhere to be found. The songs' protagonists are alone, marginal, usually nameless. They have no family or social support. Their living conditions are precarious, and they are in deep emotional pain. But although they are beyond the pale of respectability, the songs they inhabit pass no moral judgmenton them. (Martín Gaite "Cuarto a espadas" 174). On the contrary: there is an outside voice, that of the third-person narrator, who *bears witness to* the protagonist's suffering and who *validates* rather than judges the protagonist's point of view. In everyday life, the defeated were told daily that they were "scum," so all such validation was lacking. Thus, for the brief period that the defeated were singing these *coplas,* the regime's relentless moralizing was suspended, and space for a more complex exploration of values was opened up.

But León and Quiroga's most famous *coplas* did more than this. They created a special kind of narrative that could ring true even to traumatized people. For if narrative is the means that human beings most commonly use to interpret the ordinary events of their lives and to understand the reasons why others act the way they do, trauma challenges narration at many levels. Not only are traumatic events often so horrific that they defy representation through language (we say that they are "unspeakable,") but they cannot be assimilated into conventional ideas of human motivation; it becomes impossible to answer the question of "why" such evil is occurring. The meaning that in an ordinary story would link characters to one another and to events is shattered by trauma; the links that compose a narrative are absent (Neimeyer "Narrative Disruptions" 212). This constitutes a threat to survival because articulation of the trauma in language is one crucial avenue toward the resolution of the symptoms of post-traumatic stress. Pierre Janet, working with hysterical patients in the early twentieth century, described the need to put experience into language in order to assimilate it:

> A situation has not been satisfactorily liquidated ... until we have achieved, not merely an outward reaction through our movements, but also an inward reaction through the words we address to ourselves, through the organization of the recital of the event to others and to ourselves, and through the putting of this recital in its place as one of the chapters in our personal history.[11]

Traumatic memories are not encoded in the brain like ordinary memories. Though some trauma survivors remember all too vividly what happened to them, others dissociate from their horrific experiences; they cannot verbalize them or make them successive. Those experiences are frozen, fixed in time, often "encoded in the form of vivid sensations and images," without a memory of the events that caused them (Herman 38). This means that survivors often lack the ability to articulate their own experience.

The narrative form of the *coplas* provided a crucial vehicle for restoring meaning in such cases because in these songs, events unfold in time, in linear fashion. This restores a sense of forward movement, of the meaning of the passage of time, whereas in ordinary life, time may bring no change. Music, too, unfolds in time, reinforcing the idea that time can indeed bring changes in feelings and circumstances. This is crucial because human emotions, too, unfold in time and have a narrative dimension.[12] Feelings change as the listener moves through both the narrative plot and the progression of the music. Singing *coplas* thus gave the defeated a precious opportunity to articulate a coded version of their own experience in narrative form, making it successive in time and combating its frozen compartmentalization as trauma.

Rafael de León's *coplas* are narratives with a beginning, middle, and end; however, they do not conclude with a pat "happy ending" in which all injustice is resolved. The suffering is usually ongoing. The "Other Woman" is still ostracized at the end of "Romance de la Otra" ("Ballad of the Other Woman"). The prostitute in "Ojos verdes" ("Green Eyes") is still heartbroken at the loss of her green-eyed horseman. La Parrala is still fending off the neighbours as well as the justice system that is trying to investigate her secrets. The nameless heroine of "Tatuaje" ("Tattoo") is still wandering from port to port seeking news of her missing sailor. Yet in each *copla* a process has occurred that has affirmed the dignity of each protagonist and the worth of her feelings, her suffering. The protagonist has gone through a transformation, even if only emotionally. The passage of time, the movement through the song's narrative, has created meaning even though the causes of the suffering and the injustice have not been removed. These *coplas* are thus *unresolved narratives.* And that is what enables them to ring true as fictional mirrors of a situation in which there is no possible end to the injustice or the suffering, but in which meaning must be found nonetheless.

The defeated in Franco's Spain faced chronic terror and ongoing grief. The music of these *coplas* provided a strong defence against both, and had other benefits as well. When chronic fear puts the body in an ongoing state of hyperarousal, music brings the body back to homeostasis by a process called entrainment, in which the body's heart rate and respiration rate automatically take on the rhythm of the music.[13] Music also reduces anxiety, lowering blood pressure and the production of stress hormones.[14] It is a powerful mood-modulator, effective against depression.[15] And music reduces physical pain and boosts the immune system.[16]

Quiroga's music reinforced the evolution of the protagonist in each narrative, which helped restore a sense of change over time in *copla* listeners. For like narrative, music is temporal in nature. According to E.T. Gaston,

> The unique structure of music – it exists only through time – requires the individual to commit himself to the experience moment by moment ... Music ... cannot be interrupted without losing its intent ... Once begun, music must be continued without interruption in order that a completed idea or expression may result; regardless of its length or complexity or type and degree of skill it requires, the music must be carried through in its time order.[17]

Carmen Martín Gaite writes that León and Quiroga's *coplas* had a narrative structure that needed to be respected and that Piquer as performer had to be attentive to "la dosificación atinada de la emoción que el texto intentaba transmitir." ("the precise dosing out of the feeling that the text was trying to convey") ("Cuarto a espadas" 170). León's lyrics told a story in which the emotions gradually intensified to a climax; Quiroga's music was critical both in conveying the increasingly intense feelings and in helping manage and contain them. As shown in the previous chapters, light *pizzicatos* and playfulness at the beginning of a *copla* like "La Parrala" helped the listener engage with a plot that would turn out to be heartrendingly tragic. Ritards at climactic points allowed the listener to come to rest on the painful emotions that were the core of what the song was really about. Changes from the tonic major to the tonic minor key, frequent in these *coplas,* again served to manage the grief so that it did not become overwhelming. They also could serve to help reformulate the trauma by allowing the brain to associate traumatic feelings with a major chord instead of a minor one.

Most importantly, although the plot often remained unresolved, the music did have a clear resolution, coming to a close on the tonic chord; sometimes a clash of cymbals reinforced the closure. This brought the listeners' exposure to their own traumatic feelings to a definite end, creating a clear separation between the alternative reality of the *copla* and everyday life. Such clear musical closure provided the comforting sense that the feelings might have an end, just like the music. The music thus existed in tension with the words at the end of each of these *coplas,* helping provide relief for what the lyrics acknowledged to be a predicament without a solution.

I contend that as the defeated sang these *coplas* along with Piquer, and as they interpreted them later, they were recapturing a sense of meaning. My hypothesis is that, as they sang along, they took the shards of their fragmented traumatic experience, which they may have been unable to articulate directly, and projected them onto the analogous fictional stories of the protagonists. They mended their own sense of self through the fact that the protagonist's experience, although tragic, constituted a continuous narrative.[18] This meant that those who sang along achieved what researchers have determined to be the condition for healing traumatic feelings: the opportunity to reformulate them, and to do so in narrative form; this in turn could help them recapture (or formulate for the first time) a sense of self. Jill Littrell explains that therapy clients suffering from post-traumatic stress are not necessarily helped by simply being made to *re-experience* the feelings associated with the trauma; indeed, this can exacerbate their symptoms. Positive outcomes occur when the client is exposed to the painful stimulus long enough to acquire a new response to it, rather than simply repeating his old traumatic response, and when he can develop a new cognitive perspective on the trauma. Revisiting painful emotion, then, must involve *recasting, restructuring* the emotional memory, combining it with new associations that are not traumatic.[19] This may have been what was occurring as many among the defeated sang the story of a fictional protagonist and associated their own painful feelings with the protagonist's story and with the song's melody and orchestration.

In the act of singing, and especially in the act of performing a theatrical genre like the *copla* along with the radio, people had the chance to exercise agency, choosing the nuances to give to each line of song. They could sing with great feeling, yet they could also be attentive to their performance. The fact that *coplas* were not just songs, but miniature plays, made the listener's participation in performing them even more active, for she could throw her whole body into imitating the performer, or into creating her own original gestures to enact the unfolding drama. Those who sang along with Piquer, absorbed in the songs, may have gotten the benefits of the state of "flow" described by Daniel Goleman. The term refers to those times when one performs at one's peak in a state that is highly focused, yet relaxed, appearing effortless:

> Flow is a state of self-forgetfulness, the opposite of rumination and worry: instead of being lost in nervous preoccupation, people in flow are so absorbed in the task at hand that they lose all self-consciousness, dropping the small preoccupations of daily life. In this sense moments of flow are egoless. Paradoxically, people in flow exhibit a masterly control of what they are doing, their responses perfectly attuned to the changing demands of the task. And although people perform at their peak while in flow, they are unconcerned with how they are doing, with thoughts of success or failure; the sheer pleasure of the act itself is what motivates them. (91)

Flow combines the beneficial effects of forgetting one's daily circumstances, feeling a sense of great mastery, and experiencing mild ecstasy. This makes it an antidote to feelings of chronic anxiety, helplessness, and hopelessness. In postwar Spain, people rarely got the experience of being spontaneous and masterful. *Coplas* gave them a unique opportunity to do so as they threw themselves into performing along with Piquer a genre that was at once poetry, song, theatre, and movement.

The voiceover in Patino's *Canciones para después de una guerra* insists:

"Las sabíamos. Las vivíamos. Las cantábamos" ("We knew them. We lived them. We sang them"). The narrative structure of León and Quiroga's *coplas* helps explain Patino's equation between singing and living. Putting their inchoate feelings into language may have given the defeated a greater sense of being alive rather than spiritually dead. But as well, Piquer's *coplas* provided a vehicle for *accessing, creating, or reconstituting* a damaged sense of self, for weaving the fragments back into a whole. Thus, I would argue that songs were not simply part of the fabric of life; they recreated, or at least helped to mend, the fabric that had been ripped apart. The fact that *coplas* were narratives *in song* made them an especially effective way for those who sang them to recover their sense of self, because in singing (unlike in reading or writing), the fabric of the self is reconstituted audibly, through the voice. To sing was to mend the fabric and to live.[20]

Thus, the listener did not simply passively receive the effects when Piquer's *coplas* were broadcast on the radio. Rather, she was, as Manuel Vázquez Montalbán says, a co-creator, who participated actively in creating and interpreting the song, producing its sounds, creating its nuances (*Crónica* 40). She exercised agency, something consistently denied her in everyday life under Franco. This gave her an enhanced sense of control over her life, a feeling that she could create some change in it.

But the use-value of a *copla* was not limited to the moments when the defeated were actually singing it. Martín Gaite asserts that, rather than consuming a song quickly, people in postwar Spain would "ruminate on it, suck all its juice out of it." *Webster's Dictionary* defines the term "ruminate." As a transitive verb, it means: "1. To go over in the mind repeatedly and often casually or slowly. 2. To chew repeatedly for an extended period" (1012). Just as one gets maximum physical nourishment by chewing food thoroughly, so one could get maximum spiritual nourishment by mulling over the meaning of a song. Food was largely missing in postwar Spain, so the nourishment that songs could provide took on special importance. Indeed, both food and music trigger the production of endorphins, so music could perhaps quite literally have substituted for the pleasurable feeling of having eaten.[21]

According to drama therapist Robert Landy, when a client plays a fictional role, emotional healing occurs in the back-and-forth movement between the world of fiction and the world of everyday reality (46). But there is also a back-and-forth movement involved in the later act of standing back and reflecting on the meaning of the fictional text, interpreting it, and connecting it to one's own life. When Piquer's listeners ruminated on her songs, they constituted themselves as subjects in several ways. First, they created their own interpretation of the story. What did it mean that the protagonist of "Tatuaje" had tattooed her body with the name of a sailor in love with someone else? How was the listener to interpret the death of La Ruiseñora? What were La Parrala's secrets? The listener created her own interpretation of such questions through her own original mental activity, at a time when independent thinking was discouraged.

Second, listeners could establish a dialogue between the fictional story and their own experience. Martín Gaite does this as she recalls the mixture of feelings that she, as a middle-class girl, had toward Piquer's heroines (*El cuarto* 152–4). On the one hand, she pitied them for their poverty, their marginality, their helplessness. On the other, she envied them the intensity of their passion, something that she herself had been denied as a "respectable," middle-class girl destined for a tepid, colourless marriage whose purpose was not personal happiness but to raise new citizens to carry out the state's wishes. By actively interpreting the similarities and differences between her own situation and that of the protagonist, Martín Gaite gained insight into her own experience. In this way, individual thinking was created through the listener's response to the text.

Third, listeners could complete the unresolved story. As John Robinson and Linda Hawpe put it, *coplas,* and other stories without resolution, are "puzzlements": "accounts in search of explanations ... Such cases require generation rather than replacement of information. In effect, the narrative task has been transferred to someone else" (123). The "rumination" to which Martín Gaite refers was likely an attempt to complete the story, to imagine the *why.* The *copla,* by fictionalizing conditions analogous to the listener's own in such an enigmatic way, begged for her to complete it by mulling it over, perhaps commenting on it, and "living it" intensely. Thus it invited listeners to begin to engage with their own traumatic material, using the protection of the mask of fiction, which meant that they didn't have to acknowledge the similarities between the protagonist's predicament and their own traumatic story. To get relief, the listeners didn't have to do the impossible and solve the insoluble predicament. Says Bruner:

> Nor is it required of narrative ... that the Trouble with which it deals be resolved ... What Frank Kermode calls the "consoling plot" is not the comfort of a happy ending but the comprehension of plight that, by being made interpretable, becomes bearable. ("Narrative Construction" 16)

Azar Nafisi recounts that she and the students in her secret class in the Islamic Republic of Iran were never sure which was more real, the fictional world into which they had retreated, or the nightmare world outside. The truth, she says, was to be found in the act of trying "to imaginatively articulate these two worlds and, through that process, give shape to our vision and identity" (26). Many Spanish writers, such as Juan Marsé and Terenci Moix, have confirmed Nafisi's insight: under dictatorship, the dissident self ekes out a life *in between* the felt reality of the fictional text and the scary, restricted, and grey reality of everyday life under dictatorship. The self comes into existence and maintains itself in between the two spaces, which are each fictional in different ways. As the defeated moved between the reality of their circumstances and feelings and those of the fictional character, they constructed a narrative. And that narrative helped give shape to a self that might previously have been experienced as fragmented, dangerously painful, or unspeakable.[22]

In sum, I hypothesize that in Franco's Spain, a principal reason why people ruminated on *coplas* was because they suggested ways to pose and to answer existential questions about their suffering that were not addressed in any other social discourse (Church, school, political speeches, newspapers, magazines, and so on). *Coplas* were "fundamental tools for survival" because they were one of a very few places one could go to get answers – if only partial, if only metaphorical – to the question of the meaning of one's life and suffering.

As they sang the *coplas* explored in this book, the defeated affirmed along with each protagonist something that would lend meaning to their present suffering and to their future, thus achieving Viktor Frankl's necessary conditions for survival. As they sang "Tatuaje," they articulated with the protagonist a meaningful narrative for the future built around the image of the tattoo. As they sang along with La Parrala, they said in essence: "You can hunt me down, but even though I am suffering, you will not break my spirit. I'll keep singing despite the fear, and use all my ingenuity to outwit you." As they acted the part of La Otra, they proclaimed that even though the regime wanted to make them invisible and deny them citizenship, they still existed in the present moment, and they had dignity and personhood even though they had been marginalized. And in the role of La Ruiseñora, they proclaimed in full voice that they were talented, and born to express those talents, and that forcing them to choose between silence and death was a denial of their basic human rights.

León's tragic *coplas* were a priceless resource in the years of terror in Franco's Spain because they created a stable and regularly available fictional world where people's suffering and their questions could be addressed by analogy. The songs created a space where the defeated could find a pool of possible responses to their plight rather than pat, unconvincing answers. Everything that had to be kept hidden in the rest of life had, in certain tragic *coplas*, a space where it could be explored under the safe cover of a fictional code. It was powerful just to hear Piquer putting words to the void on the radio. But for those who had to keep their identity hidden, it was exceptionally powerful and healing for them to be able to raise their voices in songs that articulated the hidden material in code.

Conclusion

Our exploration of the *copla* in its historical and emotional context has enabled us to answer the questions posed in the Introduction to this book: How could a song help the defeated survive? What were the mechanisms by which it did so? What were the characteristics of Piquer's *coplas* that made people single them out as the period's most important survival tools? And how could these songs, created by people on the winning side, meet the needs of the losers?

We have seen that certain of the *coplas* written by León, Quiroga, and Quintero and performed by Conchita Piquer allowed the defeated to refer in code to their own reality and experience, which the Franco regime had rendered otherwise invisible and inaudible. When they played the role of the protagonists, who suffered analogous problems, they could express their terror at being constantly watched and investigated. They could speak of the loved ones who had disappeared and about whom they could obtain no information. They could say goodbye to those who lay in mass graves. They could protest their impoverished, clandestine existence and the prohibition on using both their talents and their voices.

These *coplas* created an alternative world that kept the defeated safe from political danger through the alibis the fictional stories provided. The distance provided by the fictional roles also kept them safe emotionally, for they did not have to acknowledge that the intense pain of the characters was also their own. Yet at the same time, the fictional world created in Piquer's tragic *coplas* was experienced as more real than the deformed "reality" the regime had created. This fictional universe named and expressed feelings that had otherwise been erased from the social surface. Francoist rhetoric proposed false solutions to people's real suffering; in the world of the *copla*, there was no false resolution of the protagonist's suffering at the end.

This book has defined survival as comprising physical, psychological, and existential factors that work together. Each of the *coplas* examined in this study addressed a crushing emotional burden the defeated were carrying. By playing the role of each fictional protagonist, the defeated learned to manage their fear and thus to retain a sense of play and resilience despite their suffering. Led by Conchita Piquer, they performed ritual acts of mourning in which they did gradual, piecemeal working-through of some of their grief, but with sufficient control and distance not to become overwhelmed by it. By telling the characters' stories, they recovered a sense of change over time and learned to associate their own traumatic feelings with those contained in the songs. Because the music matched their despondent mood, they were able to feel understood, and this helped them manage and even change that mood. And after singing, they could ruminate on their own lives by reflecting on the meaning of the songs. The *coplas* of León and Quiroga combined poetry, narrative, music, theatre, and sometimes dance. They were thus extremely potent means for establishing new associative networks for traumatic feelings. All of this worked to keep the defeated psychologically alive, rather than becoming overwhelmed by despair, emotionally deadened, or withered away by silencing.

The ideological ambiguity of Conchita Piquer's tragic *coplas* was critical to their function as survival tools. These songs had been created by people who benefited directly from being on the winning side. Yet the personal lives of those creators did not match the model of marriage and sexual repression imposed under Franco, so those creators experienced some of the pain of forbidden love, absence, and clandestinity that were the constant experience of the losers. Born under the Republic but developed under Franco, *coplas* could be read in different ways by winners and losers alike; both could sing them with all their hearts. This made them safe tools for the emotional work of survival, which the defeated carried out as they sang along. As Vázquez Montalbán said, more than the political views of their creators or of the Francoist media that broadcast them, the most important factor in determining their meaning is how they were used by the people to meet their needs. One crucial aspect of that use was that *coplas* allowed people to sing together, telling each other in coded singing the crucial events and feelings that they did not dare tell each other in speech.

There are a number of directions that I hope future research on the *copla* will take. We need a sociological overview of the genre along the lines of Salaün's study of the *cuplé*, one that considers the roles and working conditions of those who performed in *copla* shows. Archival research on the political and social ties and iconic roles of the major *copla* stars would enhance our understanding of the workings of popular music in the period. Also needed is a comprehensive study of Piquer's performances that examines her costumes and stage sets, as well as the reviews her shows and film performances garnered, both in urban centres and provincial capitals. It would be especially fruitful for scholars to conduct an oral history of those who remember singing *coplas* in the postwar period (this would be along the lines of the study of cinemagoing directed by Jo Labanyi). We also need much more close reading of the *coplas* performed by Piquer and other stars. Finally, if scholars were to lift the veil of secrecy over Rafael de León's personal life, it would contribute much to our understanding of the *copla* and of the history of gay life in Spain.

The method proposed in this book, of examining certain songs as instruments of psychological change through role play, ritual, narrative, and music, has implications for the study of how popular music helps people around the world cope with repressed grief, fear, and trauma. These four modalities are used in psychotherapy in many countries. Therapists in Argentina under the military junta developed bereavement rituals for the disappeared (Kohen). Group rituals have helped Vietnam veterans in the United States cope with the deaths of close friends in that war (Lubin and Johnson). Psychodrama and drama therapy are widely used in the United States, the British Commonwealth, Europe, and Latin America. Music therapy developed in the context of the Second World War, when musicians entertaining wounded servicemen discovered that the benefits of music went far beyond distraction; patients became less depressed, socialized more, expressed their feelings more, and had greater contact with reality (Gaynor 78). This suggests that the four modalities may be key to understanding the effects of popular music in many countries.

The beneficial effects of song are illustrated in a documentary film called *Sierra Leone's Refugee All-Stars* (2005). During the brutal civil war in Sierra Leone (1991–2002), many fled for their lives to refugee camps in Guinea, having witnessed the butchering of their relatives or having had limbs amputated themselves. Inside the refugee camps, musicians came together and formed a band. They toured the many camps, performing songs that, like *coplas*, had content related to the experiences that people were living; the songs dealt with war, conditions in the camps, and related themes. The band leader explains in the documentary that the purpose of the songs he writes is to "detraumatize the people."

It would be fruitful to apply the method used in this book not only to countries suffering under dictatorship and terror, but also to democratic countries. The links between emotional states and survival that ground my argument have been researched in the United States. Given that Americans spend more money on music than on prescription drugs (Levitin 7), and that today's young people take the trouble to load thousands of songs on their iPods, it is important to explain how and why people use music when they are not in imminent danger of death, but still facing significant emotional burdens as well as political and social pressure to keep those burdens under wraps. It would be particularly fruitful to explore the role of popular music in grieving in the United States, where the dominant culture largely tries to erase death from the social surface (Didion 60).

Conchita Piquer died on 12 December 1990. Her last wish was to be buried in the costume of La Parrala, her first postwar hit. Loyal to her characters to the end, she was buried in role (Manuel Román 142, Plaza, *Conchita Piquer* 135).[1] Spain's leading writers, who had grown up "sucking all the juice" out of Piquer's songs, were deeply affected by her death. Terenci Moix recalls:

> El día que falleció, Carmen Martín Gaite interrumpió una de las sesiones de un congreso en el extranjero para entonar una *copla* de la Piquer. Yo mismo me hallaba en Santa Cruz de Tenerife, pronunciando una conferencia sobre la Biblioteca de Alejandría y pedí al público un minuto de silencio para aquel recuerdo que se nos iba con el lento escabullirse de las generaciones.
>
> The day she died, Carmen Martín Gaite interrupted a panel at a conference in a foreign country to sing one of Piquer's *coplas*. I myself was in Santa Cruz de Tenerife, giving a lecture about the Library of Alexandria, and I asked for a moment of silence for the memory of all that was leaving us as the generations slowly slipped away. (*Suspiros* 61)

Conchita Piquer defined an entire era. But she also became the standard and the reference point for a genre that outlived that era and that is now flourishing again in a very different Spain. When Piquer's coffin came out of her apartment on the Gran Vía, a voice cried out to her daughter: "Debes estar orgullosa de tu madre. Deja generaciones de huérfanos y sobre todo, huérfanos que aún no han nacido" ("You should be proud of your mother. She leaves behind generations of orphans, and especially, orphans who haven't even been born yet") (Plaza, *Conchita Piquer* 136).

Time is proving that woman right. In the 1960s, anti-regime dissidents dismissed the *copla* as Francoist. Many young people, having heard those songs their whole lives on the state-controlled radio stations, judged the whole genre on that basis. Furthermore, the *coplas'* use of Andalusian pronunciation, musical forms, and characters was considered oppressive by Catalan and Basque singers, whose own forms of expression had been repressed. The peculiarly Spanish *coplas* were also regarded as the supreme expression of an isolationist Spain. In the 1960s, the anti-Franco opposition was internationalist; it preferred foreign music – American and British rock and French protest songs – reflecting its desire for political and sexual freedom and for Spain to reopen its doors to the rest of the world. The *copla* was stigmatized as *españolada*, or Spanish jingoism.

But already in the early 1970s, leading left-wing intellectuals like Martín Gaite, Vázquez Montalbán, Moix, and Martín Patino were beginning to insist on the value of certain *coplas* they had first heard as children in the 1940s. And beginning in the 1990s and continuing until the present day, the *copla* has enjoyed a renaissance. Enough time has gone by since Franco's death that the best *coplas* can be embraced by singers of all political persuasions, who create wonderful new versions of the genre's classics. In 1999 a group of left-wing singers who had become famous in the 1970s for singing protest songs against the dictatorship came together to create an album called *Tatuaje*, in which each artist performed a *copla* from the 1930s or 1940s; the leaders of the musical opposition to Franco had now appropriated the *copla* as their own. Today, performers like Martirio and Miguel Poveda continue the tradition. And Concha Buika, born in Spain to parents from Equatorial Guinea, dazzles audiences worldwide with her performances of *coplas* like "Ojos verdes." The nuanced performances of these contemporary *copla* singers indicate that they have studied Concha Piquer's own performances in great detail. And her songs have pride of place in the *coplas* they select to record.

Meanwhile, Piquer's original recordings are readily available today on remastered discs. Many of today's young people, born after Franco's death, know the lyrics to her songs, more than sixty years after their creation. Vázquez Montalbán may have been right when he said that nothing has ever replaced Piquer's *coplas* as the expression of something authentic, not only about Spain's past, but also about its present (*Can-*

cionero 21). These *coplas,* like our jazz standards, will survive because of the beauty of their music and lyrics alone. This book has suggested, however, that the emotional urgency that Piquer conveyed so compellingly as she incarnated her fictional protagonists continues to be relevant today, now that many survivors of Franco's terror and their grandchildren are demanding a resolution of the real pain and injustice that began in the "time of silence" and that their families have carried with them to this day.

Notes

Introduction

1 Francoist rhetoric and practice divided Spanish society into the "winners," on the one hand, and the "losers," or "defeated," on the other; I will use these terms throughout this study. The terms "winners" and "losers" ("vencedores" and "vencidos") continue to be used today to refer to the divided society of the Franco dictatorship.

2 All translations in this book are mine, unless otherwise noted.

3 Another key vehicle was Hollywood film, whose effects on young people growing up in the 1940s are thematized in works by Juan Marsé, Terenci Moix, and Martín Gaite herself.

4 "No tengo ley que me abone / ni puerta donde llamar" are lines from "Romance de la otra" ("Ballad of the Other Woman"), discussed in chapter 6.

5 In Spain, several anecdotal histories of the genre have been published, as well as biographies and autobiographies of some *copla* performers. (Manuel Román; Ignacio Román; Plaza; Miguel de Molina; Moix, *Suspiros*). There is also an excellent philological study of Rafael de León's poetic technique and tropes in the prologue by Josefa Acosta Díaz, Manuel José Gómez Lara, and Jorge Jiménez Barrientos to their edition of León's poems and songs. As this book went to press, two new popular books had just appeared: one on Rafael de León and his collaborators (Romualdo Molina), and a memoir by Conchita Piquer's daughter, Concha Márquez Piquer (*Yo misma*).

As far as the interpretation of specific *coplas*, Silvia Bermúdez's foundational 1997 article on "Tatuaje" and Emilio Alarcos Llorach's philological reading of the same song are lone exceptions. José Colmeiro has emphasized the importance of these songs in recovering historical memory ("Canciones con historia"). However, the issue of the *Journal of Spanish Cultural*

Studies on Spanish popular music begins with the 1960s (see Bermúdez and Pérez). A recent television documentary on Piquer, in the series, "Imprescindibles del siglo XX," attests to the ongoing interest in the star and her songs, fully fifty years after she retired from the stage ("Concha Piquer"). The *copla* genre as a whole was the subject of an exhibit at the Biblioteca Nacional in 2009. Contemporary stars like Martirio and Miguel Poveda have done moving new renditions of Piquer's classic songs. And each month on a Sunday evening, a crowd packs the bar La Fídula on Madrid's Calle de las Huertas to hear Manuel Rey and his accompanists do wonderful performances of the old *cuplés* and *coplas.*

6 Colmeiro emphasizes that these songs reflected a collective experience, not just individual stories of sorrow and misery ("Canciones con historia" 33–4). See also Colmeiro's chapter, "Canciones con historia: en busca de la memoria perdida," in *Memoria histórica e identidad cultural,* 78–104.) Martín argues that during Spain's transition to democracy, the tears and the pain contained in these postwar songs became epistemological tools, ways to transmit a different history from the official one to future generations (*Gramática* 200).

7 For some key texts in recent scholarship on historical memory in Spain, see Paloma Aguilar Fernández, *Memoria y olvido de la guerra civil española*; Resina, ed., *Disremembering the Dictatorship*; Resina and Winter, eds., *Casa encantada*; the special issue of *Journal of Spanish Cultural Studies* on "The Politics of Memory in Contemporary Spain", ed. Jo Labanyi; Carlos Jerez-Farrán and Samuel Amago's edited volume, *Unearthing Franco's Legacy*; and Santos Juliá, *Memoria de la guerra y del franquismo.* Scholars also debate whether the representation of the Spanish transition as having involved an agreement to forget is historically accurate (Molinero, Loureiro).

8 Gina Herrmann has pointed out how the important documentaries by Montse Armengou and Ricard Belis function as substitute judicial trials, in which the filmmakers are cast as detectives and prosecutors and spectators as "would-be jurors" (Herrmann 195). Jo Labanyi notes that memory is notoriously inaccurate and that the value of the testimonies of survivors "is not the legal function of establishing what happened ... but the insight they give us into emotional attitudes toward the past in the present time of the speaker" ("Testimonies" 193). She notes that unlike Armengou and Belis's work, some books and documentaries present these testimonies as transparent representations of historical truth (195).

9 See, for example, Woods, "Radio Free *Folklóricas*"; "Performance in Theory and Practice"; and "Identification and Disconnect"; Colmeiro, "Nationalising Carmen"; Labanyi, "Musical Battles"; and Vernon, "Theatricality." The

round table on *folklóricas* organized by Silvia Bermúdez and Roberta Johnson for the 2012 MLA Convention involved seven scholars, indicating current critical interest in the genre.

10 See, for example, Annabel Martín's *La gramática de la felicidad.* In the third chapter, Martín analyses Francoist melodramatic films not involving *folklóricas.* Such scholarship on emotion within Hispanic studies comes at a time when the field of cultural studies in general has turned to the emotions as socially constructed (see Harding and Pribram; Ahmed; Berlant). In another major trend, affect theory has looked at emotions as pre-subjective, corporeal, autonomic processes (Leys "The Turn to Affect" 437; see Melissa Gregg and Gregory J. Seigworth, eds., *The Affect Theory Reader*). My own study lines up rather with those of critics who, following Freud, see emotions as "intentional states governed by our beliefs, cognitions, and desires" (Leys 437).

11 The fact that in *folklórica* films, the protagonist, a singer herself, is first dishonoured but then rises to fame and takes vengeance on her aristocratic seducer invites the audience to identify with the narrative of suffering, justice, and vindication, even if the film then contains the rebellion through a conservative ending (Woods "Excess, Affect" 292). Annabel Martín, proposes that melodrama, by raising feelings and hopes to a fever pitch, creates a "critical epistemology," founded on the gap between the spectator's desire for justice and the solution the film coerces him into accepting at the end (29, 200).

12 This oral history project allows us to establish how the spectators themselves remember the films. It also reveals their rituals around filmgoing: how they dressed up to go to the cinema, how they imitated film stars in their dress and hairstyles, to whom they told the plots of the films afterwards, how they used the cinema as a safe place to cry, and much more. On the aims and scope of the project, see Labanyi, "The Mediation of Everyday Life," in *Studies in Hispanic Cinemas,* 2.2. That volume also contains articles by Marsh, Martin-Márquez, Woods Peiró, and Vernon that present some of the fascinating findings of the project.

13 Conversations with researchers involved in the cinemagoing project over the years have indicated that their interviews have underscored the importance of the same categories that I am using here based on psychological theory: role play, narrative, ritual, and music making (the interviewees sometimes burst into song as they recalled a particular film featuring a singer; see Woods, "Identification and Disconnect," 129).

14 "No te mires en el río" ("Don't Look at Yourself in the River") is a song about survival if there ever was one, albeit under the code of a fictional

story. Vázquez Montalbán also refers to songs like "Yo no me quiero enterar" ("I Don't Want to Know"), a song that enabled people to say out loud that reality was so unremittingly awful that they needed to dissociate to some degree in order to stay alive. And there are many more, by León and Quiroga and by others. Piquer's prewar hit "En tierra extraña" ("In a Strange Land") is about a Christmas Eve party for Spanish expatriates that she held during her years in New York in the 1920s; everyone there, upon hearing the song, "Suspiros de España," began to cry with nostalgia. These lyrics, sung in the 1940s, a time when hundreds of thousands of Spaniards had relatives in exile, must have been emotional indeed. And there are many other songs by Rafael de León, such as "La Lirio" ("The Lily") and "Vamos a dejarnos" ("Let's Leave One Another", which I believe begs for a gay reading), that call for further study.

15 Salvador Valverde co-authored "Ojos verdes" with Rafael de León; it was not originally written for Piquer. Piquer first performed it in 1940, but it is her version that is remembered today. León co-authored "La Parrala" and "Tatuaje" with Xandro Valerio. In all cases the music is written by Quiroga.

1 Camouflage

1 While I discuss physical, emotional, and existential threats separately in this chapter, research has shown that what we refer to as mind (the brain and nervous system), body (the internal organs, immune system, etc.,) and heart (feelings) are actually inseparable. When we feel an emotion, chemical messengers are released that affect every cell in our bodies. Emotions, then, are at once psychological and physiological processes. See Damasio, *Descartes' Error,* and *The Feeling*; Pert, *Molecules of Emotion*; Pert, Dreher, and Ruff, "The Psychosomatic Network"; Gaynor 62; Thaut and Davis; and Weiss. The existential threat to survival, the sense that life lacks meaning, is inseparable from emotional states such as numbness or despair.

2 *ABC* (Sevilla), 26 July 1936, 6; quoted in Reig Tapia, 145.

3 Radio broadcast of 17 August 1936, qtd. in Reig Tapia 155.

4 This meant that forty years later, when their widows finally tried to claim their right to a pension, they ran into the bureaucratic problem that their husbands had never been certified as dead. Some of these widows were still listed officially as "married" in 1978 and later (Reig Tapia 101–5).

5 Today, thanks to the work of historians such as Julián Casanova, Santos Juliá, Angela Cenarro, Javier Rodrigo, and Helen Graham, we have a clear and detailed understanding of the perfectly coordinated apparatus of repression that the Francoists used to try to annihilate the defeated, both physically

and psychologically. Graham has situated these methods of repression in a broader European context (*The Spanish Civil* War, ch. 6.). Casanova has detailed how social networks of denunciation were created that involved large swathes of the civilian population in the repression (Casanova "Una dictadura" 28). The terror and the penal system have been further explored by historians such as Reig Tapia and Mir. Rodrigo has given us the first comprehensive account of Franco's concentration camps. For the blurring of the boundaries between penal institutions and ostensibly "charitable" ones, see Cenarro, and Vinyes et. al. For the attempts to "re-educate" prisoners by stamping out their former ideals, see the documentary film *Rejas en la memoria,* in which these and other historians are interviewed.

6 Such treatment found its "scientific" justification in the theories of Antonio Vallejo Nájera, Franco's Head of Psychiatric Services. See *Els nens perduts,* Part One.

7 Moreno Gómez 63. See also pp. 63–7 for the stories of the persecution that motivated such suicides.

8 Many survivors of the period recall vividly how they were addressed by the victors. In *Els nens perduts del franquisme,* Carme Riera recalls how the women prisoners were called whores by the chaplain at the first mass she was forced to attend in jail. Francisca Aguirre and her sister Susana were taken as children to the orphanages of Auxilio Social, Franco's Social Services organization, when their father was condemned to death. Francisca recalls that the women of Auxilio Social, who ran the orphanage, told them upon their arrival that they were scum, the daughters of Reds, murderers, atheists, and criminals, and that they therefore deserved nothing (*Els nens perduts,* Part Two).

9 Parkes, Benjamin and Fitzgerald, "Broken Heart." See also O'Connor et al. 183–5; Kemeny 203.

10 See also Gerrity, Keane, and Tuma.

11 See, for example, Caruth's Introduction to her edited volume, *Trauma.* See also her *Unclaimed Experience.* I do not take a position on the current debates within trauma theory on the nature of trauma, such as whether trauma is a bodily phenomenon (a neurological change in the brain) or a psychological one (a case of dissociation or repression). These debates are usefully reviewed by Ruth Leys (*Trauma*). However, I do not concur with Caruth that trauma resists representation and remains literal in dreams and flashbacks, nor do I agree with her that it "resists cure" (Caruth *Trauma* 7). Rather, I focus on the kinds of treatment that have proven effective at helping survivors work through the traumatic experience and gain relief from the symptoms of PTSD. As Leys indicates, such therapies are often eclectic and do not line

up with one particular theory of what trauma is (307). My goal in using the clinical literature on trauma is to better understand what might be the psychological effects of using the four modalities involved in singing along with Conchita Piquer – that is, to ascertain what kinds of role play, rituals, and so on have proven effective in treating the symptoms of traumatic stress, and how the clinicians understand what is happening unconsciously as the survivors perform such operations.

12 As Ruth Leys has pointed out, the trauma of Holocaust survivors could not be properly understood until the Vietnam period, when the diagnosis of PTSD was developed (*Trauma* 15–16). The same is true of traumatic stress during and after the Spanish Civil War, as José María Ruiz Vargas has noted. It seems particularly fruitful to apply the knowledge of trauma that developed under the dictatorships in Chile and Argentina, where the mechanisms and goals of repression were quite similar to those of Franco, but where therapists could build on the new developments in the treatment of trauma that developed in the 1970s.

13 Linda Chapman, personal communication, 6 June 2011.

14 Jodie Waisberg, personal communication, 7 June 2011.

15 Vinyes, Armengou, and Belis, 136. In her article on the television documentaries of Montse Armengou and Ricard Belis, Gina Herrmann notes that "in all of the scenes featuring Álvarez, he recounts his traumatic experiences with an unchanging sombre facial expression and ashen complexion." Herrmann cites Shoshana Felman, who reads this absence of expression as a trait of trauma survivors, "'those who ... have been historically made faceless ... Those whom violence has paralysed, effaced, or deadened, those whom violence has treated in their lives as though they were *already dead*'" (Herrmann 198). Herrmann is quoting Shoshana Felman, *The Juridical Unconscious: Trials and Trauma in the Twentieth Century* (Cambridge, MA: Harvard UP, 2002), 13–14.

16 See Pennebaker (1990, 1993, 1995), and his articles co-authored with Sussman; and with Kiecolt-Glaser and Glaser. See also Smyth and Pennebaker; and Traue and Pennebaker.

17 Azar Nafisi, an English literature professor who gave clandestine literature classes to female students in fundamentalist Iran, describes the psychological effect of this self-erasure: "The worst crime committed by totalitarian mind-sets is that they force their citizens, including their victims, to become complicit in their crimes ... Participating in your own execution, that is an act of utmost brutality. My students ... enacted it every time they went out into the streets dressed as they were told to dress ... [The regime] invaded all private spaces and tried to shape every gesture, to force us to become

one of them, and that in itself was another form of execution" (76–7). Nafisi describes how her female students eradicated their own individuality every time they prepared to go out on the street, covering up their hair, their nail polish, and the clothing they had chosen to wear under their obligatory black robes and scarves.

18 *Semillas*, a documentary in the CD-DVD set called *Recuperando memoria: Concierto-Homenaje a los Republicanos.*

19 For a description of how this occurred, and of the kinds of roles and qualities women were expected to take on, see Domingo, *Coser y cantar;* and Morcillo, *True Catholic Womanhood.* See also Graham, "Gender and the State."

20 Juan Manuel Fernández Soria notes that writer Alvaro Cunqueiro compared Franco to El Cid ("cabalgador y espadero, paladino y campeador") and to Julius Caesar. Alvaro Cunqueiro, "Necesidad de un César," en *Arriba España,* 4, marzo 1938 (Fernández Soria 159n88). Franco was also compared to El Cid in verse, by Eduardo Marquina, "A nuestro Caudillo" in *Obras completas* (Madrid: Aguilar, 1951, VI, 1132–4 ("Cid Francisco Franco el Justo," etc.). Fernández Soria 160 and n91.

21 See Arrarás Iribarren and Sáenz de Tejada. Lush colour illustrations by Carlos Sáenz de Tejada show a medieval knight galloping across the fields of Castile.

22 The recourse to medieval roles in the 1930s and 1940s was not unique to Spain. See Helen Solterer, *Medieval Roles for Modern Times,* on how right and left alike brought to life medieval theatre in prewar and wartime France.

23 This contrasted with the exceptionally brutal repression of the defeated in rural areas; see Moreno Gómez; Mir; Ruiz Vargas 325, 329.

24 The communal radio was a common phenomenon in the 1940s and beyond.

25 Vázquez Montalbán, *Cancionero,* xvii. See also Labanyi's use of Gramsci in "Musical Battles," 210. Carmen Martín Gaite's *El cuarto de atrás,* and Terenci Moix's *El cine de los sábados* are extended meditations on this phenomenon.

26 Says Martin-Márquez: "in the Spanish context, where the repression of sexuality was ostensibly so ferocious, any expression of sexual desire within the cinema must be seen as politically charged." Indeed, under Francoism, in the words of social historian Clive Beadman, "political and sexual deviancy were bound together." Beadman, "'Cimentada en el sillar firmísimo de la familia cristiana' and 'Viudas de medio pelo': Illicit prostitution in 1940s Spain," *International Journal of Iberian Studies* 13.3: 157–66 at 160). Quoted in Martin-Márquez, 118.

27 For an illustration of how such a process worked in fundamentalist Iran using highbrow literary texts, see Nafisi, ch. 1.

28 I had hoped to provide the reader with images from the wealth of popular magazines of the 1940s held at the Biblioteca Nacional. However, these magazines are currently classified as "orphaned works" (i.e., works not yet in the public domain but for which the rights cannot be located), and cannot legally be reproduced. I can only encourage my reader to explore this rich archive.

29 References to photographs of these gestures and activities can be found in the Bibliography as follows: "Mujer con uniforme de la Sección Femenina con insignia de yugo y flechas" [Woman wearing the Women's Section Uniform with Falange yoke-and-arrows insignia]; "Equipo femenino de hockey haciendo saludo falangista" [Women's hockey team making the fascist salute]; "Mujeres haciendo el saludo falangista ante la bandera" [Women making the Fascist salute as the flag is raised]; "Mujer leyendo en aula con cruz" [Woman reading in classroom with cross]; "Oración ante la Cruz de los Caídos en el campamento 'Pinar de Villarreal'" [A prayer before the Cross of the Fallen at the Pinar de Villarreal Camp]; "Mujer cosiendo con uniforme de Talleres José Antonio" [Woman sewing with uniform of the José Antonio Factory]; "Mujeres hacienda calcetines" [Women making socks]; "Clase de cocina en la Escuela de Hogar 'Santa Ana'" [A cooking lesson at "Saint Anne" Housekeeping School].

30 Durbin, in a dress showing no cleavage, smiles sweetly as she wishes the readers of *Primer plano* a Happy Easter. ("Deanna Durbin").

31 In an article on Francoist folkloric film musicals, Labanyi shows how the female protagonist, who comes from the common people, is invariably a performer who uses role play to achieve her own tactical ends, which include seducing the wealthy male protagonist. The films, she argues, self-consciously thematize the idea of everyday life as performance ("Musical Battles" 213–14).

32 Psychologist Terry Vance, consultation session with the author.

33 Vance, consultation session.

34 See also Greenberg and van der Kolk.

2 An Introduction to the *Copla*

1 On whites' appropriation and domestication of black music, and the role of radio, see chapter 4, "Tuning in to Jazz," in Douglas, *Listening In,* 83–99.

2 Miles Davis recognized in flamenco something analogous to the blues in 1950 (Arbelos 7).

3 On the development of flamenco, see Arbelos and Hoyos, ch. 3; and Gamboa Rodríguez, pts 4 and 5. For a critique of the ideologies ascribed to fla-

menco by historians, see Washabaugh. On the cathartic value of *cante jondo,* see Mitchell, chapter 9, "Deep Song as Psychodrama," in Mitchell, *Flamenco Deep Song,*126–42.

4 Cristina Hoyos, "Prólogo," in Arbelos and Hoyos, 5–6, esp. 6.

5 Blas Vega, *Los cafés cantantes,* 15. Blas Vega defines the *café cantante* as an "establecimiento público en el que se ofrecían sesiones con bailes y cante flamenco, además de otras manifestaciones artísticas, mientras los espectadores consumían vino, café o licores" ("a public establishment in which spectators could watch flamenco songs and dances and other artistic offerings while consuming wine, coffee, or liquor") (16).

6 Martirio, arguably the best of today's *copla* performers, notes that León, Quintero, and other great *copla* creators loved jazz and that there are structural similarities between the two genres. And thematic ones: "los temas: el amor-pasión, el desgarro, la ausencia, el encuentro ... son los grandes temas que unen a Ella Fitzgerald o a Billie H. con esas figuras representativas de la copla" ("the themes: passionate love, heartbreak, absence, the amorous encounter ... these are the great themes that unite Ella Fitzgerald or Billie H. with the representative figures of the *copla*") (letter to Marta Valdés in *Coplas de madrugá,* trans. mine).

7 For a comprehensive introduction to the formal features of Rafael de León's *coplas,* see Acosta Díaz et al., 31–53.

8 The study of Spanish folklore, and of flamenco in particular, had been formalized in the late nineteenth century by Antonio Machado y Álvarez (Demófilo), the father of the poets Manuel and Antonio Machado. It was Machado y Álvarez who introduced the word "folklore" into the Spanish language (Antonio Gil, prologue to Demófilo, *Cantes flamencos* 8). In 1881 he founded the Spanish Folklore Society, as well as a regional one in Andalucía; in the following years he would work to create other such societies in regions across Spain. He also founded a journal, *El Folk-Lore Andaluz,* in 1882. Demófilo did foundational fieldwork on flamenco, collecting examples of each kind of flamenco song known at the time, interviewing the flamenco legends of his day, and explaining flamenco terms and traditions (see *Cantes flamencos* and *El folk-lore andaluz*). Both of his sons would use in their poetry some of the popular poetic forms they had encountered in their father's work (Acosta Díaz 32). The poets of the Generation of 1927 would follow in Demófilo's footsteps, again collecting songs and poetry directly from the common people. See Naval, 15, 30–3.

9 Francisco Umbral, *Memorias de un niño de derechas* (Barcelona: Destino, 1972), 36. Quoted in Colmeiro, "Canciones con historia," 35.

10 Female *copla* singers in the 1940s were still referred to as *tonadilleras.*

11 Many chroniclers of the *copla* present it as the opposite of the *cuplé.* But there is more continuity between the two genres than is often acknowledged. As Acosta Díaz and her colleagues note, the two musical genres have the same structure (40). And while generally, *cuplés* were erotic songs without reference to any national context, some *cuplé* stars had begun singing more typically Spanish songs very early on. Famous examples are Raquel Meller's renditions of "El relicario" (1918) and "La violetera" (1919) (Salaün 272, 293). Furthermore, the *cuplé* performers La Goya and Raquel Meller laid the groundwork for Conchita Piquer by wearing a different costume for every number. They also turned each song into a polished melodrama that evoked the deep feelings of the audience (111–12). La Goya is considered to be the star who "dignified" the *cuplé.* The same was later said of Piquer, who elevated the *copla* by adding perfectionism, superb acting, and a large dose of class and seriousness to a genre that could too often become tacky (Moix 42).

12 Acosta Díaz and her colleagues include in their anthology two prologues by Rafael de León in which he refers to his art as *copla.* See esp. 61.

13 For more on the history of the *copla* form, see Manuel Román, Ignacio Román, Miguel de Molina, Imperio Argentina, Martín de la Plaza, and Acosta Díaz et al. In 2009, Spain's National Library offered an exhibit on the genre, with a catalogue containing several articles on it. See *La Copla en la Biblioteca Nacional de España.*

14 La Argentinita was the stage name of Encarnación López. See the recording "Colección de Canciones Populares Españolas."

15 The famous trunks that transported Piquer's costumes, with all their stickers from different provinces and countries, are on view at the Casa-Museo Concha Piquer in Valencia.

16 Federico Grafe, personal communication.

17 For a comprehensive history of Spanish radio, see Balsebre's two-volume *Historia de la radio en España.*

18 Carmen Ortiz and Manuel Rey, personal communication. I have had conversations with several Spaniards who remember hearing women singing *coplas* in the courtyards in their youth, or in their houses while they were doing housework. (Leonardo Romero [b. 1941] and Juan Urrutia [b. 1944], personal communications.) But this practice continued well beyond the 1940s. About ten years ago in Madrid, I heard a jazz trio play improvisations on famous *coplas.* One of the members of the trio, Manolo Martínez, explained that as a child he had been ill and had to miss school for months at a time. He remembers waking up every morning to the sound of women singing *coplas.* I calculate that this would have been in the late 1950s or early 1960s.

19 Casanova, personal communication.

20 Leonardo Romero, personal communication; Carmen Ortiz, personal communication.

21 León wrote the lyrics to "Tatuaje," the most famous *copla* of the entire period, in collaboration with Xandro Valerio.

22 On the use and study of Spanish folklore under Franco, see Ortiz.

23 See, for example, "Como en España, ni hablar," or "Sombrero en mano," in Vázquez Montalbán, *Cancionero*, 7–8.

24 Popular legend has it that in 1931, when Rafael de León went to Piquer's dressing room to introduce himself after a show, he asked her: –¿Es usted Conchita Piquer?– And she replied –¿Y usted es maricón? (Plaza 50)

25 A multitude of complex factors contributed to Lorca's murder, as is made clear in Emilio Ruiz Barrachina's 2006 documentary, *Lorca, el mar deja de moverse*. However, it is also clear that Lorca was hated in part because of his homosexuality. In the film, Ian Gibson recounts how Juan Luis Trescastro, one of the men who participated in Lorca's execution, later boasted, "Yo le he puesto dos balas en el culo por maricón" ("I put two bullets up his ass for being a faggot"). And Félix Grande describes how, at the moment of Lorca's death, one of the murderers hit him with the butt of his rifle and called him "rojo maricón" ("Red faggot"). Rafael de León would not have been aware of these particulars, but certainly he knew the extent of the hypermasculinity of his native Andalucía.

26 Not surprisingly, gay men identified deeply with Rafael de León's *coplas* throughout the Franco dictatorship. See Mira 347. Acosta Díaz and her colleagues have noted that León wrote his most memorable hits in the 1940s, and that in the 1950s his songs repeated the same kinds of themes without much further development. They wonder why his most fundamental work was so concentrated in that decade, and conclude that this was the time when León had reached artistic maturity by creating his own amalgam of highbrow poetry and popular song (27). This is undoubtedly true, but I believe there is another reason. In the 1940s, half of Spain was being vilified, beaten, ostracized, excluded, terrorized, condemned to a clandestine existence, and generally treated as subhuman, in much the same way that gay people had long been treated. And heterosexuals were finding out what it meant to be jailed, fined, or publicly shamed for the tiniest displays of sexual expression. In the 1940s, then, the kinds of emotional and physical suffering that León knew from gay life resonated with a huge sector of the population.

27 We might think of the gritty cynicism of the American *film noir* of the 1940s, which by the 1950s had yielded to the domesticated films of Doris Day.

28 As Leroi Jones put it: "The God spoken about in the black songs is not the same one in the white songs. Though the words might look the same." Jones, *Black Music* (New York: William Morrow, 1968), 183, qtd in Cone, 4.
29 *El cuarto de atrás* 132, 115.
30 Deep feeling in popular culture is often later considered excessive and parodied as camp. But Patrick Garlinger, reading Almodóvar's *Todo sobre mi madre* (*All About My Mother*), shows how the theatrical excess of the transvestite Agrado is not a form of insincerity. In Agrado's monologue, he says, "artificiality, as well as theatricality, is shown to be authenticity" (Garlinger 102). Excess, in other words, is not necessarily parodic, even in camp. Furthermore, as Annabel Martín has shown, although Western culture has devalued tears and constructed them as the opposite of reason, deep feelings, born of injustice, also contain a critique of the unjust political order. Tears are then tears of *reason*, a form of knowledge, a way to get to the truth (Martín 29, 200). On the capacity of melodramatic excess to provide a critique of ordinary life, see Vernon, "Theatricality," 186–7.
31 Carmen Martín Gaite pays special homage to Piquer in *El cuarto de atrás.* Manuel Vázquez Montalbán loved her so much he wrote a poem called "Conchita Piquer," published in José María Castellet's famous 1970 anthology, *Nueve novísimos* (61–4). He also titled one of his detective novels after her most famous hit, "Tatuaje" (1976). Terenci Moix calls her, "La emperatriz de la copla ... el modelo al que todas han intentado parangonarse" ("The empress of the *copla* ... the model whom all the others tried to equal" (*Suspiros* 42). And filmmaker Basilio Martín Patino has his fictional character, the Marqués de Almodóvar, compare Piquer's rendition of "Ojos verdes" to the Song of Songs (*Ojos verdes*). For a fuller account of Piquer's life, see Plaza and Manuel Román.
32 Manuel Román places her first in his chapter "La edad de oro" ("The Golden Age"), stating that she brought the "canción española" to its peak (121). Terenci Moix, in *Suspiros de España,* follows his general introduction with a chapter on Piquer called "La emperatriz de la copla" ("The Empress of the *Copla*") (42). Piquer is the only *copla* singer named by Martín Gaite in *El cuarto de atrás.* In Patino's *Canciones para después de una guerra,* it is when "Tatuaje" is playing that the voiceover says, "Eran canciones para sobrevivir" ("They were songs for survival"). And all the songs named by Vázquez Montalbán as capturing the experience of the people in postwar Spain were sung by Piquer.
33 Ángel Zúñiga and Santiago Castelo, quoted in Plaza 118.
34 Jo Labanyi, in reference to the high–low hybridization of the Francoist film musicals called *folklóricas,* refers to Rowe and Schelling, who "note that,

when the culture industry coincides with the nation-formation process, as it has in countries where modernization occurred late, the former takes on some of the 'aura' of high culture." Labanyi, "Musical Battles," 218n8, referring to W. Rowe and V. Schelling, *Memory and Modernity: Popular Culture in Latin America* (London: Verso, 1991), 8. This was certainly the case with Conchita Piquer's performances of the songs by León and Quiroga, which helped establish the formula for the Spanish pop song.

35 As a child, Piquer had spoken *valenciano*, the language of her native region. She learned English as a teenager in the United States. She had to learn Spanish quickly when she returned to Spain in 1927 (Plaza 38).

36 S.N. Eisenstadt, ed., *Max Weber on Charisma and Institution Building* (Chicago: University of Chicago Press, 1968), 329; quoted in Dyer, "Charisma," 57.

37 E.A. Shils, "Charisma, Order and Status," *American Sociological Review* 30 (1965): 199–213. Quoted in Dyer, 57.

38 "Concha Piquer" is the creation of J. Solano Pedrero, J.A. Ochaíta García, and A. Rodríguez Gómez (Valerio). ISRC:ES614900214. Lyrics used by permission. English translation mine.

39 According to Terenci Moix,

> El acontecimiento que suponía el estreno de un espectáculo de la Piquer no tuvo rival. Lejos de la pléyade de folklóricas que montaron compañia por cuatro chavos y pergeñaron tristes parodias de clavel y pandereta, ella fue una de las grandes dignificadoras del género (*Suspiros* 42).

> The opening of a new show by Piquer was an event without parallel. Unlike the herd of *folklóricas* who created a company on the cheap, and put together pathetic parodies of bread and circus, she was one of the great dignifiers of the genre.

40 Vance, consultation session with the author.

41 Thomas Scheff, *Catharsis in Healing, Ritual and Drama* (Berkeley, CA: University of California Press, 1979), p. 62. Quoted in Andersen-Warren and Grainger, 89.

3 Coping with Terror

1 Piquer first recorded the song in 1940 with La Voz de su Amo. In the early 1950s, she took advantage of the new stereo technology to record what became the definitive versions of her most famous hits. In the 1954 recording with EMI-Odeón that I am using here, there are a few variations on the lyrics copyrighted by León, Valerio, and Quiroga. Here, Piquer sings "supo"

rather than "pudo." In each case, I have translated what Piquer sings rather than the copyrighted lyrics.

2 Piquer sings, "nadie comprendía."

3 Corradi and colleagues describe the Uruguayan regime as "a society that was silent, atomized, and, at times, without hope" (6).

4 See Arnalte; Olmeda.

5 The prison population was at its peak in January 1940. The regime's statistics for April 1939 show a prison population of 100,262. By January 1940 it had reached 270,719; in January 1941, it was 233,373. It then dropped to 124,423 by December 1942. Much of that drop would have been due to executions, which were being carried out daily. *Anuario estadístico de España*, 1943, 1100-1.

6 In Piquer's 1954 recording, one can almost hear an aspirated Andalusian "s" on the word "lo," implying that more than one person was killed.

7 The use of the *pasodoble*, the rhythm used in the music of the bullfight (Spain's "pasión nacional"), reinforces this interpretation.

8 Carmen Martín Gaite, who grew up in a middle-class, liberal family, recalls how her mother froze in terror whenever she heard a truck stop outside their house at night (*El cuarto* 193).

9 The rise in suicides during the postwar years indicates that many did give in to despair.

10 Fraiberg, 20; Kelly, ch. 8, "Fixed-role Therapy," in *The Psychology of Personal Constructs*, I:360–51.

11 Verónica Feliú, personal communication with the author. Azar Nafisi, writing about life in Iran's fundamentalist Islamic regime, notes how she and her students used humour in telling stories almost every day of incidents in which they had been oppressed: "It was as if the sheer act of recounting those stories gave us some control over them," she says. The deprecating tone we used, our gestures, even our hysterical laughter seemed to reduce their hold over our lives" (Nafisi 30–1).

12 On the use of music for reducing anxiety and stress, see Reynolds; Davis and Thaut (1989); Smith and Morris.

13 The term refers to those times when one performs at one's peak in a state that is highly focused yet relaxed, appearing effortless. The feeling associated with flow is that of mild ecstasy, in which people lose all track of time and space. The emotions, says Daniel Goleman, are used in the most productive possible way: "not just contained and channelled, but positive, energized, and aligned with the task at hand." (Goleman 91)

14 The fact that music listening in itself has been amply shown to function as a powerful anxiety reducer indicates that "La Parrala," which adds activity

to the listening, could have acted as a very potent survival tool indeed. See Gaynor, 83–84; Robb 4; Spintge; Guzzeta; Jill White.

4 Paradise Lost

1 On the concept of "working through," see Freud, "Remembering, Repeating, and Working Through."
2 Robert Pogue Harrison has declared, "to be human means above all to bury" (xi).
3 Testimony of Isabel González in *Les fosses del silenci*, Part Two. Armengou and Belis, *Las fosas del silencio*, 189.
4 I will explore the concept of disenfranchised grief in chapter 6, in connection with the *copla* "Romance de la Otra" ("Ballad of the Other Woman").
5 Piquer sings "*y* yo fuego te daré."
6 Piquer sings "y *sonar* el alba *en* la Torre la Vela." In all cases, my translation is of the words Piquer actually sings.
7 Most importantly, Piquer sings, "Te fuiste de mí" rather than "y un beso te di." This emphasizes the theme of abandonment that is key to the song's emotional anguish.
8 Manuel Román, 25. Before becoming an immortal hit in Piquer's version, "Ojos verdes" was performed by a number of singers, including Blanquita Suárez, Estrellita Castro, Miguel de Molina, and Consuelo Heredia. According to Salvador Valverde Calvo, son of the composer of the lyrics, it was actually first performed by Rafael Nieto during the war in the second act of the play "María Magdalena" (personal communication, 22 July 2012). It was first recorded by Consuelo Heredia in 1939. Conchita Piquer first performed it on stage in January 1940, and recorded it in May of that year. Later, she would sing it in the film *Filigrana* (1949).
9 Molina himself was tortured and beaten by the Francoists and left for dead after his first postwar performance in Madrid. He went into exile in Argentina and never returned to Spain. The persecution was due to his sexual orientation (Molina 150–6).
10 Lorca's discs were originally recorded for La Voz de su Amo, and consisted of ten songs from the Colección de Canciones Españolas Antiguas, collected and arranged by Lorca and accompanied by him on the piano. They are available today on remastered CD: "Colección de Canciones Populares Españolas," Federico García Lorca (piano); La Argentinita (voz). 1994, Madrid, Sonifolk, SA. 20105.
11 It is ironic that the mention of a brothel should be censored, since prostitution was legal under Franco until 1956, and reached epidemic proportions

during the 1940s as poor Republican widows turned to prostitution in order to eat. Government-supervised houses of prostitution were instituted in 1941 (Martin-Márquez 117, 120–1). Yet it could not be mentioned in song.

12 Only when she sang the song in a film, *Filigrana* (1949), was Piquer forced to sing the censored version. See Martín de la Plaza, 113.

13 On the Franco regime's propaganda warning young women in 1940s Spain against expressions of sexual desire, and the threat of losing their reputation, see Martín Gaite, chapter 5, "Entre santa y santo, pared de cal y canto," in *Usos amorosos de la posguerra española*, 91–117.

14 See Richards (24) on government policy. Fernando Fernán-Gómez recalls how, when Franco's troops finally entered Madrid at the end of the civil war, his planes flew over the city, "bombing" it this time not with bombs, but with white bread. Fernán-Gómez explains: "[El pan] fue fabricado especialmente para esta ocasión, para dar la sensación a la población cercada y hambrienta de la abundancia de los sitiadores, pero en realidad ya no existía en sus filas. Fue el último pan blanco que vieron los madrileños hasta pasados muchos años" ("The bread was made especially for this occasion, to give the hungry population which had been living under siege for so long the idea that [the Francoists] would bring prosperity. But in fact this was not the case. It was the last white bread the population of Madrid would see for many years") (Fernán-Gómez 182n28).

15 See "Restricciones eléctricas."

16 In what follows, I am not making any attempt to provide a balanced or scholarly view of the Republic. This has been done by historians. (See, for example, Jackson; Casanova, *La República y la Guerra Civil.*) The important thing for my purposes is to recapture the *project* of the Republic, which many people have remembered so vividly, and which until the last few years has been relegated to oblivion even by left-wing governments in Spain's post-1975 democracy. Because that is so, people's lived experiences have been denied, in a continuation of the dictatorship's policy of denying their postwar suffering and blaming them for the war's destruction. A song like "Ojos verdes," may have served in postwar Spain as a symbolic validation for people who knew they had lost something precious, at a time when the value of the Republic was everywhere denied.

17 *II República Española*, 75 Aniversario 1931–2006. Edición facsimilar de la Constitución Española de 1931, 49.

18 Carlos Elordi reading the manifesto of the organizers of the concert "Homage to the Republicans" in 2004. (*Recuperando memoria: Concierto-Homenaje a los Republicanos*, concert DVD).

19 See Blanca Calvo, "Memoria de la modernidad," and the catalogue, *Biblioteca en guerra.* The Republic brought culture and literacy to the people under

the auspices of organizations such as the Misiones Pedagógicas and Cultura Popular.

20 Pilar Bardem read an unpublished text by José Luis Sampedro containing these words at the "Concierto-Homenaje a los Republicanos." (*Recuperando memoria)*

21 Among the exiles was one of the authors of "Ojos verdes," Salvador Valverde, a fervent Republican who spent the entire war in Barcelona with Rafael de León. As the Nationalists approached, Valverde hugged León goodbye, not knowing that they would never see each other again. He crossed the border into France and then managed to get on a ship for Argentina, where he remained. Valverde had written all the major hits of the 1930s with León and Quiroga, but when those songs were broadcast in Franco's Spain, his name was suppressed, so that throughout the Franco dictatorship and even afterwards, people believed that only León and Quiroga had written them. For León and Quiroga themselves, hearing "Ojos verdes" after the war must have filled them with sadness at the irrevocable absence of their dear friend and co-creator.

22 Speeches at the "Concierto-Homenaje a los Republicanos."

23 The major effort in this regard was the 2007 Ley de Memoria Histórica ("Historical Memory Law") which made some reparations but still left the exhumation of the remains of Franco's victims to the families and to volunteer associations.

24 Alonso's pictures are projected while Pedro Guerra sings the song "Huesos."

25 See Van der Hart; Van der Hart and Ebbers.

26 See Linda and Michael Hutcheon, *Bodily Charm*, 154, on the "sensory overload" of opera, which we find in miniature in "Ojos verdes."

27 Therapists who use ritual with Vietnam veterans tell us that a ritual is effective when it achieves what Thomas Scheff has called "aesthetic distance." The participant in the ritual must be neither "underdistanced" (overwhelmed by emotion) nor "overdistanced" (not emotionally involved). (Johnson et al. 285, 286.) Therese Rando expresses this another way, specifying that the ritual must allow the individual to be both participant and observer.

28 Landy, 46. See also Andersen-Warren and Grainger, 87.

29 *Anuario Estadístico de España*, 1943, 38.

5 "Tatuaje" (Tattoo)

1 So enamoured was Vázquez Montalbán of "Tatuaje" that he named one of his popular detective novels after it (*Tatuaje*, 1976). He also cited its lyrics

in his poem "Conchita Piquer," published in José María Castellet's famous anthology *Nueve novísimos.*

2 The song's enormous impact continues in today's Spain. In 1999 a group of left-wing singers that included some of the most famous singers of protest songs against the dictatorship released an album of the most famous *coplas* of the 1930s and 1940s. It was called "Tatuaje." And Martirio, one of the most innovative and talented contemporary singer-actresses of the *copla,* includes "Tatuaje" in her remarkable album *Coplas de madrugá* (*Coplas for the wee hours*), in which she is accompanied by the Chano Domínguez jazz trio.

3 I will be referring throughout this chapter to Silvia Bermúdez's foundational study of "Tatuaje." See also Graham, "Popular Culture"; Colmeiro, "Canciones"; Alarcos Llorach.

4 Bermúdez has pointed out the phallic nature of this imagery (39).

5 This permanent mark on the soul is a far cry from the regime's rhetoric about cheerfulness. According to Carmen Martín Gaite:

> Las dos virtudes más importantes eran la laboriosidad y la alegría ... Carmen de Icaza, portavoz literario de aquellos ideales, había escrito en su más famosa novela, "Cristina Guzmán" ...: "La vida sonríe a quien le sonríe, no a quien le hace muecas."
>
> The two most important virtues were ... cheerfulness and activity ... Carmen de Icaza, spokeswoman for those ideals, had written in her most famous novel, *Cristina Guzmán* ...: "Life smiles at those who smile at it, not at those who make a face at it." (*El cuarto* 94)

6 As Bermúdez has pointed out, this alternative world is introduced directly into the listener's own house through the radio (46, 50).

7 This song was extremely important for men as well as women. Here, I choose to call the listener *she* because in 1940, there were 1 million more women than men, according to the regime's statistics (*AEE,* 1943, 38). In Madrid alone, there were 55,000 more single women than single men and 60,000 more widows than widowers. And many more women whose husbands were still alive were nevertheless single mothers because their husbands were in jail. Patino and Vázquez Montalbán concur in representing it as the paradigmatic expression of the women of postwar Spain (*Canciones para después de una guerra; Crónica* 43).

8 Conchita Piquer's voice itself was associated with those absent caresses. Rafael de León wrote a poem about her in which he said: "cantando te acaricia / con su voz de apasionado terciopelo" ("as she sings she caresses you / with her voice of passionate velvet"). Quoted in Bermúdez 37, from

Anacleto Rodríguez Moyano, *Conchita Piquer: El nombre de la copla* (Madrid: Cofás, 1988), 11.

9 Alarcos Llorach specifies that the song recalls the *jarchas* and the *canciones de amigo* (9).

10 There is another important possible reading for "Tatuaje" that involves the protagonist as well as the foreigner – the gay reading. This reading had to be kept secret from right and left alike. Alberto Mira Nouselles explains:

> "Tatuaje" es un placer para millones de oyentes, fue cierto tipo de goce para unos pocos que entiendieron su verdad emocional: la de la pasión en la penumbra, en tugurios, por hombres exóticos que están de paso, desde una perspectiva de irredimible marginalidad ... Diversos elementos en esta canción remiten a tradiciones homosexuales: el sexo efímero, los marineros, la noche, lo ilícito, el desgarro.
>
> "Tatuaje" is a pleasure for millions of listeners. It was a special kind of pleasure for the few who understood its emotional truth: that of passion in the twilight, in seedy rooms (*tugurios*), by exotic men just passing through, and from the perspective of irredeemable marginality ... Several elements of the song allude to homosexual traditions: ephemeral sex, sailors, the night, the illicit, the heart-rending passion. (348)

Mira also notes that the song's structural symmetry makes the woman's desire every bit as strong as the man's, which hardly conformed to the dominant stereotypes of sexuality at the time. For him, this reinforces the reading of the woman at the port as a gay man.

Mira's reading adds yet one more reason to the ones I will offer below for the continued relevance of "Tatuaje" today. Although the recent laws permitting gay marriage are a huge step forward, gay people in Spain still are not free to be open about their relationships in the workplace. And as discussed in the next chapter, the personal life of Rafael de León himself is still stigmatized enough that it has been silenced by those who have studied it (Mira 346).

11 The bulk of the atrocities committed on the Republican side were carried out in the first several months of the Spanish Civil War, when the working-class syndicates controlled many cities and towns and conducted revenge killings of landholders, priests, and Fascist sympathizers. Later, the central government regained control and the killings abated. (Jackson, *Breve historia*, 69–73). On the Republican terror, see Casanova, "'Abajo la Iglesia."

12 Many were simply economic conservatives; others were Fascist revolutionaries who wanted to keep the Church in a subordinate role.

13 See Hoaken; Barbara Smith.
14 See www.foroporlamemoria.info for the database "Desaparecidos y víctimas del franquismo," on which users can post the names of the missing or executed and request information from others.
15 For January 1943 the regime's records show 104,286 prisoners in jail "for crimes associated with the Marxist rebellion." *Anuario estadístico de España*, 1944, 1096.
16 Ferres, *Los vencidos*. This novel was written in 1960 and was published outside Spain in several foreign languages. The first version in Spanish was published in Paris in 1965. It was not published in Spain until 2005.
17 On concentration camps in Franco's Spain, see Rodrigo. Dulce Chacón's novel *La voz dormida* (*The Sleeping Voice*) is based on interviews with survivors of the Francoist repression. In it, the protagonist, Pepa, receives a letter from her boyfriend, Jaime, from France. This results in her being interrogated and tortured (170 ff).
18 See also Vinyes, Armengou, and Belis.
19 See Cenarro Lagunas on the history of Auxilio Social.
20 Bermúdez asserts that by singing out the longing of the sailor for the other woman, and the longing of the protagonist for the sailor, the defeated gave the lie to the Francoist propaganda about Spain's transcendent mission and exposed "the waiting and wanting condition in which many women and men actually lived" (39).
21 See Junquera.
22 We may think here of Sophocles' *Antigone* or Shakespeare's *Hamlet.* Jordi Ibáñez Fanés' philosophical reflection on the incapacity of some in Spain to recognize the mourning of others is titled *Antígona y el duelo*. This same tradition informs a popular expression, "wandering like a lost soul," which exists in many languages, Spanish included, to describe someone who has died with an unsolved problem and who is now wandering either in purgatory or in the world.
23 Virgil, *The Aeneid,* 154. One of Aeneas' crew, Palinurus, is in this unburied category, having fallen overboard by accident. He pleads with Aeneas to take him over the river so that he can rest in peace. The seer tells him this is not to be, but consoles him:

> But hear what I say and remember it,
> It will console you in your hard misfortune:
> For all the neighbouring cities shall be roused
> By heavenly portents to appease your bones.
> They will erect a tomb and to that tomb

> Will send their solemn offerings, and the place
> Shall be called Palinurus, and for ever. (155)

This is effectively what the families of the Republicans executed so long ago are doing for them in today's Spain.

24 This is movingly illustrated in Patricio Guzmán's documentary *Nostalgia de la luz* (2010), a meditation on how Chileans are eager to learn about the distant past of astronomy and archaeology, by contrast with the recent past they prefer not to remember. In it, we see elderly women who dig daily in the Atacama Desert, looking for the bones of their sons, murdered decades earlier during the Pinochet dictatorship.

25 My reading of the tattoo complements that of Silvia Bermúdez, who reads the tattoo as a gesture of rebellion, as part of the struggle against the cultural and sexual mores that the Franco regime tried to impose in the 1940s. She reads it as a defiant declaration of a desire that will not be contained by the terms of marriage and procreation. Where Bermúdez reads the tattoo primarily in terms of sex, I read it in terms of violence. Where she explores the meaning of tattoos on the body, I use them as metaphors for tattoos on the soul, tattoos that asserted agency over the traumas imposed on the defeated.

26 See Littrell.

27 How this worked narratively and musically in "Tatuaje" and other *coplas* is the subject of chapter 8.

28 I am grateful to Harriet Turner for this formulation.

6 The "Other Woman"

1 On the obsessive, puritanical attempt by the Church and the authorities to stamp out all sexual behaviour from public spaces, see Juan Eslava Galán, *Coitus interruptus*.

2 The impact of these *coplas* on the gay community remained strong throughout Spain's transition to democracy, when the *copla* genre was out of favour with everyone else, and this continues even today (Mira 348).

3 This reading is buttressed by Eva Woods's argument that film spectators of the period often identified with the characters on the screen across gender lines. See Woods, "Identification and Disconnect," 132.

4 *All of Spain Was a Jail* is the title of one book by Rodolfo and Daniel Serrano: *Toda España era una cárcel*. The title is an exaggeration; that said, we should recall the orphaned children of Auxilio Social, forbidden from going out on the streets; women's obligation to put in endless hours at the Women's

Section institutions of Social Service; compulsory attendance at mass; and so on. People spent a lot of time in closed spaces being indoctrinated against their will.

5 See Vázquez Montalbán, *Cancionero,* xx.

6 See also Nathan Kollar, "Rituals and the Disenfranchised Griever."

7 Reasserting Personhood

1 See Carmen Martín Gaite, *El cuarto de atrás,* 152.

2 © 1953 by Antonio Quintero Ramírez, Rafael de León y Arias de Saavedra, y Manuel López-Quiroga y Miquel, Madrid (España). Reservados todos los derechos. English translation mine. "Yo soy…Esa" was first performed by Juanita Reina in the movie *Aeropuerto* and the show *El Puerto de los amores* in 1952, and was later taken up by Piquer (Plaza, *Conchita Piquer* 176).

3 This is why these *coplas* were such a precious resource for gay people, as discussed by Mira (347).

4 The beautiful statue of La Macarena, a sorrowful Virgin, is one of the most important objects of Marian devotion in Spain. The statue is carried through the streets on Good Friday as one of the culminations of Seville's Holy Week processions.

5 See *Oxford English Dictionary,* XI, 596–7. I owe this insight to Harriet Turner.

6 Piquer sings, "*la* cantaora."

7 Piquer sings, "que yo *le di la* lisencia"

8 Maslow, *Motivation and Personality,* 46.

9 Paco routinely comes home at dawn, and he kills La Ruiseñora "between nightfall and dawn." The resonance of these hours during the postwar years raises the issue of whether Paco, in addition to committing adultery, is using his pistol on anyone besides his wife.

10 I owe the formulation of "expression plus protection" to clinical psychologist Terry Vance.

8 When a Radio Song Is the Meaning of Life

1 This quotation appeared in a 1957 interview with Dinesen (Bent Mohn, *New York Times Book Review,* 3 November 1957). It was then quoted by Hannah Arendt in *The Human Condition* (1958). Visit http://en.wikiquote.org/wiki/Isak_Dinesen. I first came across it as quoted by Sue Monk Kidd in the *Penguin Reader's Guide* at the end of her novel, *The Secret Life of Bees,* p. 8.

2 Frankl, *Unheard Cry,* 133; *Man's Search for Meaning,* 115–26.

3 Jerome Bruner, *Making Stories,* 64–5; "The Narrative Construction of Reality," 5.

4 Julia Manzanal tells her story in the 2002 documentary *Els nens perduts del franquisme,* also prepared by the authors of the book version.

5 One book calls this moment "The End of Hope." Juan Hermanos, *El fin de la esperanza.*

6 Human beings need their experience to be recognized and validated by others in order to know they are not insane. That is why solitary confinement is considered the worst of punishments. The self, in Jerome Bruner's words, is "profoundly relational" (*Making Stories* 86). Under totalitarian regimes, receiving such validation was not easy. Martín Gaite refers to a feeling of schizophrenia between what people were told was happening and what was really going on (*Usos* 25). When most of Spain was living in hunger, a newspaper headline proclaimed, "Vivimos con diez años de adelanto a otros pueblos." ("We are ten years ahead of other countries.") *El Alcázar* 29 March 1948, 1.

7 Juan José Carreras Ares, historian at the University of Zaragoza, recalled these terms in conversation with me. 1 June 2005.

8 As Nafisi says of fundamentalist Iran, "the past was dead, the present a sham, and there was no future" (144).

9 The *copla* form is thus very different from the other major popular music genre of the day, the *bolero,* in which a nameless "I" addresses a nameless "you" about a situation whose time, place, and exact circumstances are never made explicit (Zavala, ch. 1).

10 Martín Gaite points out that despite the distance that separated her own middle-class life from that of the marginal characters in these *coplas,* they seemed much more real than the characters in other songs, precisely because of their suffering ("Cuarto a espadas" 173–4).

11 Pierre Janet, *Psychological Healing* [1919], vol. 1, trans. E. Paul and C. Paul (New York: Macmillan, 1925), 661–3. Quoted in Herman 37.

12 Martha Nussbaum, arguing for philosophers to take better account of the emotions in moral philosophy, says: "if emotions are as Proust describes them, they have a complicated cognitive structure that is in part narrative in form, involving a story of our relation to cherished objects that extends over time ... Past loves shadow present attachments, and take up residence within them. This, in turn, suggests that in order to talk well about them we will need to turn to texts that contain a narrative dimension" (*Upheavals,* 2–3).

13 See Gaynor, 49, 58–9, 71–6; Cook, 257–8; Bonny, 6–7.

14 Gaynor, 83–4, Robb et al., 4. See also Guzzeta; Davis and Thaut; Gross and Swartz; Jill White.

15 See Bailey; Hanser and Thompson.

16 On pain reduction, see Brown et al.; Good et al.; Maslar. On music's effect on the immune system, see Bartlett et al.

17 E.T. Gaston, ed., *Music in Therapy* (New York: Macmillan Co., 1968), 35; qtd in Brown et al., 56.

18 Here I am following narrative therapist Robert Neimeyer, who used a system of cards to help traumatized clients take their fragmented memories ("jigsaw memories," as one client called them) and turn them into a continuous story. Each flash of memory was written on a card; the client was then asked to compose a story that linked the cards together in a narrative (Neimeyer "Narrative Disruptions" 223). For more on narrative therapy, see Neimeyer and Stewart, "Trauma, Healing, and the Narrative Emplotment of Loss"; Neimeyer, "Reauthoring Life Narratives"; and Óscar F. Gonçalves, "Cognitive Narrative Psychotherapy."

19 Littrell, 71, 95–6. See also Foa et al. and Schauer et al. on narrative exposure therapy, especially 23–5.

20 On the concept of repair, see Gheith.

21 See Davidson; Blood and Zatorre.

22 I see the acts of singing and reflecting here as having similar effects to writing as a therapeutic medium. See DeSalvo; Lepore and Smyth; Lepore and Greenberg.

Conclusion

1 This kind of symbiosis between performers and songs already existed in the era of the *cuplé*. See Vernon, "Theatricality," 190.

Bibliography

100 Años. Concha Piquer canta junto a Concha Márquez Piquer. CD and DVD. EMI Music Spain, 2006.

"40.000 españoles sueñan con trabajar en el cine." *Cámara* II, 4. January 1942: 14.

"Abastecimientos." *El Alcázar,* 3 April 1948: 4.

Abella, Rafael. *La vida cotidiana en España bajo el régimen de Franco.* Barcelona: Argos Vergara, 1985.

Acosta Díaz, Josefa, Manuel José Gómez Lara, and Jorge Jiménez Barrientos, eds. *Poemas y canciones de Rafael de León.* 3rd ed. Sevilla: Ediciones Alfar, 1997.

Agger, Inger, and Søren Buus Jensen. *Trauma and Healing under State Terrorism.* Atlantic Highlands: Zed Books, 1996.

Aguilar Fernández, Paloma. *Memoria y olvido de la guerra civil española.* Madrid: Alianza Editorial, 1996.

Ahmed, Sara. *The Cultural Politics of Emotion.* New York: Routledge, 2004.

Alarcos Llorach, Emilio. "Tatuaje: Un acercamiento a la copla." *Clarín* 65 (2006): 3–11.

"Algunas de las maestras opositoras que toman parte en este curso" [Some of the teachers being trained in this course]. Photograph. "Tareas de la S.F." *Medina,* 28 January 1945: 14.

Andersen-Warren, Madeleine, and Roger Grainger. *Practical Approaches to Dramatherapy: The Shield of Perseus.* Preface. Anna Seymour. London: Jessica Kingsley Publishers, 2000

Anuario estadístico de España. 1943. Madrid: Presidencia del Gobierno. Instituto Nacional de Estadística. Sucesores de Rivadeneyra, 1943.

Anuario estadístico de España. 1944. Madrid: Presidencia del Gobierno. Instituto Nacional de Estadística. Sucesores de Rivadeneyra, 1944.

Anuario estadístico de España. 1948–9. Madrid: Presidencia del Gobierno, Instituto Nacional de Estadística, Sucesores de Rivadeneyra, 1949.

Arbelos, Carlos, and Cristina Hoyos. *El flamenco cantado con sencillez.* Madrid: Maeva, 2003.

Armengou, Montse, and Ricard Belis. *Las fosas del silencio: ¿Hay un holocausto español?* Barcelona: Plaza y Janés, 2004.

Arnalte, Arturo. *Redada de violetas: La represión de los homosexuales durante el franquismo.* Madrid: La Esfera de los Libros, 2003.

Arrarás Iribarren, Joaquín, and Carlos Sáenz de Tejada. "Frontispiece," image. *Historia de la cruzada española.* Vol. 3. Madrid: Eds. Españolas, 1940–1.

Bailey, Lucanne Magill. "Music Therapy in Pain Management." *Journal of Pain and Symptom Management* 1.1 (1986): 25–8.

Balsebre, Armand. *Historia de la radio en España.* 2 vols. Madrid: Cátedra, 2001.

Bartlett, Dale, Donald Kaufman, and Roger Smeltekop. "The Effects of Music Listening and Perceived Sensory Experiences on the Immune System as Measured by Interleukin-1 and Cortisol." *Journal of Music Therapy* 30.4 (1993): 194–209.

Beadman, Clive. "'Cimentada en el sillar firmísimo de la familia cristiana' and 'Viudas de medio pelo': Illicit prostitution in 1940s Spain." *International Journal of Iberian Studies* 13.3: 157–66.

Becker, David. "The Deficiency of the Concept of Posttraumatic Stress Disorder When Dealing with Victims of Human Rights Violations." *Beyond Trauma: Cultural and Societal Dynamics.* Ed. Rolf J. Kleber, Charles R. Figley, and Berthold P.R. Gersons. New York: Plenum Press, 1995. 99–110.

Berlant, Lauren Gail. *The Female Complaint: The Unfinished Business of Sentimentality in American Culture.* Durham: Duke University Press, 2008.

Bermúdez, Silvia. "'Music to My Ears': *Cuplés*, Conchita Piquer, and the (Un) making of Cultural Nationalism." *Siglo XX / 20th Century* 15.1–2 (1997): 33–54.

Bermúdez, Silvia, and Jorge Pérez, eds. Special Issue. Spanish Popular Music Studies. *Journal of Spanish Cultural Studies* 10. Oxford: Routledge, 2009.

Biblioteca en guerra. Catalogue. Ed. Blanca Calvo and Ramón Salaberría. Madrid: Biblioteca Nacional, 2005.

Blas Vega, José. *Los cafés cantantes de Madrid (1846–1936).* Madrid: Guillermo Blázquez, 2006.

Blatner, Adam. *Acting-In: Practical Applications of Psychodramatic Methods.* New York: Springer, 1973.

– *Psychodrama, Role-Playing, and Action Methods: Theory and Practice.* Thetford: H. Blatner, 1970.

Blood, A.J., and R.J. Zatorre. "Intensely Pleasurable Responses to Music Correlate with Activity in Brain Regions Implicated in Reward and Emotion."

Proceedings of the National Academy of Sciences of the United States of America 98.20 (2001): 11818–23.

Bonny, Helen Lindquist. "Music and Healing." *Music Therapy* 8A.1 (1986): 3–12.

Brown, Carlene J., Andrew C.N. Chen, and Samuel F. Dworkin. "Music in the Control of Human Pain." *Music Therapy* 8.1 (1989): 47–60.

Bruner, Jerome. *Acts of Meaning*. Cambridge, MA: Harvard University Press, 1990.

– *Making Stories: Law, Literature, Life*. Cambridge, MA: Harvard University Press, 2003.

– "The Narrative Construction of Reality." *Critical Inquiry* 18.1 (1991): 1–21.

"Calendario del ama de casa 1941." *Y: Revista de la mujer nacionalsindicalista* 36, January 1941: 38–9.

"Camaradas que asisten a este curso, en una de las clases" [Comrades attending this course, in one of the classes]. Photograph. "Tareas de la S.F." *Medina*, 29 April 1945: 18.

Calvo, Blanca. "Memoria de la modernidad." *La lectura pública en España durante la II República*. Madrid: Biblioteca Nacional, 1991. 9–12.

"El campamento del SEU ..." [At the University Student Union camp ...]. Photograph. "Florece el trabajo de todas las Secciones Femeninas." *Medina*, 14 January 1945: 45.

Canciones para después de una guerra. Dir. Basilio Martín Patino. 1971. DVD. Diario El País, 2003.

Caruth, Cathy. *Trauma: Explorations in Memory*. Baltimore: Johns Hopkins University Press, 1995.

– *Unclaimed Experience: Trauma, Narrative, and History*. Baltimore: Johns Hopkins University Press, 1996.

Casanova, Julián. "'Abajo la Iglesia, que caiga el poder': la violencia desde abajo." *Víctimas de la guerra civil*. Ed. Santos Juliá. Madrid: Temas de hoy, 1999. 117–57.

– "Una dictadura de cuarenta años." *Morir, matar, sobrevivir*. Ed. Julián Casanova. Barcelona: Crítica, 2002. 3–52.

– *República y guerra civil*. Josep Fontana and Ramón Villares, dir. *Historia de España*. Vol. 8. Barcelona: Crítica/Marcial Pons, 2007.

Cenarro Lagunas, Ángela. *La sonrisa de Falange: Auxilio Social en la guerra civil y en la posguerra*. Barcelona: Crítica, 2006.

Chacón, Dulce. *La voz dormida*. Madrid: Alfaguara, 2002.

"El cigarrillo, personaje del cinema" [The cigarette, a character in film]. *Primer Plano* II, 15, 26 January 1941: 7.

"Clase de cocina en la Escuela de Hogar 'Santa Ana'" [A cooking lesson at "Saint Anne" Housekeeping School]. Photograph. "Florece el trabajo en todas las Secciones Femeninas." *Medina*, 14 January 1945: 4.

"Clase de corte y confección" [Tailoring Lesson]. Photograph. "Tareas de la S.F." *Medina,* 28 January 1945: 14.

Colección de Canciones Populares Españolas. Federico García Lorca (piano) and La Argentinita (voice). Remastered CD. Madrid: Sonifolk, 1994.

Colmeiro, José F. "Canciones con historia: Cultural Identity, Historical Memory, and Popular Songs." *Journal of Spanish Cultural Studies* 4 (2003): 31–46.

– *Memoria histórica e identidad cultural: De la postguerra a la postmodernidad.* Barcelona: Anthropos, 2005.

– "Nationalising Carmen: Spanish Cinema and the Spectre of Francoism." *Journal of Iberian and Latin American Research* 15 (2009): 1–26.

"Concha Piquer." *Imprescindibles.* RTV2, Madrid. 4 November 2010. Televisión.

Concha Piquer, *La copla, siempre.* BMG Music Spain, S.A., with RCA, 2000.

"Conchita Piquer." Photograph by "Campúa." *Espectáculos,* 5 April 1944: Cover.

"Conchita Piquer triunfa en Barcelona." *Espectáculos,* 16 March 1944: 14.

"Conchita Piquer with guitar." Photograph. "Galería de fotos." Track 16 of DVD *100 Años: Concha Piquer canta junto a Concha Márquez Piquer.* CD and DVD. EMI Music Spain, 2006.

"Los concursos de 'Espectáculos.'" *Espectáculos,* 24 February 1944: 16.

Cone, James H. *The Spirituals and the Blues: An Interpretation.* New York: Orbis Books, 1991.

Cook, Janet D. "The Therapeutic Use of Music: A Literature Review." *Nursing Forum* 20.3 (1981): 252–66.

La Copla en la Biblioteca Nacional de España. Catalogue. Ed. Alicia García Medina and Nieves Iglesias Martínez. Madrid: Biblioteca Nacional, 2009.

Corradi, Juan E., Patricia Weiss Fagan, and Manuel Antonio Garretón, eds. *Fear at the Edge: State Terror and Resistance in Latin America.* Berkeley: University of California Press, 1992.

Damasio, Antonio R. *Descartes' Error: Emotion, Reason, and the Human Brain.* New York: G.P. Putnam, 1994.

– *The Feeling of What Happens: Body and Emotion in the Making of Consciousness.* New York: Harcourt Brace, 1999.

Davidson, Terry L. "Endorphins." *Encyclopedia of Psychology.* Ed. Alan E. Kazdin. Vol. 3. New York: Oxford University Press, 2000.

Davis, William B., and Michael H. Thaut. "The Influence of Preferred Relaxing Music on Measures of State Anxiety, Relaxation, and Physiological Responses." *Journal of Music Therapy* 26.4 (1989): 168–87.

"Deanna Durbin" [Photograph, autograph, and Easter greetings from Deanna Durbin]. "Felicitaciones para nuestros lectores." *Primer Plano,* 19 December 1948.

DeSalvo, Louise. *Writing as a Way of Healing: How Telling Our Stories Transforms Our Lives.* San Francisco: Harper San Francisco, 1999.

Desaparecidos y víctimas del franquismo. Foro por la Memoria y despage. April 2005, March 2008.

"El 'Día de la Canción' y el Frente de Juventudes" [The "Day of the Song" and the Youth Front]. Article and photograph. *El Alcázar,* 1 March 1948: 7.

Díaz, Lorenzo. *La radio en España: 1923–1997.* Madrid: Alianza, 1997.

Didion, Joan. *The Year of Magical Thinking.* New York: Alfred A. Knopf, 2005.

Doka, Kenneth J. "Disenfranchised Grief." *Disenfranchised Grief: Recognizing Hidden Sorrow.* Ed. Kenneth J. Doka. Lexington: Lexington Books, 1989. 3–12.

Domingo, Carmen. *Coser y cantar.* Barcelona: Lumen, 2007.

Douglas, Susan J. *Listening In: Radio and the American Imagination, from Amos 'n' Andy and Edward R. Murrow to Wolfman Jack and Howard Stern.* New York: Times Books, 1999.

Dualde Gil, Josefa. "Diana Durbin." *Radiocinema,* 30 May 1940.

DuBois, W.E.B. *The Souls of Black Folk.* New York: Fawcett, 1961.

Dyer, Richard. "Charisma." *Stardom: Industry of Desire.* Ed. Christine Gledhill. London and New York: Routledge, 1991. 57–9.

Ebert, Angela, and Murray J. Dyck. "The Experience of Mental Death: The Core Feature of Complex Post-Traumatic Stress Disorder." *Clinical Psychology Review* 24 (2004): 617–35.

"Equipo femenino de hockey haciendo el saludo falangista" [Women's hockey team making the fascist salute]. Photograph. "Tareas de la S.F." "El equipo de San Sebastián." *Medina,* 1 April 1945: 18–19.

Eslava Galán, Juan. *Coitus interruptus: la represión sexual y sus heroicos alivios en la España franquista.* Barcelona: Planeta, 1997.

"Las estrellas nos muestran el camino de la naturalidad" [The stars show us how to look natural]. *Cámara,* 15 January 1948: 40.

Felman, Shoshana. *Testimony: Crises of Witnessing in Literature, Psychoanalysis, and History.* New York: Routledge, 1992.

Fernán-Gómez, Fernando. *Las bicicletas son para el verano.* 17th ed. Madrid: Espasa-Calpe, 1995.

Fernández Soria, Juan Manuel. *Educación, socialización y legitimación política (España 1931–1970).* Valencia: Tirant lo Blanch, 1998.

Ferres, Antonio. *Los vencidos.* Madrid: Gadir, 2005.

Filigrana. Dir. Luis Marquina. Prod. Manuel del Castillo. Perfs. Conchita Piquer, Fernando Granada, and Luis Hurtado. Music: Manuel Quiroga. Songs: Juan Quintero, Rafael de León, Manuel L. Quiroga. DVD. 1949.

Foa, E.B., T.M. Keane, and M.J. Friedman, eds. *Effective Treatments for PTSD:*

Practice Guidelines from the International Society for Traumatic Stress Studies. New York: Guilford Press, 2000.

Foa, E., G. Steketee, and B. Rothbaum. "Behavioral/Cognitive Conceptualizations of Post-Traumatic Stress Disorder." *Behavior Therapy* 20 (1989): 155–76.

Les fosses del silenci. Part 2. Dir. Montse Armengou and Richard Belis. DVD. Enciclopedia Catalana and Televisió de Catalunya, 2003.

"Fotoreportaje: Conchita Piquer." Series of photographs. *Cámara,* December 1941: 30.

Fraiberg, Selma. *The Magic Years.* New York: Scribner, 1959.

Frankl, Victor. *Man's Search for Meaning: An Introduction to Logotheraphy.* New York: Pocket Books, 1963.

– *The Unheard Cry for Meaning: Psychotherapy and Humanism.* New York: Simon and Schuster, 1978.

Freud, Sigmund. "Mourning and Melancholia." 1915. *The Standard Edition of the Complete Psychological Works of Sigmund Freud.* Trans. James Strachey. Vol. XIV. London: Hogarth and the Institute of Psychoanalysis, 1962. 243–58.

– "Remembering, Repeating, and Working-Through." 1914. *The Standard Edition of the Complete Psychological Works of Sigmund Freud.* Trans. James Strachey. Vol. XII. London: Hogarth and the Institute of Psychoanalysis, 1953–1974. 147–156.

Friedman, Matthew J., and Bruce S. McEwen, "Posttraumatic Stress Disorder, Allostatic Load, and Medical Illness." *Trauma and Health: Physical Health Consequences of Exposure to Extreme Stress.* Ed. Paula P. Schnurr and Bonnie L. Green. Washington: American Psychological Association, 2003. 157–88.

"Galería de fotos: Concha Piquer." *100 Años. Concha Piquer canta junto a Concha Márquez Piquer.* DVD. EMI Music Spain, 2006.

Gamboa Rodríguez, José Manuel. *Una historia del flamenco.* Madrid: Espasa, 2005.

García Piedra, Juan Carlos, and Joan Carles Gil Siscar. "Lunares que entienden: márgenes eróticos de la copla erótica española." *Diàlegs gais, lesbians, queer. Diálogos gays, lesbianos, queer.* Ed. Julián Acebrón and Rafael M. Mérida. Lleida: Edicions de la Universitat de Lleida, 2007.

Garlinger, Patrick Paul. "All About Agrado, or the Sincerity of Camp in Almodóvar's Todo sobre mi madre." *Journal of Spanish Cultural Studies* 5.1 (2004): 117–34.

Garretón, Manuel Antonio. "Fear in Military Regimes: An Overview." *Fear at the Edge: State Terror and Resistance in Latin America.* Ed. Juan E. Corradi, Patricia Weiss Fagan, and Manuel Antonio Garretón. Berkeley: University of California Press, 1992. 13–25.

Gaston, E.T., ed., *Music in Therapy* New York: Macmillan, 1968.

Gaynor, Mitchell L. *Sounds of Healing: A Physician Reveals the Therapeutic Power of Sound, Voice, and Music.* New York: Broadway Books, 1999.

Gennep, Arnold van. *The Rites of Passage.* Chicago: University of Chicago Press, 1960.

Gerrity, Ellen, Terence M. Keane, and Farris Tuma, eds. *The Mental Health Consequences of Torture.* New York: Kluwer/Plenum, 2001.

Gheith, Jehanne. "'Collecting Crumbs': Memory, Rupture, and Repair for Children of the Gulag." *Proceedings from the History and Legacy of the Gulag Conference,* Harvard University, 1 November 2006, Ed. Steven Barnes. Forthcoming.

"Gilda" [advertisement]. Photograph. *Fotogramas,* 1 January 1948: 2.

"'Gilda,' la mujer que despertó la admiración del mundo entero" [Gilda, the woman the whole world admires]. Article and photographs. *Primer Plano,* 4 January 1948.

Goldfried, Marvin R., and Gerald C. Davison. "Systematic Desensitization." *Clinical Behavior Therapy.* Expanded ed. New York: John Wiley and Sons, 1994. 112–35.

Goleman, Daniel. *Emotional Intelligence.* New York: Bantam, 1995.

Gonçalves, Oscar F. "Cognitive Narrative Psychotherapy: The Hermeneutic Construction of Alternative Meanings." *Cognitive and Constructive Psychotherapies: Theory, Research, and Practice.* Ed. Michael J. Mahoney. New York: Springer, 1995. 139–62.

Good, M., et al. "Relief of Postoperative Pain with Jaw Relaxation, Music and Their Combination." *Pain* 81.1–2 (1999): 163–72.

Graham, Helen. "Gender and the State." *Spanish Cultural Studies: An Introduction.* Ed. Helen Graham and Jo Labanyi. Oxford: Oxford University Press, 1995. 182–95.

– "Popular Culture in the Years of Hunger." *Spanish Cultural Studies: An Introduction.* Ed. Helen Graham and Jo Labanyi. Oxford: Oxford University Press, 1995. 237–245.

– *The Spanish Civil War: A Very Short Introduction.* Oxford: Oxford University Press, 2005.

Grainger, Roger. *Drama and Healing: The Roots of Drama Therapy.* London: Jessica Kingsley, 1990.

Gramsci, Antonio. *Selections from the Prison Notebooks.* Ed. Quintin Hoare and Geoffrey Nowell Smith. New York: International, 1971.

Grandes creaciones de Conchita Piquer. Songbooks. 3 vols. Madrid: Ediciones Quiroga, 2004.

Green, Bonnie L., and Rachel Kimerling. "Trauma, Posttraumatic Stress

Disorder, and Health Status." *Trauma and Health: Physical Health Consequences of Exposure to Extreme Stress.* Ed. Paula P. Schnurr and Bonnie L. Green. Washington: American Psychological Association, 2003. 13–42.

Greenberg, Mark S., and Bessel A. van der Kolk. "Retrieval and Integration of Traumatic Memories with the 'Painting Cure.'" *Psychological Trauma.* Ed. Bessel van der Kolk. Washington: American Psychiatric Press, 1987. 191–216.

Gregg, Melissa, and Gregory J. Seigworth, eds. *The Affect Theory Reader.* Durham: Duke University Press, 2010.

Gross, Jodi-Levine, and Robert Swartz. "The Effects of Music Therapy on Anxiety in Chronically Ill Patients." *Music Therapy* 2.1 (1982): 43–52.

Guzzetta, Cathie E. "Effects of Relaxation and Music Therapy on Patients in a Coronary Care Unit with Presumptive Acute Myocardial Infarction." *Heart and Lung* 18.6 (1989): 609–16.

Hanser, Suzanne B., and Larry W. Thompson. "Effects of a Music Therapy Strategy on Depressed Older Adults." *Journal of Gerontology* 49.6 (1994): 265–69.

Harding, Jennifer, and E. Deidre Pribram. *Emotions: A Cultural Studies Reader.* New York: Routledge, 2009.

Harrison, Robert Pogue. *The Dominion of the Dead.* Chicago: University of Chicago Press, 2003.

Herman, Judith Lewis. *Trauma and Recovery.* New York: Basic Books, 1997.

Hermanos, Juan. *El fin de la esperanza.* Madrid: Oberón, 2004.

Herrmann, Gina. "Documentary's Labours of Law: The Television Journalism of Montse Armengou and Ricard Belis." *Journal of Spanish Cultural Studies* 9 (2008): 193–212.

Hoaken, Paul. "Resolution of Complicated Grief through Vicarious Grieving." *Canadian Journal of Psychiatry* 44.6 (1999): 606.

Hutcheon, Linda, and Michael Hutcheon. *Bodily Charm: Living Opera.* Lincoln: University of Nebraska Press, 2000.

Ibáñez Fanés, Jordi. *Antígona y el duelo: Una reflexión moral sobre la memoria histórica.* Barcelona: Tusquets, 2009.

Una inmensa prisión. Dir. Carlos Ceacero Ruiz y Guillermo Carnero Rosell. Prod. Insularia S.L. y 14 Pies Audiovisual. Impulso Records, S.I., 2005. Part of Imágenes contra el olvido: Lo que nunca se contó del franquismo. [Madrid]: [Suevia Films], 2006.

Jackson, Gabriel. *Breve historia de la guerra civil española.* Trans. José Antonio Bravo. Barcelona: Grijalbo, 1986.

Jacobs, Selby, and Holly Prigerson. "Psychotherapy of Traumatic Grief: A Review of Evidence for Psychotherapeutic Treatments." *Death Studies* 24.6 (2000): 479–95.

Janet, Pierre. *Psychological Healing* [1919], vol. 1, trans. E. Paul and C. Paul. New York: Macmillan, 1925.

Janoff-Bulman, Ronnie. *Shattered Assumptions: Towards a New Psychology of Trauma.* New York: Maxwell Macmillan International, 1992.

Jennings, Sue. *Introduction to Developmental Playtherapy: Playing and Health.* London: Jessica Kingsley, 1999.

– *Introduction to Dramatherapy: Theatre and Healing, Ariadne's Ball of Thread.* Philadelphia: Jessica Kingsley, 1998.

– *Theatre, Ritual, and Transformation.* London: Routledge, 1995.

Jerez-Farrán, Carlos, and Samuel Amago, eds. *Unearthing Franco's Legacy: Mass Graves and the Recovery of Historical Memory in Spain.* Notre Dame: University of Notre Dame Press, 2010.

Johnson, David Read. "The Role of the Creative Arts Therapies in the Diagnosis and Treatment of Psychological Trauma." *The Arts in Psychotherapy* 14 (1987): 7–14.

Johnson, David Read, et al. "The Therapeutic Use of Ritual and Ceremony in the Treatment of Post-Traumatic Stress Disorder." *Journal of Traumatic Stress* 8.2 (1995): 283–98.

Juliá, Santos, ed. *Memoria de la guerra y el franquismo.* Madrid: Taurus Ediciones, 2006.

– ed. *Victimas de la Guerra Civil.* Madrid: Temas de Hoy, 1999.

Junquera, Natalia. "¿Y mi padre, cuál es?" *El País,* 11 September 2006: 24.

Kelly, George Alexander. *A Theory of Personality.* Vol. 1 of *The Psychology of Personal Constructs.* 2 vols. New York: W.W. Norton, 1955.

Kemeny, Margaret. "Emotions and the Immune System." *Healing and the Mind.* Ed. Bill Moyers, Betty S. Flowers, and David Grubin. New York: Doubleday, 1993. 195–211.

Kidd, Sue Monk. *The Secret Life of Bees.* New York: Penguin, 2002.

Kohen, Cecilia. "Political Traumas, Oppression, and Rituals." *Rituals in Families and Family Therapy.* Ed. Evan Imber-Black, Janine Roberts, and Richard Alva Whiting. New York: W.W. Norton, 1988. 363–83.

Kollar, Nathan R. "Rituals and the Disenfranchised Griever." *Disenfranchised Grief: Recognizing Hidden Sorrow.* Ed. Kenneth J. Doka. Lexington: Lexington Books, 1989. 271–85.

Labanyi, Jo. "The Mediation of Everyday Life: An Oral History of Cinema-Going in 1940s and 1950s Spain: An Introduction to a Dossier." *Studies in Hispanic Cinemas* 2.2 (2005): 105–8.

– "Musical Battles: Populism and Hegemony in the Early Francoist Folkloric Film Musical." *Constructing Identity in Contemporary Spain.* Ed. Jo Labanyi. New York: Oxford University Press, 2002. 206–21.

– "Testimonies of Repression: Methodological and Political Issues." *Unearthing Franco's Legacy: Mass Graves and the Recovery of Historical Memory in Spain.* Ed. Carlos Jere and Samuel Amago. Notre Dame: University of Notre Dame Press, 2010. 192–205.

– ed. Special Issue. "The Politics of Memory in Contemporary Spain." *Journal of Spanish Cultural Studies* 9. Oxford: Routledge, 2008.

"Lana Turner" [Lana Turner, portrait]. Photograph. *Vestuario* 25 February 1948: 39.

Landy, Robert. *Persona and Performance: The Meaning of Role in Drama, Therapy, and Everyday Life.* New York and London: Guilford Press, 1993.

Lechner, Norbert. "Some People Die of Fear: Fear as a Political Problem." *Fear at the Edge: State Terror and Resistance in Latin America.* Ed. Juan E. Corradi, Patricia Weiss Fagan, and Manuel Antonio Garretón. Berkeley: University of California Press, 1992. 26–35.

Lepore, Stephen J., and Melanie A. Greenberg. "Mending Broken Hearts: Effects of Expressive Writing on Mood, Cognitive Processing, Social Adjustment, and Health Following a Relationship Breakup." *Psychology and Health* 17.5 (2002): 547–60.

Lepore, Stephen J., and Joshua M. Smyth, eds. *The Writing Cure: How Expressive Writing Promotes Health and Emotional Well-Being.* Washington: American Psychological Association, 2002.

Levitin, Daniel. *This Is Your Brain on Music.* London: Dutton, 2006.

Leys, Ruth. *Trauma: A Genealogy.* Chicago: University of Chicago Press, 2000.

Lira, E., and M. Castillo. *Psicología de la Amenaza Política y del Miedo.* Santiago: Instituto Latinoamericano de Salud Mental y Derechos Humanos, 1991.

Littrell, Jill. "Is the Re-experience of Painful Emotion Therapeutic?" *Clinical Psychology Review* 18.1 (1998): 71–102.

Lo mejor de Conchita Piquer. Madrid: EMI-Odeón, 1987.

Lorca. El mar deja de moverse. Dir. Emilio Ruiz Barrachina. 2006. DVD. Impacto Films; Ircania Producciones; Divisa Home Video.

Lotman, Jurij. *The Structure of the Artistic Text.* Trans. G. Lenhoff and R. Vroon. Ann Arbor: Department of Slavic Languages and Literature, University of Michigan, 1977.

Loureiro, Ángel G. "Pathetic Arguments." *Journal of Spanish Cultural Studies* 9 (2008): 225–37.

Lubin, Hadar, and David Read Johnson. "Use of Ceremony in Multiple Family Therapy for Psychological Trauma." *Action Therapy with Families and Groups: Using Creative Arts Improvisation in Clinical Practice.* Ed. Daniel J. Wiener and Linda K. Oxford. Washington: American Psychological Association, 2003. 75–100.

Machado y Álvarez, Antonio (Demófilo), ed. *Cantes flamencos.* Barcelona: DVD Ediciones, 1998.

– *El folk-lore andaluz.* Seville: Ediciones Andaluzas Unidas, 1986.

Maercker, Andreas, et al. "Prediction of Complicated Grief by Positive and Negative Themes in Narratives." *Journal of Clinical Psychology* 54.8 (1998): 1117–36.

Márquez Piquer, Concha. *Yo misma: Memorias de Concha Márquez Piquer.* https://itunes.apple.com/us/book/memorias-concha-marquez-piquer/id569238705?l=es&ls=1.

Marsé, Juan. *Teniente Bravo.* Barcelona: Seix Barral, 1987.

Marsh, Steven. "The Haptic in Hindsight: Neighbourhood Cinema-Going in Post-War Spain." *Studies in Hispanic Cinemas* 2.2 (2005): 109–15.

Martín, Annabel. *La gramática de la felicidad.* Madrid: Ediciones Libertarias, 2005.

Martín-Baró, Ignacio. *Poder, ideología y violencia.* Madrid: Editorial Trotta, 2003.

Martín Gaite, Carmen. "Cuarto a espadas sobre las coplas de posguerra." *La búsqueda de interlocutor y otras búsquedas.* Barcelona: Destino, 1982. 167–80.

– *El cuarto de atrás.* Madrid: Ediciones Destino, 1990.

– *Usos amorosos de la posguerra española.* Barcelona: Editorial Anagrama, 1987.

Martin-Márquez, Susan. "Sex in the Cinema: Film-Going Practices and the Construction of Sexuality and Ideology in Franco's Spain." *Studies in Hispanic Cinemas* 2.2 (2005): 117–24.

Martirio. *Coplas de Madrugá.* Ed. Borja Casani. Madrid: Colección LCD El Europeo, 1999.

– "Carta a Sra. Marta Valdés." *Coplas de Madrugá.* Ed. Borja Casani. Madrid: Colección LCD El Europeo, 1999. 103.

Maslar, Patricia M. "The Effect of Music on the Reduction of Pain: A Review of the Literature." *The Arts in Psychotherapy* 13 (1986): 215–19.

Maslow, Abraham H. *Motivation and Personality.* New York: Harper and Row, 1970.

Melham, Nadine M., et al. "Comorbidity of Axis I Disorders in Patients with Traumatic Grief." *Journal of Clinical Psychiatry* 62.11 (2001): 884–7.

Mir, Conxita. "El sino de los vencidos: La represión franquista en la Cataluña rural de posguerra." *Morir, matar, sobrevivir.* Ed. Julián Casanova. Barcelona: Crítica, 2002. 123–96.

Mira Nouselles, Alberto. *De Sodoma a Chueca: Una historia cultural de la homosexualidad en España en el siglo XX.* Barcelona: Editorial Egales, 2004.

Mitchell, Timothy. *Flamenco Deep Song.* New Haven: Yale University Press, 1994.

Moix, Terenci. *El cine de los sábados* (Memorias. El Peso de la Paja/1). Barcelona: Planeta, 1998.

– *Suspiros de España: La copla y el cine de nuestro recuerdo.* Barcelona: Plaza y Janés, 1993.

Molina, Miguel de, Salvador Valverde Calvo, y Alejandro Salade. *Botín de guerra: Autobiografía.* La España Plural. Barcelona: Planeta, 1998.

Molina, Romualdo. *Rafael de León.* Madrid: Fundación Autor, 2012.

Molinero, Carme. "La transición y la 'Renuncia' a la recuperación de la 'Memoria Democrática.'" *Journal of Spanish Cultural Studies* 11 (2010): 33–52.

Morcillo, Aurora G. *True Catholic Womanhood: Gender Ideology in Franco's Spain.* DeKalb: Northern Illinois University Press, 2000.

Moreno, Jacob Levy. *Psychodrama.* New York: Beacon House, 1946.

– *The Theatre of Spontaneity.* New York: Beacon House, 1947.

– *Who Shall Survive? Foundations of Sociometry, Group Psychotherapy and Sociodrama.* New York: Beacon House, 1953.

Moreno, Joseph. "The Therapeutic Role of the Blues Singer and Considerations for the Clinical Applications of the Blues Form." *The Arts in Psychotherapy* 14.4 (1987): 333–40.

Moreno Gómez, Francisco. *Córdoba en la posguerra (la represión y la guerrilla, 1939–1950).* Córdoba: F. Baena, 1987.

"Mujer con uniforme de la Sección Femenina con insignia de yugo y flechas" [Woman wearing the Women's Section Uniform with Falange yoke-and-arrows insignia]. Photograph. "Labor de la Sección Femenina en 1940." *Y: Revista de la mujer nacionalsindicalista,* January 1941: 16.

"Mujer cosiendo con uniforme de Talleres José Antonio" [Woman sewing with uniform of the José Antonio Factory]. Photograph. *Y: Revista de la mujer nacionalsindicalista,* January 1941: 17.

"Mujer leyendo en aula con cruz" [Woman reading in classroom with cross]. Photograph. "Tareas de la S.F." *Medina,* 29 April 1945: 18.

"Mujeres asistiendo a un curso de la Sección Femenina" [Women attending classes given by the Women's Section]. Photograph. "Tareas de la S.F." *Medina,* 29 April 1945: 18.

"Mujeres cantando: 'En el campamento del S.E.U. de Rande-Redondela cantan las camaradas" [Women singing at University Student Union camp]. Photograph. "Florece el trabajo en todas las S.F." *Medina,* 14 January 1945: 4–5.

"Mujeres haciendo el saludo falangista ante la bandera" [Women making the Fascist salute as the flag is raised]. Photograph. "Labor de la S.F. en 1940." *Y: Revista de la mujer nacionalsindicalista* January (1941): 17.

Nafisi, Azar. *Reading Lolita in Tehran.* New York: Random House, 2003.

Naval, María Angeles. *El sentimiento apócrifo: un estudio del cantar literario en Aragón, 1880–1900.* Zaragoza: Institución Fernando el Católico, 1990.

Neimeyer, Robert A. "Narrative Disruptions in the Construction of the Self." *Constructions of Disorder: Meaning-Making Frameworks for Psychotherapy*. Ed. Robert A. Neimeyer and Jonathan D. Raskin. Washington: American Psychological Association, 2000. 207–42.

– "Reauthoring Life Narratives: Grief Therapy as Meaning Reconstruction." *Israel Journal of Psychiatry and Related Sciences* 38.3–4 (2001): 171–83.

Neimeyer, Robert A., and Alan E. Stewart. "Trauma, Healing, and the Narrative Emplotment of Loss." *Families in Society* 77.6 (1996): 360–75.

Els nens perduts del franquisme. Parts 1 and 2. Dir. Montse Armengou and Richard Belis. DVD. Enciclopedia Catalana and Televisió de Catalunya, 2003.

Nile del Río, Magdalena, and Pedro Manuel Villora. *Imperio Argentina: Malena Clara.* Madrid: Temas de Hoy, 2001.

Nostalgia de la Luz. Dir. Patricio Guzmán. Pyramide Distribution, 2010. DVD.

Nussbaum, Martha. *Upheavals of Thought: The Intelligence of Emotions.* Cambridge: Cambridge University Press, 2001.

O'Connor, Mary-Frances, John J.B. Allen, and Alfred W. Kaszniak. "Autonomic and Emotion Regulation in Bereavement and Depression." *Journal of Psychosomatic Research* 52.4 (2002): 183–5.

Ochsenius, Carlos, and José Luis Olivari. "Métodos y técnicas de teatro popular: Revisión crítica, sistematización y propuesta." Santiago: CENECA (Centro de Indagación y Expresión Cultural y Artística), 1986.

"Ojos verdes." *Lo mejor de Conchita Piquer.* Madrid: EMI-Odeón, 1987.

Ojos verdes. Dir. Basilio Martín Patino. *Andalucía: Un siglo de fascinación.* Prod. Pablo Martín Pascual and La linterna mágica. Canal Sur Televisión, 1997. DVD. Suevia Films (distributor), 2004.

Olmeda, Fernando. *El látigo y la pluma: Homosexuales en la España de Franco.* Madrid: Oberon, 2004.

"Oración ante la Cruz de los Caídos en el campamento 'Pinar de Villarreal'" [A prayer before the Cross of the Fallen at the "Pinar de Villarreal" Camp]. Photograph. "Cómo fue el trabajo de la Sección Femenina en 1944." *Medina,* 25 February 1945: 4.

Ortiz, Carmen. "The Uses of Folklore by the Franco Regime." *Journal of American Folklore* 112.446 (Fall 1999): 479–96.

"La otra Veronica Lake que usted no conoce" [The Veronica Lake you don't know]. *Primer Plano,* 14 November 1948: Cover.

"Para ser bella ante el lienzo de plata." [How to look beautiful in front of the silver screen]. Sketches, photographs, captions. *Cámara,* March 1942: 16–17.

Parkes, C.M., B. Benjamin, and R.G. Fitzgerald. "Broken Heart: A Statistical Study of Increased Mortality among Widowers." *British Medical Journal* (1969): 740–6.

"La Parrala." *Lo mejor de Conchita Piquer.* Madrid: EMI-Odeón, 1987.

Pennebaker, James W. *Emotion, Disclosure and Health.* Washington: American Psychological Association, 1995.

– *Opening Up: The Healing Power of Confiding in Others.* New York: Avon Books, 1990.

– "Putting Stress into Words: Health, Linguistic, and Therapeutic Implications." *Behaviour Research and Therapy* 31.6 (1993): 539–48.

Pennebaker, James W., Janice K. Kiecolt-Glaser, and Ronald Glaser. "Disclosure of Trauma and Immune Function Health Implications for Psychotherapy." *Journal of Consulting and Clinical Psychology* 56.2 (1988): 239–45.

Pennebaker, J.W., and J.R. Sussman. "Disclosure of Traumas and Psychosomatic Process." *Social Science and Medicine* 26 (1988): 327–32.

"Person." The Oxford English Dictionary. 2nd ed. 20 vols. Oxford: Clarendon Press, 1989.

Pert, Candace B. *Molecules of Emotion.* New York: Scribner, 2003.

Pert, Candace B., Henry E. Dreher, and Michael R. Ruff. "The Psychosomatic Network: Foundations of Mind–Body Medicine." *Alternative Therapies in Health and Medicine* 4.4 (1998): 30–41.

"Pilar Primo de Rivera." Photograph. *Y: Revista de la mujer nacional-sindicalista,* no. 36 (1941): 16.

Plaza, Martín de la. *Conchita Piquer.* Madrid: Alianza Editorial, 2001.

– *Maestro Quiroga, compositor. De la A a la Z.* Discografía y filmografía comentadas. Madrid: Alianza Editorial, 2002.

Preston, Paul. *The Spanish Civil War.* New York: W.W. Norton, 2006.

Prigerson, Holly G., et al. "Rates and Risks of Complicated Grief among Psychiatric Patients in Karachi, Pakistan." *Death Studies* 26.10 (2002): 781–92.

– "Traumatic Grief as a Risk Factor for Mental and Physical Morbidity." *American Journal of Psychiatry* 154.5 (1997): 616–23.

Primo de Rivera, Pilar. *Discursos. Circulares. Escritos.* Madrid: Sección Femenina de F.E.T. y de las J.O.N.S., n.d.

Rando, Therese A. *Treatment of Complicated Mourning.* Champaign: Research Press, 1993.

Recuperando memoria: Concierto-Homenaje a los Republicanos. Dir. Diego Sabanés and Cristian Perenyi. Prod. Contamíname Discos. DVD and CD. El Diablo Distribución, 2004.

Reig Tapia, Alberto. *Ideología e historia: Sobre la represión franquista y la Guerra Civil.* Madrid: Akal, 1986.

Rejas en la memoria. Dir. Manuel Palacio. Prod. Canal+ y Pirámide S.A. DVD. Dist. Sogecable y Pirámide S.A., 2004.

Resina, Joan Ramón, ed. *Disremembering the Dictatorship: The Politics of Memory in the Spanish Transition to Democracy.* Amsterdam: Rodopi, 2000.

Resina, Joan Ramón, and Ulrich Winter, eds. *Casa encantada. Lugares de memoria en la España constitucional (1978–2004).* Frankfurt am Main: Vervuert; Madrid: Iberoamericana, 2005.

"Restricciones eléctricas." *El Alcázar,* 27 August 1948: 8.

Reynolds, Scottie Blake. "Biofeedback, Relaxation Training, and Music: Homeostasis for Coping with Stress." *Biofeedback and Self-Regulation* 9.2 (1984): 169–79.

Richards, Michael. *A Time of Silence: Civil War and the Culture of Repression in Franco's Spain, 1939–1945.* New York: Cambridge University Press, 1998.

Robb, Sheri L., Ray J. Nichols, Randi L. Rutan, Bonnie L. Bishop, and Jayne C. Parker. "The Effects of Music Assisted Relaxation on Preoperative Anxiety." *Journal of Music Therapy* 32.1 (1995): 2–21.

Robinson, John A., and Linda Hawpe. "Narrative Thinking as a Heuristic Process." Chapter 6 in Theodore R. Sarbin, ed., *Narrative Psychology: The Storied Nature of Human Conduct.* New York, Westport, and London: Praeger, 1986. 111–24.

Rodrigo, Javier. *Cautivos. Campos de concentración en la España franquista, 1936–1947.* Barcelona: Crítica, 2005.

Rodríguez, José Manuel. *"Rodri," Una historia de la censura musical en la Radio española.* RTVE Música: Casa de la Radio, 2007.

Rodríguez Kauth, Ángel. "Psicosociología del miedo: La experiencia argentina reciente." *El miedo, motor de la historia individual y colectiva.* Theoria: Proyecto Crítico de Ciencias Sociales-Grupo de Investigación UCM, 2005. 20 October 2006. 1–14.

Rogin, Michael. *Ronald Reagan, the Movie: And Other Episodes in Political Demonology.* Berkeley: University of California Press, 1987.

Román, Ignacio. *Crónicas de la copla.* Madrid: Fundación Autor, 2006.

Román, Manuel. *Memoria de la copla. La canción española de Conchita Piquer a Isabel Pantoja.* Madrid: Alianza Editorial, 1993.

"Romance de la otra." *Lo mejor de Conchita Piquer.* Madrid: EMI-Odeón, 1987.

"Romance de valentía." *La copla, siempre: Concha Piquer.* BMG Music Spain, 2000. Reissue under RCA label.

"La Ruiseñora." *Lo mejor de Conchita Piquer.* Madrid: EMI-Odeón, 1987.

Ruiz Vargas, José María. "Trauma y memoria de la guerra civil y la dictadura franquista." *Hispania Nova* 6 (2006): 299–336.

Rycroft, Charles. *A Critical Dictionary of Psychoanalysis.* New York: Basic Books, 1968.

Salaün, Serge. *El cuplé (1900–1936).* Madrid: Espasa-Calpe, 1990. 340.

Salimovich, Sofia, Elizabeth Lira, and Eugenia Weinstein. "Victims of Fear: The Social Psychology of Repression." *Fear at the Edge: State Terror and Resistance in Latin America.* Ed. Juan E. Corradi, Patricia Weiss Fagan, and Manuel Antonio Garretón. Berkeley: University of California Press, 1992. 13–25.

Sanders, Catherine M. Grief: *The Mourning After: Dealing with Adult Bereavement.* 2nd ed. New York: John Wiley, 1999.

Santino, Jack, ed. *Spontaneous Shrines and the Public Memorialization of Death.* New York: Palgrave Macmillan, 2006.

Scanlon, Geraldine. *La polémica feminista en la España contemporánea: 1868–1974.* 2nd ed. Trans. Rafael Mazarrasa. Madrid: Ediciones Akal, 1986.

Schauer, Maggie, Frank Neuner, and Thomas Elbert. *Narrative Exposure Therapy: A Short-Term Intervention for Traumatic Stress Disorders after War, Terror, or Torture.* Cambridge, MA: Hogrefe, 2005.

Scheff, T.J. *Catharsis in Healing, Ritual, and Drama.* Berkeley: University of California Press, 1979.

Sedgwick, Eve Kosofsky. "Paranoid Reading and Reparative Reading: or, You're So Paranoid, You Probably Think This Introduction Is About You." *Novel Gazing: Queer Readings in Fiction.* Ed. Eve Kosofsky Sedgwick. Durham: Duke University Press, 1997. 1–37.

II República Española. 75 aniversario, 1931–2006. Edición facsimilar de la Constitución Española de 1931. Zaragoza, Grupo Socialista de la Diputación Provincial de Zaragoza, 2006.

Semillas. Dir. Cristian Perenyi. *Recuperando memoria: Concierto-Homenaje a los Republicanos.* Prod. Contamíname Discos. DVD. El Diablo Distribución, 2004.

Senie, Harriet F. "Mourning in Protest: Spontaneous Memorials and the Sacralization of Public Space." *Spontaneous Shrines and the Public Memorialization of Death.* Ed. Jack Santino. New York: Palgrave Macmillan, 2006. 41–56.

Serrano, Rodolfo, and Daniel Serrano. *Toda España era una cárcel: Memoria de los presos del franquismo.* Madrid: Aguilar, 2002.

Shils, E.A. "Charisma, Order and Status." *Heavenly Bodies: Film Stars and Society.* Ed. Richard Dyer. New York: Routledge, 2004. 199–213.

Sierra Leone's Refugee All Stars. Dir. Zach Niles and Banker White. DVD. New York: Docurama, 2007.

Silva, Emilio. *Las fosas de Franco: Crónica de un desagravio.* Madrid: Temas de Hoy, 2005.

Smith, Barbara J. "Uncovering and Healing Hidden Wounds: Using Guided Imagery and Music to Resolve Complicated and Disenfranchised Grief." *Journal of the Association for Music and Imagery* 5.1 (1997): 1–23.

Smith, Carol A., and Larry W. Morris. "Effects of Stimulative and Sedative Music on Cognitive and Emotional Components of Anxiety." *Psychological Reports* 38 (1976): 1187–93.

Smyth, Joshua M., and James W. Pennebaker. "What Are the Health Effects of Disclosure?" *Handbook of Health Psychology*. Ed. A. Baum, T.A. Revenson, and J.E. Singer. Hillsdale: Lawrence Erlbaum, 2001. 339–48.

Solterer, Helen. *Medieval Roles for Modern Times: Theater and the Battle for the French Republic*. University Park: Pennsylvania State University Press, 2010.

Sophocles. *Antigone*. Trans. David Franklin and John Harrison. Cambridge: Cambridge University Press, 2003.

Spintge, Ralph K.W. "The Anxiolytic Effects of Music." *Rehabilitation, Music, and Human Well-Being*. Ed. Matthew H.M. Lee. Saint Louis: MMB Music, 1989.

Strachey, James, ed. *The Standard Edition of the Complete Psychological Works of Sigmund Freud*. London: Hogarth Press and the Institute of Psycho-Analysis, 1953.

"Tatuaje." *Lo mejor de Conchita Piquer*. Madrid: EMI-Odeón, 1987.

"Tatuaje." Perf. Ana Belén et al. BMG Music Spain, 1999.

Thaut, Michael H., and William B. Davis. "The Influence of Subject-Selected versus Experimenter-Chosen Music on Affect, Anxiety, and Relaxation." *Journal of Music Therapy* 30.4 (1993): 210–23.

Tichi, Cecelia. *High Lonesome: The American Culture of Country Music*. Chapel Hill: University of North Carolina Press, 1994.

Traue, Harald C., and James W. Pennebaker. *Emotion, Inhibition and Health*. Seattle: Hogrefe and Huber, 1993.

Umbral, Francisco. *Memorias de un niño de derechas*. Barcelona: Destino, 1972.

– *Memorias de un hijo del siglo*. Madrid: El País, 1987.

Van der Hart, Onno. *Rituals in Psychotherapy*. New York: Irvington, 1983.

Van der Hart, Onno, and Jos Ebbers. "Rites of Separation in Strategic Psychotherapy." *Psychotherapy: Theory, Research, and Practice* 18.2 (1981): 188–94.

Van Gennep, Arnold. *The Rites of Passage*. Trans. Monika B. Vizedom and Gabrielle L. Caffe. Chicago: University of Chicago Press, 1960.

Vázquez Montalbán, Manuel. *Cancionero general del franquismo, 1939–1975*. Barcelona: Crítica, 2000.

– "Conchita Piquer." *Nueve novísimos*. Ed. José María Castellet. Barcelona: Barral, 1970. 61–4.

– *Crónica sentimental de España*. Madrid: Espasa-Calpe, 1986.

– *Tatuaje*. Barcelona: Planeta, 1997.

Vernon, Kathleen M. "Material Culture and the Cinema Collector: A Case Study from Franco-Era Spain." *Studies in Hispanic Cinemas* 2.2 (2005): 137–44.

– "Theatricality, Melodrama, and Stardom in *El último cuplé*." *Gender and Spanish Cinema*. Ed. Steven Marsh and Parvati Nair. Oxford: Berg, 2005. 183–99.

"Veronica Lake." Photograph. *Revista Semana,* 15 July 1947: Cover.

Víctimas todavía. Dir. Joaquín Sánchez Martínez and Pablo Sánchez Torres. Prod. Antonio Quílez Tomás and Castilla-La Mancha Noticias SL. Collifilms Diffusion, 2003.

"'La vida empieza a los 40,' dice Joan Crawford" [Life begins at 40, says Joan Crawford]. *Primer Plano,* 24 October 1948.

Villarroya i Font, Joan, and Josep Mª Solé i Sabaté. "El castigo a los vencidos." *La Guerra Civil.* Ed. M. Tuñon de Lara et al. Vol. 24. *Historia 16*: Barcelona (1986). 54–67.

Vinyes, Ricard, Montse Armengou, and Ricard Belis. *Los niños perdidos del franquismo.* Barcelona: Plaza y Janés, 2002.

Virgil. *Aeneid.* Trans. C.H. Sisson. Manchester: Carcanet, 1986.

Washabaugh, William. *Flamenco: Passion, Politics, and Popular Culture.* Washington: Berg, 1996.

Webster's New Collegiate Dictionary. Springfield: Merriam, 1977.

Weiss, Jay M. "Psychological Factors in Stress and Disease." *Scientific American* 226.6 (1972): 104–13.

White, Jill M. "Music Therapy: An Intervention to Reduce Anxiety in the Myocardial Infarction Patient." *Clinical Nurse Specialist* 6.2 (1992): 58–63.

Witztum, Eliezer, and Ilana Roman. "Psychotherapeutic Intervention with Complicated Grief: Metaphor and Leave-Taking Ritual with the Bereaved." *Traumatic and Nontraumatic Loss and Bereavement: Clinical Theory and Practice.* Ed. Ruth Malkinson, Simon Shimshon Rubin, and Eliezer Witztum. Madison: Psychosocial Press, 2000. 143–71.

Woods, Eva. "Excess, Affect, and Emergent Classes: Melodramatic Modes in Mariquilla Terremoto (Benito Perojo 1939) and Filigrana (Luis Marquina 1949)." *Letras Peninsulares* 16 (2003): 291–315.

– "Identification and Disconnect through Popular Melodrama." *Studies in Hispanic Cinemas* 2.2 (2005): 125–35.

– "Performance in Theory and Practice: The Folklórica as the Internal Other in *María de la O* and *Morena Clara.*" Ed. and intro. George Cabello-Castellet, Jaume Martí-Olivella, and Guy H. Wood. *Cine-Lit III: Essays on Hispanic Film and Fiction.* Corvallis: Oregon State University, 1998. 48–60.

– "Radio Free *Folklóricas*: Cultural, Gender and Spatial Hierarchies in *Torbellino.*" In Steven Marsh and Parvati Nair, *Gender and Spanish Cinema.* Oxford and New York: Berg, 2004. 201–18.

Zavala, Iris M. *El bolero: Historia de un amor.* Madrid: Celeste, 2000.

Zeitlin, Steve. "Oh Did You See the Ashes Come Thickly Falling Down? Poems Posted in the Wake of September 11." *Spontaneous Shrines and the Public Memorialization of Death.* Ed. Jack Santino. New York: Palgrave Macmillan, 2006. 99–111.

Index

TORONTO IBERIC

1 Anthony J. Cascardi, *Cervantes, Literature, and the Discourse of Politics*

2 Jessica A. Boon, *The Mystical Science of the Soul: Medieval Cognition in Bernardino de Laredo's Recollection Method*

3 Susan Byrne, *Law and History in Cervantes' Don Quixote*

4 Mary E. Barnard and Frederick A. de Armas (eds.), *Objects of Culture in the Literature of Imperial Spain*

5 Nil Santiáñez, *Topographies of Fascism: Habitus, Space, and Writing in Twentieth-Century Spain*

6 Nelson Orringer, *Lorca in Tune with Falla: Literary and Musical Interludes*

7 Ana M. Gómez-Bravo, *Textual Agency: Writing Culture and Social Networks in Fifteenth-Century Spain*

8 Javier Irigoyen-García, *The Spanish Arcadia: Sheep Herding, Pastoral Discourse, and Ethnicity in Early Modern Spain*

9 Stephanie Sieburth, *Survival Songs: Conchita Piquer's* Coplas *and Franco's Regime of Terror*

www.ingramcontent.com/pod-product-compliance
Lightning Source LLC
LaVergne TN
LVHW090155080826
844660LV00013B/815/J

* 9 7 8 1 4 4 2 6 4 4 7 3 1 *